BRAZIL IN FOCUS: ECONOMIC, POLITICAL AND SOCIAL ISSUES

Brazil in Focus: Economic, Political and Social Issues

Jorge T. Almeida
Editor

Nova Science Publishers, Inc.
New York

NOTICE TO THE READER

The Publisher has taken reasonable care in the preparation of this book, but makes no expressed or implied warranty of any kind and assumes no responsibility for any errors or omissions. No liability is assumed for incidental or consequential damages in connection with or arising out of information contained in this book. The Publisher shall not be liable for any special, consequential, or exemplary damages resulting, in whole or in part, from the readers' use of, or reliance upon, this material.

Independent verification should be sought for any data, advice or recommendations contained in this book. In addition, no responsibility is assumed by the publisher for any injury and/or damage to persons or property arising from any methods, products, instructions, ideas or otherwise contained in this publication.

This publication is designed to provide accurate and authoritative information with regard to the subject matter covered herein. It is sold with the clear understanding that the Publisher is not engaged in rendering legal or any other professional services. If legal or any other expert assistance is required, the services of a competent person should be sought. FROM A DECLARATION OF PARTICIPANTS JOINTLY ADOPTED BY A COMMITTEE OF THE AMERICAN BAR ASSOCIATION AND A COMMITTEE OF PUBLISHERS.

LIBRARY OF CONGRESS CATALOGING-IN-PUBLICATION DATA
Brazil : economics, politics and sociology / Jorg T. Almeida (editor).
        p. cm.
Includes bibliographical references and index.
ISBN 978-1-60456-165-4(hbk. : alk. paper)
1. Brazil—Economic conditions—21st century. 2. Brazil—Economic policy—21st
century.3.Brazil—Politics and government—21st century.4.Brazil—Social conditions—21st
century. I. Almeida, Jorge, prof.
HC187.B8696 2008
330.981—dc22
                2008019444

Published by Nova Science Publishers, Inc. New York

CONTENTS

PREFACE

Brazil is located on the east coast of the South America, along the Atlantic Ocean. With its area of 8,511,965 km^2, it constitutes one of biggest countries of the world in territorial extension. It possesss vast natural water holds; the biggest land forest ; and flora, fauna, air, land, minerals and waters of inestimable value for the planet. It posesses around 169 million inhabitants, distributed in 26 States and a Federal District, in which the capital, Brasilia , is located. Brazil has a Gross Internal Product (GIP) close to US$ 800 billion, and the per capita GIP is close to US$ 4,719.76. It has the biggest economy of Latin America, and well developed sectors in the areas of agriculture, industry, commerce and jobs. In agriculture, it is distinguished by coffee, soy, rice, meat, sugar cane, citric, and cocoa. Its industrial park is distinguished by the production of chemicals, shoe products, cement, iron, steel, airplanes, engines and automobiles, buses, machines, implements and equipment. It exports and imports around US$ 50 billion per year; it has around 50 million television sets, 40 million fixed and cellular telephones, and 70 million radios. This new book presents important analyses of this dynamic country.

Chapter 1 - On January 1, 2007, Luis Inácio "Lula" da Silva, of the leftist Workers' Party (PT), was inaugurated for a second four-year term as President of Brazil. President Lula defeated Geraldo Alckmin, former governor of the state of São Paulo, of the Brazilian Social Democratic Party (PSDB), in a run-off presidential election held on October 29, 2006. Lula captured 61% of the votes as compared to Alckmin's 39%, winning handily in the poorer north and northeastern regions of the country but failing to carry the more prosperous southern and western states or São Paulo, the country's industrial and financial hub.

President Lula has been working to make cabinet appointments and to form a governing coalition capable of pushing his agenda through Brazil's notoriously fractured legislature. His immediate tasks are to boost Brazil's lagging economic growth and to address the issues of crime and violence. Some analysts predict that ongoing corruption investigations involving President Lula's PT party may undermine the strength of his second term in office.

Relations with the United States have been generally positive, although President Lula has made relations with neighboring countries in the Southern Common Market (Mercosul) his first priority, and has sought to strengthen ties with nontraditional partners, including India and China. Many analysts believe Brazil-U.S. cooperation may increase during President Lula's second term, particularly on energy issues. Brazilian and U.S. officials are currently negotiating an agreement to promote greater ethanol production and use throughout Latin America, the details of which are expected to be announced after two upcoming meetings between President Bush and President Lula. President Bush is scheduled to visit Brazil on March 9, which will be followed by a visit from President Lula to Camp David on March 31.

In recent years, congressional interest in Brazil has focused on the U.S.-Brazilian bilateral trade relationship, as well as Brazil's role in sub-regional, regional, and global trade talks in the Doha round of the World Trade Organization (WTO) negotiations. In December 2006, Congress extended trade preferences for Brazil under the Generalized System of Preferences (GSP), but set thresholds that may limit trade preferences for some Brazilian exports compared to previous years. Interest in Brazil also centers on its role as a stabilizing force in Latin America, especially with respect to Venezuela and Bolivia. Brazil's role as an ethanol producer has generated growing interest in Congress. In addition, Brazil is a key U.S. ally whose cooperation is sought on issues that include counternarcotics and counterterrorism efforts; human rights concerns, such as race relations and trafficking in persons; the environment, including protection of the Amazon; and HIV/AIDS prevention.

Chapter 2 - In late 2002, Brazil initiated a World Trade Organization (WTO) dispute settlement case (DS267) against specific provisions of the U.S. cotton program. On September 8, 2004, a WTO dispute settlement (DS) panel ruled against the United States on several key issues in case DS267. On October 18, 2004, the United States appealed the case to the WTO's Appellate Body (AB) which, on March 3, 2005, confirmed the earlier DS panel findings against U.S. cotton programs.

Key findings include the following: (1) U.S. domestic cotton subsidies have exceeded WTO commitments of the 1992 benchmark year, thereby losing the protection afforded by the "Peace Clause," which shielded them from substantive challenges; (2) the two major types of direct payments made under U.S. farm programs — Production Flexibility Contract payments of the 1996 Farm Act and the Direct Payments of the 2002 Farm Act — do not qualify for WTO exemptions from reduction commitments as fully decoupled income support and should therefore count against the "Peace Clause" limits; (3) Step-2 program payments are prohibited subsidies; (4) U.S. export credit guarantees are effectively export subsidies, making them subject to previously notified export subsidy commitments; and (5) U.S. domestic support measures that are "contingent on market prices" have resulted in excess cotton production and exports that, in turn, have caused low international prices and have resulted in "serious prejudice" to Brazil.

What happens next? On March 21, 2005, the AB and panel reports were adopted by the WTO membership, initiating a sequence of events, under WTO dispute settlement rules, whereby the United States will bring its policies into line with the panel's recommendations or negotiate a mutually acceptable settlement with Brazil. First, the panel recommended that all "prohibited" U.S. export subsidies (i.e., Step 2 payments and exports of unscheduled commodities — including cotton —made with GSM export credit guarantees) must be withdrawn by July 1, 2005. Second, as concerns a ruling on "actionable" subsidies under a finding of serious prejudice caused by "price contingent" subsidies (e.g., loan deficiency payments, marketing loss assistance payments, counter-cyclical payments, and Step-2 payments), the United States is under an obligation to "take appropriate steps to remove the adverse effects or withdraw the subsidy."

It is noteworthy that the panel finding that U.S. direct payments do not qualify for WTO exemptions from reduction commitments as fully decoupled income support (i.e., they are not green box compliant) appears to have no further consequences within the context of this case and does not involve any compliance measures. This is because direct payments were deemed "non-price contingent" and were evaluated strictly in terms of the Peace Clause violation.

Chapter 3 - Brazil is a major world producer and exporter of agricultural products. In 2004, Brazil exported $30.9 billion worth of agricultural and food products, making it the world's third-largest exporter of agricultural products after the United States and the European Union. Brazil's major agricultural exports include soybeans, poultry, beef, pork, orange juice, and coffee.

Highlights of Brazil's agricultural production and exports include:

- Soybeans: In 2005, Brazil, the world's second largest producer, became the world's leading exporter, with 39% of global export market share. The United States, the world's leading producer of soybeans, had a 37% share of the world soybean market, although forecasts are for the United States to return to its leading position in 2006.
- Poultry (Broilers): Brazil, the world's third largest producer of broilers, was the leading exporter in 2005, with 41% of the world's export market. The United States, the world's leading producer, was the second largest exporter, with 35% of the world's export market.
- Beef and Veal: Brazil was the world's second largest producer and the leading exporter of beef and veal in 2005. In 2005, the United States, the top global producer of beef and veal, fell to eighth place in terms of exports, due to the discovery of a cow with BSE in late 2003.
- Orange Juice: Brazil is the world's leading producer (59% share) and exporter (83% share) of orange juice.
- Coffee: Brazil is the world's leading producer and exporter of coffee. Its share of world coffee production in 2005 was 32%, while its share of world coffee exports was 28%.
- Sugar: Brazil is the world's leading producer and exporter of sugar. The United States is a major producer, but a minor exporter of sugar.
- Cotton: Brazil is the world's fifth largest producer and exporter of cotton. The United States, the world's second largest producer, is the world's leading exporter of cotton, with 41% of world exports.

Chapter 4 - The paper makes use of an event study to test the Efficient Market Hypothesis and its variant, the Uncertain Information Hypothesis, for the Brazilian stock market. Previous literature has associated inefficiencies generated by thin markets with investor overreaction or underreaction, thereby refuting the Efficient Market Hypothesis. However, the arrival of new information introduces a period of increased risk and uncertainty to the rational agents. The Uncertain Information Hypothesis was devised to be a more realistic variation of the efficiency theory, since it accounts for investor reactions to unexpected surprises. The evidence found here indicates that neither the Efficient Market nor the Uncertain Information Hypotheses are supported by the Brazilian data. Actually, the authors found evidence that the Brazilian stock market overreacts to positive shocks and underreacts to negative shocks, which suggests the prevalence of institutional inefficiency.

Chapter 5 - What are the dynamics of the political crisis of the post-64 Brazilian dictatorship? What place do intra-military processes have in the configuration of these broader dynamics? What types of divisions took shape within the military field during the dictatorship? These are the questions that guided my research on the political processes of the Brazilian dictatorship in the period of its consolidation (1964-69). The approach that I propose here focuses specifically on the political dynamics of the regime. The relationship between these two terms – political dynamics and regime form – both defines the field where my general concerns lay and calls for a review of the most relevant literature about the Southern Cone military regimes of the 1960s and 1970s. In this regard I will suggest that the dominant theses on those military governments lead to a series of difficulties in our understanding of the political process of the dictatorships, insofar as they underestimate the role that military processes played within them.

Chapter 6 - As the largest and one of the most influential countries in Latin America, Brazil has emerged as a leading voice for developing countries in setting regional and multilateral trade agendas. The United States and Brazil have cultivated a constructive relationship in pursuit of their respective efforts to promote trade liberalization, including attempting to broker a compromise with the European Union in the World Trade Organization (WTO) Doha Round and forming bilateral working groups on trade (and other) issues. Still, they approach trade policy quite differently, are at odds over how to proceed regionally with the Free Trade Area of the Americas (FTAA), and share concerns over specific trade policies and practices.

Brazil's trade strategy can be explained only in part by economic incentives. Its "trade preferences" also reflect deeply embedded macroeconomic, industrial, and foreign policies. Whereas U.S. trade strategy emphasizes the negotiation of comprehensive trade agreements on multiple fronts, Brazil is focused primarily on market access issues as they pertain to its economic dominance in South America. Brazil exercises this priority in all trade arenas, such as pursuing changes to agricultural policies in the WTO, expanding the Southern Common Market (Mercosul) in South America, and resisting the FTAA for lack of a balance conducive to Brazilian interests.

Brazil has a modern, diversified economy in which services account for 53% of GDP, followed by industry and manufacturing at 37%, and agriculture at 9%. Agribusiness (commodity and processed goods) account for some 30% of GDP, explaining Brazil's emphasis on agricultural policies in trade negotiations. Brazil is the world's largest producer of sugar cane, oranges, and coffee, and the second largest of soybean, beef, poultry, and corn. It is also a major producer of steel, aircraft, automobiles, and auto parts, yet surprisingly, a relatively small trader by world standards. The United States is Brazil's largest single-country trading partner.

Brazil is critical of U.S. trade policies such as the Byrd Amendment (repealed, but program in effect until October 1, 2007), which directs duties from trade remedy cases to affected industries, the administration of trade remedy rules, and what it considers to be discriminatory treatment in the U.S. expansion of free trade agreements in Latin America. It also objects to product-specific barriers such as tariff rate quotas on sugar, orange juice, ethanol, and tobacco; subsidies for cotton, ethanol, and soybeans; and prolonged antidumping orders on steel and orange juice. U.S. concerns focus on Brazil's comparatively high tariff structure, especially on industrial goods, Mercosul's common external tariff program, and Brazil's refusal to address issues of critical importance to the United States such as services trade, intellectual property rights, government procurement, and investment.

Despite these differences, both countries recognize the potential for important gains to be had from mutually acceptable trade liberalization at all levels. As a developing country with an opportunity for considerable growth in both exports and imports, however, Brazil may have the most to gain from addressing both foreign barriers to its trade, and unilaterally opening its economy further.

Chapter 7 - Although labor unions are considered one of the most important institutions of modern capitalism (Freeman, 2000), the literature shows that their mode of operation and impact on the economy vary from country to country. Although there is a wide variety of systems, institutions, and union action strategies in the different countries, an important stylized fact in the literature is that labor unions reduce wage dispersion through collective bargaining processes. This has led Metcalf et al. (2000) to refer to them as a "sword of justice." According to Freeman (2000), this phenomenon is actually more widespread than the more thoroughly researched effect of unions on wages, namely their ability to raise the relative wages of their members. The literature shows that: (i) the distribution of wages among unionized workers and/or those covered by collective bargaining is more concentrated than the wage distribution for other workers, even when demographic and productive characteristics are controlled for in the corresponding regressions; and (ii) collective bargaining diminishes the importance of merit in wage formation, thereby narrowing the wage spread between jobs.

Estimates of the impact of unions on the labor market in Brazil are still very preliminary. The few results available include those obtained by Arbache (1999), who investigates the wage and income-distribution effects of unions among male manufacturing workers; Arbache and Carneiro (1999), who examine the importance and effects of unions on collective bargaining; Arbache (2000), who studies the effects of trade liberalization on unions and collective bargaining; Menezes-Filho et al. (2002) who assesses the impact of trade unions on the economic performance of Brazilian establishments; and Amorim (2000), who analyzes the relationship between unions and indirect pay. Little is known about the effect of unions on employment, productivity or labor market rigidity, and especially on wages and income distribution. Knowledge of the impact of unions on pay dispersion is particularly important for Brazil, given its highly unequal income distribution. If the legal framework that regulates labor relations is a decisive factor in the functioning of unions and collective bargaining processes, then knowing this could help us to understand the effects of unions on the overall economy.

This chapter seeks to answer the following questions: (i) How do employment and union laws affect collective bargaining processes? (ii) Do unions affect wage formation and income distribution? (iii) Do unions increase the rigidity of the labor market? The authors conclude by making some suggestions for enhancing collective bargaining and unions in Brazil.

The chapter is organized as follows: Section 2 describes labor laws and union legislation in Brazil. Section 3 describes the characteristics of unionized and non-union workers, union density, and the determinants of unionization. Section 4 investigates the effects of unions on wages and income distribution. Section 5 discusses the results obtained and seeks to demonstrate the effects of employment and union laws on collective bargaining processes and union behavior. Section 6 offers some recommendations for improving labor relations in Brazil.

In: Brazil in Focus: Economic, Political and Social Issues   ISBN: 978-1-60456-165-4
Editor: Jorge T. Almeida, pp. 1-26   © 2008 Nova Science Publishers, Inc.

Chapter 1

BRAZIL-U.S. RELATIONS[*]

Clare M. Ribando

ABSTRACT

On January 1, 2007, Luis Inácio "Lula" da Silva, of the leftist Workers' Party (PT), was inaugurated for a second four-year term as President of Brazil. President Lula defeated Geraldo Alckmin, former governor of the state of São Paulo, of the Brazilian Social Democratic Party (PSDB), in a run-off presidential election held on October 29, 2006. Lula captured 61% of the votes as compared to Alckmin's 39%, winning handily in the poorer north and northeastern regions of the country but failing to carry the more prosperous southern and western states or São Paulo, the country's industrial and financial hub.

President Lula has been working to make cabinet appointments and to form a governing coalition capable of pushing his agenda through Brazil's notoriously fractured legislature. His immediate tasks are to boost Brazil's lagging economic growth and to address the issues of crime and violence. Some analysts predict that ongoing corruption investigations involving President Lula's PT party may undermine the strength of his second term in office.

Relations with the United States have been generally positive, although President Lula has made relations with neighboring countries in the Southern Common Market (Mercosul) his first priority, and has sought to strengthen ties with nontraditional partners, including India and China. Many analysts believe Brazil-U.S. cooperation may increase during President Lula's second term, particularly on energy issues. Brazilian and U.S. officials are currently negotiating an agreement to promote greater ethanol production and use throughout Latin America, the details of which are expected to be announced after two upcoming meetings between President Bush and President Lula. President Bush is scheduled to visit Brazil on March 9, which will be followed by a visit from President Lula to Camp David on March 31.

In recent years, congressional interest in Brazil has focused on the U.S.-Brazilian bilateral trade relationship, as well as Brazil's role in sub-regional, regional, and global trade talks in the Doha round of the World Trade Organization (WTO) negotiations. In December 2006, Congress extended trade preferences for Brazil under the Generalized

---

[*] Excerpted from CRS Report RL33456, dated February 28, 2007.

System of Preferences (GSP), but set thresholds that may limit trade preferences for some Brazilian exports compared to previous years. Interest in Brazil also centers on its role as a stabilizing force in Latin America, especially with respect to Venezuela and Bolivia. Brazil's role as an ethanol producer has generated growing interest in Congress. In addition, Brazil is a key U.S. ally whose cooperation is sought on issues that include counternarcotics and counterterrorism efforts; human rights concerns, such as race relations and trafficking in persons; the environment, including protection of the Amazon; and HIV/AIDS prevention.

BACKGROUND

Brazil is a significant political and economic power in Latin America, but deep-seated social and economic problems have kept it from realizing its goal of becoming a truly global leader. A former Portuguese colony that achieved independence in 1822, Brazil occupies almost half of the continent of South America and boasts immense biodiversity, including the vast Amazon rainforest, and significant natural resources. Brazil is the fifth most populous country in the world. Brazil's188 million citizens are primarily of European, African, or mixed African and European descent.[1] With an estimated gross domestic product (GDP) of $786 billion in 2006, Brazil's diversified economy is the eleventh largest in the world, the largest in Latin America, and one of the largest in the developing world, but per capita gross national income is only $3,460, and the country has a highly unequal income distribution. Brazil has long held potential to become a major world power, but its rise to prominence has been held back by political setbacks, including twenty-one years of military rule (1964-1985), social problems, and slow and uneven economic growth. This apparent failure to live up to its enormous potential has resulted in the common adage, "Brazil is the land of the future, and always will be."[2]

Between World War II and 1990, both democratic and military governments sought to expand Brazil's influence in the world by pursuing a state-led industrial policy and an independent foreign policy. Brazilian foreign policy has recently aimed to strengthen ties with other South American countries, engage in multilateral diplomacy through the United Nations (U.N.) and the Organization of American States (OAS), and act at times as a countervailing force to U.S. political and economic influence in Latin America. In addition to its active engagement in regional and multilateral trade talks, Brazil under President Luis Inácio "Lula" da Silva has helped diffuse potential political crises in Venezuela, Ecuador, and Bolivia, and supported Colombia's ongoing struggle against terrorist organizations and drug traffickers. Brazil is also commanding the U.N. stabilization force in Haiti.

Currently, relations between the United States and Brazil are characterized as fairly warm and friendly. The United States has increasingly regarded Brazil as a significant power, especially in its role as a stabilizing force and skillful interlocutor in Latin America. U.S. officials tend to describe Brazil, similar to Chile, as a friendly country governed by a moderate leftist government that shares the U.S. commitment to democratic practices, human rights, and prudent macroeconomic policies. They assert that the United States seeks to increase cooperation with moderate leftist governments in Latin America in order to diffuse mounting tensions among the countries in South America, and to deal with populist governments in the region.

Although they share common goals for regional stability, Brazil's independent approach to foreign policy has led to periodic disputes with the United States on trade and political issues, including Brazil's vocal opposition to the war in Iraq. Despite these disagreements, Brazil and the United States have worked closely on a wide range of bilateral and regional issues. In addition to trade matters, these issues include counter-narcotics and terrorism, energy security, human rights protection, environmental issues (including protection of the Amazon), and HIV/AIDS. Brazilian and U.S. officials are currently formulating an agreement on ethanol and technology development that is expected to be signed by President Bush and President Lula in March 2007.

POLITICAL SITUATION

The Brazilian political system has several unique characteristics that distinguish it from other countries in Latin America. The country's federal structure, comprising 26 states, a Federal District, and some 5,581 municipalities, evolved from the decentralized colonial structure devised by the Portuguese in an attempt to control Brazil's sizable territory. Even during the centralizing government of Getúlio Vargas and the Estado Novo, or New State, (1937-1945), landowning remained the source of local power in Brazil and states retained considerable autonomy from the federal government. Brazil's military governments ruled from 1964-1985 and, while repressive, were not as brutal as their counterparts in other South American countries. Although nominally allowing a two-party system, judiciary, and Congress to function during its tenure, the Brazilian military stifled representative democracy and civic action in Brazil, carefully preserving its influence during one of the most protracted transitions to democracy to take place in Latin America. Brazil also stands out as one of the last countries in the region to abandon state-led economic policies in favor of market reforms. Significant pro-market reforms did not occur until the government of Fernando Henrique Cardoso (1994-2002).[3]

During the first decade after its return to democracy in 1985, Brazil experienced economic recession and political uncertainty as numerous efforts to control runaway inflation failed and two elected presidents did not complete their terms. One elected president died before taking office; the other was impeached on corruption charges. In 1994, Cardoso, a prominent sociologist of the center-left Brazilian Social Democratic Party (PSDB), was elected by a wide margin over Luis Inácio "Lula" da Silva of the Worker's Party (PT), a former metalworker and union leader who had led the PT since the early 1980s. Cardoso was elected largely on the basis of the success of the anti-inflation "Real Plan" that he implemented as Finance Minister earlier that year. The plan resulted in a new currency (the real) pegged to the dollar beginning in July of 1994. During his first term, Cardoso achieved macroeconomic stability, opened the Brazilian economy to trade and investment, and furthered privatization efforts begun in the early 1990s. Despite those achievements, the Cardoso government was unable to enact much needed political and social changes, such as social security, tax, or judicial reforms.

President Cardoso sought a second presidential term after a constitutional reform was passed in 1997 to allow for reelection, and he defeated Lula da Silva in the first presidential election round in October 1998 with 53% of the vote. President Cardoso's popularity fell towards the end of his second term, however, as Brazil faced a major financial crisis in 1998, as well as contagion effects from Argentina's financial collapse in 2001. Most analysts credit Cardoso with restoring macroeconomic stability to Brazil's economy and solidifying its role as leader of the Southern Common Market (Mercosul)[4], but fault him for failing to implement more aggressive political reforms or more effective social programs.[5]

Lula Administration

In 2002, Lula da Silva ran in his fourth campaign for the presidency of Brazil. Unlike in his previous failed campaigns, he moderated his leftist rhetoric and, while still advocating greater attention to social issues, promised to maintain the fiscal and monetary policies associated with Brazil's standing International Monetary Fund (IMF) agreements. Lula, as he prefers to be known, argued for a more aggressive foreign policy and for strengthening of Mercosul, but was often critical of the proposed Free Trade Area of the Americas (FTAA).

The 2002 presidential election proved to be a referendum on eight years of "neo-liberal" policies enacted by the Cardoso government. High unemployment rates and economic stagnation led voters to support Lula, a critic of neoliberalism. Although Lula did not win in the first round of voting, he was elected decisively in the second round with 61% of the valid vote, as compared to Cardoso's designated successor, José Serra, the Minister of Health and Senator from São Paulo, with 39%. Several factors may account for Lula's presidential victory and the PT's strong showing in the 2002 congressional elections. They include the PT's reputation as a "clean" political party untainted by corruption; the PT's promise to increase state investment in education, health care, and agrarian reform; and Lula's compelling personal story.[6]

In January 2003, Lula da Silva was inaugurated for a four-year term as President of Brazil. During his first term, President Lula maintained the restrained economic policies associated with his predecessor, even surpassing the IMF's fiscal and monetary targets. In 2003, the Lula government enacted social security and tax reforms, and in 2004, a law to allow more private investment in public infrastructure projects. President Lula launched several social programs, some of which have been more successful than others. The *Bolsa Familia* (Family Grant) program, which provides monthly stipends to 11.1 million poor families in exchange for compulsory school attendance for all school-age children, has been credited with poverty reduction. Its success has been limited, however, by bureaucratic problems and local corruption. Some argue that it has made poor households more reliant on government handouts than on earned income.[7]

By 2005, legislative progress had stalled, and President Lula was increasingly criticized for failing to develop effective programs to address Brazil's ongoing problems with land distribution and crime. Critics argued that, ironically, one of the first Lula government's only major achievements was to maintain the orthodox economic policies of the Cardoso administration. In 2006, some analysts began to dismiss President Lula's efforts to expand Brazil's international profile as a leader among developing countries as "a relatively inexpensive [tactic] to shore up domestic support"[8] that had failed to yield many concrete results.

Corruption Scandals

Many political scientists have asserted that the fragmented nature of Brazil's electoral and party systems have made the country extremely difficult to govern. They maintain that the country's institutions create incentives that encourage politicians to concentrate on delivering pork-barrel programs to their political benefactors rather than on legislating issues of national concern. In addition, Brazilian political parties tend to be more personalistic than ideological, and many are locally or regionally based rather than national in scope. As a result, forming successful governing coalitions in Brazil often has less to do with finding political parties with ideological similarities than with distributing ministries or other patronage in exchange for political support.[9] Many Brazilians had hoped that the PT would be able to clean up Brazilian politics, but those hopes seemed dashed in the wake of a series of corruption scandals involving top PT officials, the first of which erupted in May 2005.[10]

The main corruption scandal, which resulted in the resignation of several senior PT officials and the impeachment of several legislators, including President Lula's former Chief of Staff who had since returned to Congress, involved the President's party allegedly paying monthly bribes (*mensalãos*) to congressmen of the allied parties in the governing coalition to guarantee their support. Another scandal involved allegations that the PT and other parties used off-the-books accounting systems to pay for their campaigns. In late March 2006, Finance Minister Antonio Palocci was forced to resign amidst allegations of corruption. Although many believe President Lula had to be aware of the bribery and irregular financing schemes, a congressional inquiry in April 2006 cleared President Lula of any direct responsibility for the scandals.

In May 2006, Brazil's federal police released a list of 69 congressmen who were allegedly involved in another unrelated scandal involving the release of money from the health ministry for the purchase of ambulances without public notification. By December 2006, a congressional committee announced that it could not find enough evidence to indict any of those congressmen. The corruption and apparent impunity in the 2003-2006 Congress caused the Brazilian press to dismiss it as "the worst ever in Brazilian history."[11]

As a result of the corruption scandals, both President Lula and the Worker's Party have lost popular support and credibility. Despite the initial popular outrage, the PT decided not to investigate or punish any party members allegedly involved in any of the scandals until after the election campaign.

October 2006 Elections

On October 1, 2006, Brazilians headed to the polls to elect a new president and vice president, federal legislators, and governors. Months before the election, most analysts predicted that President Lula would soundly defeat his main opponent Geraldo Alckmin, former governor of the state of São Paulo of the PSDB, in the first round. The presidential race tightened, however, when top Lula advisers were accused of trying to buy a dossier with damaging information on Alckmin and then- gubernatorial candidate Jose Serra just two weeks prior to the election. Voters appeared to punish Lula for the scandal by denying him a first round victory. They also denied reelection to 61 of the legislators suspected of participating in the ambulance scandal.[12]

In the October 29 second round, Lula overcame his first-round setback, capturing 61% of the votes to Alckmin's 39%. President Lula won handily in the poorer north and northeastern regions of the country but failed to carry the more prosperous southern and western states or

São Paulo. Observers have assessed that Brazilians, though divided by class and region, effectively voted in favor of continuing macroeconomic stability under a second Lula Administration despite the corruption scandals that had involved Lula's party, including many of his closest advisers, during the first term.

The PT did not fare as well as President Lula in the legislative elections. In the Chamber of Deputies, the PT secured 83 seats, 9 less than in 2002. In the Senate, the PT suffered a loss of 4 seats. In contrast, previous ruling parties increased their congressional delegations. Some assert that election outcome shows that President Lula successfully distanced himself from the PT and its corruption scandals, relying on his personal popularity and charisma rather than his party affiliation to win the election. Many others attribute his electoral success to the success of his Bolsa Familia program and the country's macroeconomic stability, which led voters in poorer income brackets to support his reelection.[13]

Prospects for Lula's Second Term

On January 1, 2007, Lula was inaugurated for a second four-year term as President of Brazil. President Lula is struggling to make cabinet appointments and form a governing coalition capable of pushing his agenda through Brazil's notoriously fractured legislature. He is currently dealing with intra-party conflicts between the PT and the Brazilian Democratic Movement Party (PMDB), the two largest parties in his fragile coalition, as well as internal divisions within the PT. Many predict that these conflicts may complicate his immediate tasks: boosting Brazil's lagging economic growth and addressing the issues of crime and violence. Some analysts feel that ongoing investigations against President Lula's PT party may also undermine the strength of his second term in office. Many believe that President Lula will tone down his foreign policy ambition, and may focus on improving relations with the United States.[14]

ECONOMIC AND SOCIAL CONDITIONS

Brazil is a regional leader in Latin America, but its rise to global prominence has been hindered by significant economic and social problems.

Economic Conditions

Throughout the last two decades, Brazil's fiscal and monetary policies have achieved mixed results by focusing primarily on inflation control. When President Lula took office in 2003, Brazil had an extremely high level of public debt, virtually necessitating that he adopt austere economic policies. Despite his leftist political origins, President Lula has maintained restrained economic policies, even surpassing the IMF's fiscal and monetary targets. As a result, Brazil has begun to experience some benefits, including lower inflation (just over 3% in 2006) and a lower credit risk rating. In December 2005, the Lula government repaid its $15.5 billion debt to the IMF ahead of schedule. The government's overall foreign debt was reduced by 19.9% between 2003 and 2006.[15] Fiscal discipline has also been accompanied by record exports that enabled Brazil to post GDP growth of 4.9% in 2004 and record trade surpluses in 2004, 2005, and 2006.

Brazil is a major exporter of agricultural and industrial products, with each accounting for about 30% of the country's exports, and plays a significant role in the world trading system. Since 2002, Brazil has been the world's third largest exporter of agricultural products after the United States and the European Union. In 2005, Brazil was the world's leading exporter of coffee, orange juice, sugar, chicken, beef, and tobacco. It was the second biggest exporter of soybean products and the fourth largest exporter of cotton and pork. Brazil has a relatively balanced trade regime. Its main trading partners in 2005 were the European Union (22% of exports and 25% of imports), the United States (19% of exports, 17% of imports), Asia (20% of exports, 27% of imports, with China alone accounting for 6% of exports and 7% of imports), Latin America (22% of exports, 15% of imports), Africa (4% of exports, 9% of imports), and the Middle East (4% of exports and imports). In 2005, the value of Brazil's exports reached $120 billion and the country's trade surplus was $45 billion.[16]

Despite some positive economic and trade indicators, Brazil's economic growth has lagged behind other emerging economies. Since 2000, Brazil's growth rates have averaged about 2.7%, as compared to Russia with 6.7%, India with 6.5%, and China with 9.4%. In 2006, Brazil posted GDP growth of only about 2.8%, the second lowest growth rate recorded in Latin America.[17] Brazil's growth rates have been constrained by a high public debt burden, excessive taxation, and lack of investment. Investment in Brazil has been limited by the country's high interest rates, extremely complex tax system, weak regulatory framework, and lack of a competitive labor force. A November 2006 report by the Organization for Economic Co-operation and Development (OECD), which echoed the opinions voiced by most financial analysts, said that reforming Brazil's unwieldy public pension system was crucial in order for the country to boost its growth rates.

On January 22, 2007, President Lula announced a Program to Accelerate Growth (PAC) aimed at boosting Brazil's growth rates to 5% per year by 2008 through increased public and private investment in energy, logistics, housing, and water sanitation. The PAC's goal is for investments totaling some $235 billion to be made over the next four years, with state-owned companies, particularly Petrobras, Brazil's state-owned oil company, responsible for the bulk of that figure. It provides tax breaks and incentives to spur housing construction and includes measures to improve and simplify Brazil's regulatory framework. Although some have praised the PAC's focus on boosting government investment in much-needed infrastructure projects, many others have criticized it for failing to include measures to curb excessive public spending or to enact labor reform.[18]

Social Indicators

Brazil has a well-developed economy and large resource base, but has had major problems solving deep-seated social problems like poverty and income inequality. Brazil has one of the most unequal income distributions in Latin America, a region with the highest income inequality in the world, and a 2004 World Bank study reported that some 50 million Brazilians live in poverty.[19] The United Nations Development Program (UNDP) has identified 600 Brazilian municipalities, many in the north and northeastern part of the country, in which poverty levels are similar to those present in poor African countries. One major cause of poverty and inequality in Brazil is historically extreme land concentration among the country's elites. In Brazil, 1% of the population controls 45% of the farmland.[20] In addition to the country's regional income disparities and unequal land distribution, the Brazilian government has acknowledged that there is a racial component to poverty in Brazil. People of African descent in Brazil, also known as Afro-Brazilians, represent 45% of the country's population, but constitute 64% of the poor and 69% of the extreme poor.[21] Other factors that inhibit the social mobility of Brazil's poor include a lack of access to quality education, and a lack of opportunity for job training and improvement.

Brazil's endemic poverty and inequality have, until recently, not been significantly affected by the government's social programs. A March 2005 OECD study found that, even though Brazil has spent the same level or more of public spending on social programs as other countries with similar income levels, it has not achieved the same social indicators as those countries.[22] There has been more recent evidence, however, that the Lula government's Bolsa Familia (Family Stipend) program, combined with relative macroeconomic stability over the past few years, has reduced poverty rates, particularly in the north and northeast of Brazil.[23]

FOREIGN AND TRADE POLICY

Brazil's foreign policy is a byproduct of the country's unique position as a regional power in Latin America, a leader among developing countries, and an emerging world power. Brazilian foreign policy has generally been based on the principles of multilateralism, peaceful dispute settlement, and nonintervention in the affairs of other countries.[24] Brazil engages in multilateral diplomacy through the OAS and the U.N., and has increased ties with developing countries in Africa and Asia. Brazil is currently commanding a multinational U.N. stabilization force of some 8,900 police and military personnel in Haiti. Instead of pursuing unilateral prerogatives, Brazilian foreign policy has tended to emphasize regional integration, first through the Common Market of the South (Mercosul) and now the South American Community of Nations. Brazil's role as a leader in South America has recently been challenged by the rise of Hugo Chávez in Venezuela, who has used his country's vast oil wealth to gain influence in the region, particularly in Bolivia and Ecuador.

Since the mid-1990s, Brazil has had much more success in developing political cohesion than true economic integration amongst its neighbors in the Southern Cone. Mercosul was established in 1991 by Brazil, Argentina, Paraguay, and Uruguay. In 1996, Chile and Bolivia became "associate members"; Peru followed in 2003 (not implemented) and Venezuela and Mexico in 2004. Associate members have no voting rights and need not observe the common external tariff. In October 2004, after years of talks, Mercosul and the Andean Community of Nations signed a trade pact, giving all Andean countries — Bolivia, Colombia, Ecuador, Peru, and Venezuela — the equivalent of associate membership. This breakthrough led to the creation of the South American Community of Nations two months later in a pact that included 12 countries (those in Mercosul, the Andean Community, along with Chile, Guyana, and Suriname). In December 2005, Mercosul agreed to the accession of Venezuela as a full member, which some say has added a decidedly anti-American factor to the pact. In

December 2006, Bolivia expressed its intention to join Mercosul as a full member, but critics say that its accession would politicize the union unnecessarily.[25]

Recent events have not boded well for the future of Mercosul. In 2006, the weakness of Mercosul's internal dispute resolution process became apparent as it was unable to resolve a dispute between Argentina and Uruguay over whether to allow European companies to construct two paper mills along the river that demarcates their border. At the same time, Uruguay has diversified its trade with the United States and even threatened to withdraw from Mercosul, arguing that it seems to serve only the needs of Argentina and Brazil. Trade asymmetries among the Mercosul members was left unaddressed at a December 2006 Mercosul summit, but Argentina and Brazil did agree to fund new development projects in Paraguay and Uruguay through the union's Structural Convergence Fund.[26]

In addition to trying to expand its regional profile through established political and economic channels, Brazilian government and business officials have, at times, worked together to expand the country's commercial interests in the region. Petrobras, Brazil's state-owned oil company, has made extensive investments in Bolivia's natural gas sector. Most analysts predicted that since Petrobras produces some 15-20% of Bolivia's GDP, Brazil would be able to exert important economic and political leverage over the new Bolivian government led by populist Evo Morales. Analysts, government officials, and the Brazilian public have criticized President Lula for failing to more vigorously defend Brazil's energy interests in Bolivia after Morales' surprise decision to nationalize his country's natural gas industry on May 1, 2006. Those criticisms escalated after a recent presidential summit in which President Lula acceded to several of President Morales' demands — including cutting tariffs for Bolivian exports to Brazil and stepping up investments in Bolivia — in order to secure an agreement over the price of natural gas.[27] Bolivia's nationalization decision, which has been supported by the Chávez government in Venezuela, may make other sectoral initiatives that have been proposed — including a South American gas pipeline that would carry Venezuela's gas through Brazil to Argentina — less likely to be pursued.

Brazil's political, business, and military ventures are complemented by the country's trade policy. In Brazil, the Ministry of Foreign Relations continues to dominate trade policy, causing the country's commercial interests to be (at times) subsumed by a larger foreign policy goal, namely, enhancing Brazil's influence in Latin America and the world.[28] For example, while concluding meaningful trade agreements with developed economies (such as the United States and the European Union) would probably be beneficial to Brazil's long-term economic self-interest, the Brazilian government has instead prioritized its leadership role within Mercosul and expanded trade ties with countries in Africa, Asia and the Middle East.

Some analysts assert that these "south-south" initiatives have enhanced Brazil's international profile, but others have noted that they have yielded few concrete results for the country, and that they have come at the expense of Brazil-U.S. relations. Roberto Abdenur, the former Brazilian Ambassador to Washington, has recently criticized the "south-south" approach of the Brazilian Foreign Ministry for indoctrinating Brazilian diplomats with "anti-imperialist" and "anti-American" attitudes.[29]

RELATIONS WITH THE UNITED STATES

As a result of its significant political and economic clout, Brazil's leaders have traditionally preferred to cooperate with the United States on specific issues rather than seeking to develop an all-encompassing, privileged relationship with the United States. The United States, in turn, has increasingly regarded Brazil as a stabilizing force and skillful interlocutor in the hemisphere. While the two nations may disagree on trade issues, they agree on the importance of maintaining regional stability and security, fighting terrorism, and combating narcotics, arms, and human trafficking.[30]

Current bilateral relations between the countries are characterized as fairly warm and friendly, despite the differing political approaches of President Lula and President Bush on some issues. On June 20, 2003, President Lula made an official visit to the United States, and he and President Bush resolved "to create a closer and qualitatively stronger [bilateral] relationship." On November 6, 2005, President Bush visited Brasília on his return from the Summit of the Americas in Argentina, and the two leaders reaffirmed the good relations between the countries and pledged to work together to advance peace, democracy, and a successful conclusion of the Doha round of global trade talks. President Bush thanked Brazil for exercising leadership in the world and in the hemisphere, including Brazil's role in the peacekeeping force in Haiti, and worldwide efforts to control HIV/AIDS.[31]

Many analysts believe Brazil-U.S. cooperation may increase during President Lula's second term, particularly on energy issues. Brazilian and U.S. officials are currently discussing an agreement to promote greater ethanol production and use throughout Latin America, the details of which are expected to be announced after two upcoming meetings between President Bush and President Lula. President Bush is scheduled to visit Brazil on March 9, which will be followed by a visit from President Lula to Camp David on March 31.

Brazil is considered a middle-income country and does not receive large amounts of U.S. foreign assistance. In FY2006, Brazil received an estimated allocation of $13.6 million. In FY2007, the Administration requested $19.2 million for Brazil, but actual aid amounts for FY2007 are not yet available. Foreign operations programs are currently operating under the terms of a continuing appropriations resolution (P.L. 109-289, as amended) that provides funding at the FY2006 level with some adjustments. The FY2008 request for Brazil is $3.7 million. The FY2008 request for Brazil is substantially lower than in previous years. The largest cuts appear in counter-narcotics assistance, from $5.9 million in FY2006, to only $1 million in the FY2008 request. However, for the first time in several years, the FY2008 request includes some $200,000 in International Military Education and Training (IMET) for the Brazilian military due to the de-linking of IMET from American Servicemembers' Protection Act (ASPA) sanctions.[32]

SELECTED ISSUES IN U.S.- BRAZIL RELATIONS

The Bush Administration has come to view Brazil as a strong partner whose cooperation must be sought in order to solve regional and global problems. Current issues of concern to both Brazil and the United States include counter-narcotics and terrorism, energy security, trade, environmental issues, human rights, and HIV/AIDS.

Counter-Narcotics and Counter-Terrorism

Brazil is not a significant drug producing country, but is a major conduit for the transit of cocaine, marijuana, and some heroin from neighboring Andean countries destined primarily for Europe, the United States, and local markets. It is the second largest consumer (after the United States) of cocaine in the western hemisphere. The Bush Administration includes Brazil on a list of major drug-producing or drug-transit countries.[33] In FY2006 Brazil received an estimated $5.9 million in U.S. counter-narcotics assistance through the Andean Counterdrug Initiative (ACI). FY2007 ACI funds requested for Brazil totaled $4 million, mainly for interdiction and law enforcement activities. In FY2008, the Administration requested $1 million in ACI funding for Brazil.

In recent years, Brazil has cooperated extensively with neighboring countries in counter-narcotics activities, adopted a new strategy against money laundering, and implemented a law permitting the shooting down of civilian aircraft (with adequate safeguards) suspected of being engaged in the trafficking of illicit narcotics. Brazil has also constructed a $1.4 billion sensor and radar project called the Amazon Vigilance System (SIVAM from its acronym in Portuguese) in an attempt to control illicit activity in its Amazon region. Brazil has offered to share data from this system with neighboring countries and the United States. In 2005, Brazil's federal police, which generally are responsible for about 75% of total Brazilian drug seizures and detentions, captured 15.8 metric tons of cocaine and 126 kilograms of crack cocaine.[34] In May 2006, Brazilian police, participating in a coordinated law enforcement effort run by the U.S. Drug Enforcement Administration, arrested a major Colombian-born drug trafficker accused of smuggling more than 70 tons of cocaine to the United States. These seizures and arrests are likely to increase as Brazil expands it cooperation with neighboring countries by establishing joint intelligence centers.

The U.S. State Department's Country Report on Terrorism covering 2005 notes that Brazil "continues to improve its counterterrorism capabilities." The United States is working with Brazilian officials to combat money laundering and arms trafficking. These efforts include increasing penalties for terrorist financing, particularly in the Tri-Border Area (TBA) of Brazil, Paraguay, and Argentina, and helping Brazilian law enforcement officials set up special units to investigate and prosecute a variety of financial crimes.[35] In December 2006, a U.S. Treasury Department report asserted that terrorist financing is still taking place in the TBA and initiated measures to choke off the assets of two companies and nine individuals in the region that it says are funding Hezbollah. Brazil, along with Argentina and Paraguay, reacted angrily to the report, stating that it "does not provide any new elements ... to affirm the existence of terrorist activities in the region, including the financing of terrorism."[36]

Energy Security

During the 109th Congress, there was significant congressional interest in issues related to energy security. On March 2, 2006, the House International Relations Committee held a subcommittee hearing on energy security in the Western Hemisphere. On June 22, 2006, the Senate Foreign Relations Committee held a full committee hearing on the same topic. Brazil was mentioned at both hearings as a country that has successfully reduced its reliance on foreign oil by using alternative energies. Brazil has also recently attained the ability to produce large amounts of enriched uranium as part of its nuclear energy program.

Ethanol Production

In the past few years, as oil and gas prices have risen, there has been increasing attention in the United States on the importance of decreasing dependence on foreign oil. Brazil stands out as an example of a country that has become a net exporter of energy, partially by increasing its use and production of alternative energy sources, including ethanol. Brazil is the world's largest consumer and producer of ethanol from sugarcane. Its sugar-based ethanol is considered more efficient than U.S. corn-based derivatives.

Brazil's ethanol program began in 1975 but did not become competitive with gasoline until very recently. For decades, before ethanol became competitive with gasoline, the Brazilian government spent billions of dollars on subsidies and tax incentives to keep the struggling ethanol industry afloat. Now, ethanol supplies some 40% of the motor fuel used in Brazil and is extremely competitive with gasoline.

Ethanol use has accelerated since 2003, when automakers introduced "flex fuel" motors in Brazil designed to run on ethanol, gasoline, or a mixture of the two. In 2006, flex-fuel vehicles represented more than 78% of new cars sold in Brazil.[37]

Brazil's experience with ethanol has not been without its share of problems, however. For instance, Brazil has at times had to import large amounts of ethanol when its sugarcane crop has been damaged by drought or simply fallen short of rising demand. In addition, the expansion of sugarcane production has occurred in areas previously used for cattle ranching and accompanying meat production, another important Brazilian export. Finally, human rights groups argue that the increasing demand for sugarcane has put undo pressure on the peasants forced to harvest the sugar under extremely difficult working conditions.[38]

Fuel ethanol consumption in the United States has grown significantly in the past several years, particularly since the establishment of renewable fuel standards in the Energy Policy Act of 2005 (P.L. 109-58). This standard requires U.S. gasoline to contain a minimum amount of renewable fuel, including ethanol. Many observers predict that the United States will have to increase its imports of foreign ethanol this year as U.S. corn-based ethanol producers are unable to keep up with increasing demand.[39]

The United States currently allows duty-free access on sugar-based ethanol imports from many countries through the Caribbean Basin Initiative, Central American Free Trade Agreement, and the Andean Trade Preferences Act, among others.[40] Some Brazilian ethanol is processed at plants in the Caribbean for duty-free entry into the United States, but exports arriving directly from Brazil are currently subject to a 54-cent-per-gallon tax, plus a 2.5% tariff.

In the 109th Congress, legislation was introduced that would have eliminated these two taxes on foreign ethanol: H.R. 5170 (Shadegg) and S. 2760 (Feinstein), the Ethanol Tax Relief Act of 2006. However, in December 2006, Congress voted to extend the taxes on foreign oil through 2009.

Brazil-U.S. Energy Cooperation

Brazilian and U.S. officials are currently formulating a new energy partnership to promote greater ethanol cooperation, production, and use throughout Latin America. The agreement reportedly involves technology-sharing between the United States and Brazil, and with other countries; joint ethanol initiatives; and efforts to develop common ethanol standards throughout the region. It may focus on developing ethanol production in sugar cane-producing countries like Guatemala, Jamaica, and Honduras. If an agreement is reached, Brazil stands to further its goal of developing ethanol into a global traded commodity, while the United States would benefit from having more producers in the region. In addition to these economic benefits, some analysts think an ethanol partnership with Brazil could help improve the U.S. image in Latin America and lessen the influence of oil-rich Hugo Chávez of Venezuela..[41]

Nuclear Energy

Between World War II and the mid-1980s, Brazil sought to develop nuclear weapons as it competed with Argentina for political and military dominance of the Southern Cone. In 1991, Brazil and Argentina reached an agreement to use nuclear energy for peaceful purposes only, although one scientist has recently asserted that the Brazilian military continued nuclear weapons efforts into the early 1990s.[42] Brazil joined the Nuclear Nonproliferation Treaty (NPT) in 1998 and since then has participated in several multilateral nonproliferation regimes, including the Missile Technology Control Regime and the Nuclear Suppliers Group (NSG). It is also a party to the Treaty of Tlatelolco, which establishes Latin America as a nuclear-weapon-free zone. Brazil chaired the May 2006 NSG plenary at which the United States tried to convince other NSG members to adopt an exception to the NSG guidelines to allow increased U.S.-Indian nuclear cooperation. In September 2006, Brazil and South Africa publicly supported India's quest to develop nuclear energy for civil uses.[43]

Despite its nonproliferation credentials, some international observers were concerned when Brazil commissioned a uranium enrichment plant in 2004 to be located at the Resende nuclear facility outside Rio de Janeiro. Uranium enrichment can be used for peaceful purposes (such as fuel for nuclear power plants) or for military purposes (nuclear weapons). In 2005, Brazilian officials refused to give International Atomic Energy Agency (IAEA) inspectors full access to the centrifuge plant, citing security concerns and proprietary aspects of the country's nuclear technology. Negotiations between Brazil and the IAEA ended in October 2005 when the Bush Administration lent its support to Brazil by asserting that limited inspections should be enough for Brazil to comply with its international obligations.[44]

Brazil is now the ninth country in the world capable of enriching uranium to generate energy. Brazil's reluctance to allow international inspectors to fully inspect the Resende facility has caused some observers to wonder whether Brazil's "new enrichment capability ... suggests South America's biggest country may be rethinking its commitment to non-proliferation."[45] Some observers have called for Brazil to abandon its uranium enrichment plans in order to counter such concerns. The Bush Administration, however, considers Brazil to have a fully operational nuclear enrichment capability and should not be required to abandon its uranium enrichment projects.[46] Brazilian officials have rejected the notion that Brazil should be treated like Iran and prohibited from owning sensitive nuclear technology.

Trade Issues

Trade issues are central to the bilateral relationship between Brazil and the United States, with both countries being heavily involved in subregional, regional, and global trade talks. Brazil has sought to strengthen Mercosul and to establish free trade agreements with most of the countries in South America, while also pursuing efforts to negotiate a Mercosul-European Union free trade agreement and to advance the global trade talks through the Doha Development Round. The United States has been actively involved in the Doha negotiations and has pressed for action on the region-wide Free Trade Agreement of the Americas (FTAA), while simultaneously undertaking a series of bilateral or subregional agreements with many hemispheric countries.

World Trade Organization (WTO) Negotiations[47]

The WTO Doha round talks were revived in 2004 after stalling in September 2003 in Cancun, Mexico, when Brazil led the G-20 group of developing countries that insisted that developed countries agree to reduce and eventually eliminate agricultural subsidies as part of any settlement. In late July 2004, WTO members agreed on the framework for a possible Doha round agreement, and negotiators worked throughout the year to achieve preliminary agreements by the Sixth WTO Ministerial Conference in mid-December 2005 in Hong Kong. For most observers, the Hong Kong Conference produced a mixed bag with modest results. In a result that was disappointing to Brazil, the ministers, bowing to the demands of the European Union, delayed the elimination of agricultural export subsidies until 2013 (not 2010), although subsidies for cotton were to be eliminated by 2006. In a result that was disappointing to the United States, formulas for reducing tariff barriers in the manufactured goods and service sectors were largely postponed.[48]

Deadlines were established in Hong Kong for concluding negotiations by the end of 2006, but the talks were suspended indefinitely in July 2006 after key negotiating groups failed to break a deadlock on agricultural tariffs and subsidies.

The EU blamed the United States for not improving its offer of domestic support, while the United States responded that no new offers were put forward by the EU or the G-20 to make an improved offer possible. Because of the negotiating stalemate, it is considered unlikely that any agreement can be reached in time for consideration before U.S. trade promotion authority (TPA) expires on July 1, 2007.

Free Trade Area of the Americas (FTAA)

In 1994, 34 countries in the Western Hemisphere announced a plan for creating a Free Trade Area of the Americas (FTAA) at the first Summit of the Americas. Twelve years later, the FTAA has yet to be established, and negotiations for its creation have been put off indefinitely, primarily due to differences of opinion between the United States and Brazil, co-chairs of the FTAA Trade Negotiation Committee.[49]

Brazil asserts that the FTAA must include measures to curtail agricultural subsidies and to reduce the use of anti-dumping and countervailing duties, while the United States emphasizes investment and intellectual property rights and argues that agricultural subsidy issues should be resolved in the Doha round of WTO talks. Disagreements on the terms of the FTAA came to a head in the November 2003 Ministerial Meeting in Miami, Florida, where the parties finally agreed on a formula dubbed by some an "FTAA light." Under the formula, all of the countries would agree to a set of core obligations, while countries which favored a more ambitious agreement would negotiate plurilateral agreements. When the Trade Negotiations Committee (TNC) met in Puebla, Mexico, in early February 2004, the delegates were unable to agree on the FTAA common obligations, and continuing disagreements between the co-chairs, and involvement in other negotiations have prevented further meetings. A U.S. effort, in early November 2005 at the fourth Summit of the Americas in Mar del Plata, Argentina, to set a date for new FTAA negotiations was resisted by Venezuela and Mercosul countries, who argued that such talks should be put off until progress is made on agricultural subsidy issues in the global WTO Doha round talks.

Trade Disputes
Brazil won a WTO dispute settlement case against U.S. cotton subsidies in September 2004, which the United States appealed, but Brazil's position was reaffirmed by the WTO appellate body in March 2005. In keeping with the requirement that the United States modify its policies or negotiate a mutually satisfactory settlement with Brazil, the Bush Administration in early July 2005 asked Congress to modify the cotton subsidy program and Brazil agreed to temporarily suspend retaliatory action.[50]

Human Rights

The U.S. State Department's Country Report on Human Rights on Brazil covering 2005 states that while "the federal government generally respected human rights of its citizens ... there continued to be numerous, serious abuses, and the record of several state [and municipal] governments was poor." Three human rights issues of particular concern include crime and human rights abuses by police in Brazil, race and discrimination, and trafficking in persons.

Violent Crime and Human Rights Abuses by Police
Most observers agree that the related problems of urban crime, drugs, and violence, on the one hand, and corruption and brutality in law enforcement and prisons, on the other, are threatening citizens' security in Brazil. Five Brazilian cities are among the fifteen cities in Latin America, the world's most violent region, with the highest murder rates.[51] Crime is most rampant in the urban shanty towns (*favelas*) in Rio de Janeiro and São Paulo. In addition to rising crime rates, human rights groups have identified extrajudicial killings by police and prison authorities as Brazil's most pressing human rights problem.[52] Prison conditions range from "poor to extremely harsh and life threatening," and the countrywide prison system, which housed more than 361,000 inmates in 2005, had an accommodation deficit of some 90,360.[53]

The current weaknesses in Brazil's criminal justice system have become dramatically apparent in the past year as gangs have launched violent attacks that have destabilized the cities of São Paulo and Rio de Janeiro. In mid-May 2006, street combat and rioting organized by a prison-based gang network, the First Capital Command (PCC), paralyzed the city of São Paulo for several days. Formed in 1993 to protest the country's poor prison conditions, the PCC now has at least 6,000 dues-paying members and reportedly exerts control over more than 140,000 prisoners in the São Paulo prison system.[54] Officially, the violent gang attacks, which were followed by police reprisals, resulted in at least 186 deaths. Although state officials have denied that negotiations occurred, Brazilian press accounts reported that the violence did not end until a high-level truce was reached between state officials and gang leaders. The PCC launched further attacks in July and August 2006, which resulted in 19 deaths. Brazilian police have been criticized for the brutal manner in which they responded to the gang violence.[55]

Violence in Rio de Janeiro has traditionally been linked to turf wars being waged between rival drug gangs for control of the city's drug industry or to clashes between drug gangs and police officials. In late December 2006, drug gangs torched buses and attacked police stations in Rio de Janeiro, leaving some 25 dead. Recent clashes have also involved vigilante militias, composed of off-duty police and prison guards, which are now charging citizens to "protect" them from the drug gangs. Rio officials have identified the militias as criminal groups but have thus far been unable to contain them.[56]

Many analysts have placed the blame for the recent attacks on Brazilian politicians at all levels of government, who they say have failed to devote the resources and political will necessary to confront the country's serious public security problems. In particular, they maintain that there has been a lack of coordination between federal, state, and local officials, and that political calculations have often prevented state governments, which have been largely ineffective in responding to the recent violence, from seeking much-needed assistance from the federal government. Most Brazilians hope that the recent attacks in Rio will spur the country's politicians to address delinquency quickly and effectively. President Lula did not launch any major anti-crime initiatives during his first term but has pledged to address crime in a firm manner during his second mandate, while continuing to tackle poverty and drugs, root causes of violence. He has recently increased spending on public security and sent federal troops to help secure Rio de Janeiro. In response to the May riots in São Paulo, the Brazilian Senate passed 11 emergency measures to combat violent crime and improve prison security, some of which are now being considered under fast-track procedures by Brazil's Chamber of Deputies.[57]

Race and Discrimination[58]

People of African descent in Brazil, also known as Afro-Brazilians, represent 45% of the country's population, but constitute 64% of the poor and 69% of the extreme poor.[59] During the Cardoso administration, the Brazilian government began to collect better official statistics on Afro-Brazilians. These statistics found significant education, health, and wage disparities between Afro-Brazilians and Brazil's general population. Successive State Department Human Rights Reports covering Brazil in the late 1990s reported frequent discrimination against Afro-Brazilians, including abuse by police officials, and a limited access to justice. These findings and other evidence challenged the notion that Brazil was a "racial democracy,"[60] and confirmed the perception that specific public policies were needed to improve the socioeconomic status of Afro-Brazilians.

Brazil now has the most extensive anti-discrimination legislation geared towards Afro-descendants of any country in Latin America. In 2001, Brazil became the first Latin American country to endorse quotas in order to increase minority representation in government service. Since 2002, several state universities in Brazil have enacted quotas setting aside admission slots for black students. Although most Brazilians favor government programs to combat social exclusion, they disagree as to whether the beneficiaries of affirmative action programs should be selected on the basis of race or income.[61] In 2003, Brazil became the first country in the world to establish a Special Secretariat with a ministerial rank to manage Racial Equity Promotion Policies. Afro-Brazilian activists, while acknowledging recent government efforts on behalf of Afro-descendants, have noted that most universities have preferred not to implement quota systems, and that the Special Secretariat lacks the funding, staff, and clout necessary to advance its initiatives.[62] Despite these limitations, Brazil has taken a leadership role in advancing issues of race and discrimination within the Organization of American States, where it is leading the drafting of an Inter-American Convention for the Prevention of Racism and All Forms of Discrimination and Intolerance.

Trafficking in Persons[63]

Brazil is a source, transit, and destination country for people, especially women and children, trafficked for forced labor or sexual exploitation. In the State Department's *Trafficking in Persons (TIP) report, June 2006,* Brazil was listed as a Tier 2 Watch List country. In the report, the Brazilian government was cited for making only limited progress in bringing traffickers to justice and for failing to apply effective penalties for those who exploit forced labor. In its 2006 Interim Trafficking Assessment to Congress, the State Department says that Brazil has made "minimal progress" in addressing trafficking since the release of the 2006 report. It urges the Brazilian government to pass comprehensive anti-trafficking legislation and to arrest and convict more traffickers.[64]

In Brazil, more than 25,000 people have been recruited from small towns in the northeast to labor in the country's agribusiness industry.[65] Since 2003, the Brazilian government has adopted stronger penalties to punish employers caught using slave labor. It has strengthened the Special Mobile Inspection Group of inspectors within the labor ministry, which has reportedly freed some 20,000 individuals from slavery during the past decade. In 2005, the ILO cited Brazil as a positive example of a country that has made a concerted effort to combat forced labor. Despite its efforts, a recent investigation alleges that some 1,000 charcoal-making camps in the Brazilian Amazon are using slave labor to produce pig iron, a key ingredient of steel.[66]

Brazil has worked closely with U.S. officials and representatives from several different international organizations to improve its anti-trafficking programs. In July 2004, President Bush announced that Brazil was one of eight countries selected to receive $50 million in strategic anti-trafficking-in-persons assistance. Some $8.2 million in funds have been approved by the Senior Policy Operating Group (SPOG) on trafficking for Brazil. These funds support programs to prevent labor trafficking in the Southern Amazon; shelters for sex tourism victims in Rio de Janeiro, Recife, and São Paulo; reintegration and border shelters in the Tri-border region (Brazil, Paraguay, and Argentina); and strengthening mobile law-enforcement teams to fight forced labor in the interior, as well as training judges and prosecutors. The funds are supporting public awareness campaigns to deter American and other foreign travelers from engaging in child sex tourism in Brazil.

In FY2005, U.S. support helped the Brazilian government provide a variety of legal and social services to more than 1,000 trafficking victims. In addition, more than 6,530 government and NGO representatives received training on how to improve assistance to trafficking victims. Finally, Brazil, with USAID support, revised its penal code to make internal and transborder trafficking for commercial sexual exploitation federal crimes with similar penalties, and eliminated language that made the previous law applicable strictly to cases involving female victims. The legislative changes did not include provisions addressing trafficking for forced labor, which is also a major problem in Brazil.

HIV/AIDS

Successive governments in Brazil have made the fight against the spread of HIV/AIDS a national priority. In 1985, Brazil's national AIDS program began within the context of the country's transition to democracy as a result of activism from Brazilian civil society. Initially focused on disease prevention, Brazil's HIV/AIDS program expanded to providing antiretroviral (ART) drugs on a limited basis by 1991, and then to all people living with the disease by 1996. Currently some 172,000 Brazilians have access to free generic versions of ART drugs, some of which are locally produced and financed by the Brazilian government. The incidence of HIV/AIDS in Brazil has stabilized since 1997, and universal free access to ART has increased average survival times from 18 months for those diagnosed in 1995, to 58 months for those diagnosed in 1996.[67] HIV prevalence has been stable at .5% for the general population in Brazil since 2000, so most government prevention efforts are now targeted at high-risk groups where prevalence rates are still above 5%.

Brazil's decision to develop generic ART drugs to treat HIV/AIDS under the compulsory licensing provision of its patent law led to a subsequent 80% drop in the cost of treatment there. That decision brought Brazil into conflict with the United States and the international pharmaceutical industry. In May 2001, the United States submitted a complaint to the WTO, which was later withdrawn, that Brazil's practices violated the Trade-Related Aspects of Intellectual Property Rights (TRIPS) agreement and prevented companies from developing new products there. While the pharmaceutical industry argued that TRIPS was an essential tool to protect intellectual property rights, developing countries (like Brazil) countered that TRIPS inhibited their ability to fight public health emergencies in a cost-effective manner. In August 2003, a WTO decision temporarily waived part of the TRIPS rules to allow the export of generic drugs to countries confronting a grave public health challenge (such as HIV/AIDS, tuberculosis, or malaria). That temporary waiver became permanent in late 2005.[68]

Brazil currently manufactures older ART drugs both for domestic consumption and for export to several African countries but has to import newer medicines. According to Brazil's ministry of health, tough negotiations with pharmaceutical companies have resulted in $1.1 billion savings for the country's HIV/AIDS program. Despite that savings, Brazil's ART program costs have escalated in recent years, prompting some advocates to urge the government to issue compulsory licenses that would enable Brazil to make generic versions of new, brand name drugs without the patent holder's consent. The Lula government has thus far resisted licensing, reportedly fearing reprisals from the pharmaceutical companies and retaliatory trade sanctions from the U.S. government.[69]

Brazil and the United States have disagreed as to whether prostitutes should be enlisted to help combat the spread of HIV/AIDS. In 2003, Congress passed an amendment to H.R. 1298 (P.L. 108-25), which authorizes the President's Emergency Plan for AIDS Relief (PEPFAR), prohibiting U.S. funds from being distributed to any group or organization that does not have a policy "explicitly opposing prostitution and sex trafficking." Brazil has rejected U.S. support for its HIV/AIDS programs because it is opposed to the new restrictions. That decision cost Brazil some $48 million in USAID funding for HIV/AIDS programs.[70]

Environmental Concerns

Amazon Deforestation

The Amazon Basin contains over half of the world's remaining tropical rainforests and is the most biodiverse tract of tropical rainforest in the world. Some 22% of the world's known plant species exist in Brazil and 20% of the world's fresh water lies in the Amazon basin. The Amazon is also thought to be home to one third of all species in the world, including some 2.5 million types of insects, and 2,000 types of birds and mammals. Further, the Amazon rainforest is a sink for global carbon dioxide, and is considered by many to be an important asset in moderating climate change. Proper management of Brazil's portion of the Amazon rainforest holds global significance.

Throughout the last forty years, the Brazilian Amazon has been increasingly deforested for development that includes roads, settlements, logging, subsistence and commercial agriculture, as well as cattle ranching. In 1960, the Amazon was largely undeveloped, but today approximately 15%-20% of the rainforest has been deforested. Deforestation threatens the biodiversity of the Amazon region and is a concern for climate change. In the 1980s, some predicted that deforestation would decline if the Brazilian government stopped providing tax incentives and credit subsidies to settlers and agricultural producers. Those predictions have not borne out, however, as the complex and often interrelated causes of deforestation have multiplied rather than decreased.[71] Between 1990 and 2000, Brazil lost an area of rainforest twice the size of Portugal. Deforestation rates, which have been fueled by increases in cattle ranching, soybean farming, and road building, spiked in 2002 and 2004 (reaching the second-highest level ever) before declining by 32% in 2005 and another 11% in 2006.[72]

The Brazilian government attributes the recent decline in the deforestation rate to its creation of new conservation areas and stricter enforcement of environmental regulations. The Lula government created some 7 million hectares of new conservation reserves in 2004 and 2005. It also launched a special operation to combat deforestation and illegal logging that resulted in the arrest of more than 100 people between June 2005 and January 2006. In March 2006, President Lula signed the Public Forest Management Law, which is set to take effect this year, that aims to decrease illegal logging by allowing companies access to 3% of the Amazon on the condition that they carry out sustainable operations. Although some environmental groups have praised this progress, others fear that it may be too little too late.

Skeptics assert that the declining deforestation rates recorded for the past two years did not occur because of any government initiatives but because declining soybean prices coupled with the strengthening of Brazil's currency made it less profitable to clear the forests.[73]

In order to combat further deforestation, most observers agree that cooperative efforts will have to be made between the Brazilian government, private companies, landowners, and the international community (including the United States). These efforts might include funding to pay farmers not to exploit the environment, conservation projects, and environmental certification of commodities such as beef, timber, and soybeans. Coordinated efforts could significantly reduce carbon emissions and the loss of Amazon diversity that is otherwise likely to occur.[74]

USAID environment programs directly support the U.S.-Brazil Common Agenda for the Environment. USAID environment programs seek to promote proper land-use trends over large geographic areas while encouraging environmentally-friendly income generation activities for the rural poor. The FY2005 allocation for USAID environmental programs in

Brazil was $6.1 million, and the FY2006 was $5.1 million. USAID also initiated the Amazon Basin Conservation Initiative in FY2006. From FY2006-FY2011, USAID plans to make an initial investment of US $50 million to support community groups, governments, and public and private organizations working in Brazil and other countries in the Amazon Basin in their efforts to conserve the Amazon's globally important biodiversity.[75]

Land Conflicts

A related development challenge for Brazil that has caught the attention of both environmentalists and human rights groups in the United States has been how to allow the country's agribusinesses to expand while simultaneously protecting the environment and providing land to millions of landless peasants. In Brazil, 1% of the population controls 45% of the farmland. While close to half of Brazil's fertile land is used for cattle ranching, nearly one third lies uncultivated.[76] In the 1980s, landless rural workers in the south of Brazil began to organize in order to demand land redistribution. By 2004, the most powerful landless organization, the Landless Workers' Movement (MST), claimed some 1.5 million affiliates nationwide and was capable of skillfully organizing mass demonstrations and land invasions to pressure the Brazilian government to fulfill its promises of land distribution. As the MST became more mobilized throughout the 1990s, land disputes between loggers, ranchers, and peasants increased, and dealing with land reform and land invasions became a major challenge for the Cardoso government.[77]

In 2002, partially because of overlapping membership and good relations at the local level between MST and PT leaders, landless leaders backed the Lula da Silva presidential campaign in hopes that he would pursue more effective agrarian reform policies than President Cardoso did. In fact, during his first two years in office, President Lula da Silva spent 24% less on land reform than the Cardoso administration had in the previous two years. The Lula government has recently reported that it resettled 381,419 families between 2003 and 2006, just short of its 400,000 target, but landless associations have disputed that figure. Moreover, the government has acknowledged that the number of peasants waiting in temporary camps to be resettled has increased from 60,000 in 2003 to 171,000 in 2006. Resettlements may have contributed to an increasing number of land conflicts between peasants, farmers, and land speculators, which peaked in 2005 when 1,900 land conflicts occurred. Some 38 people were thought to be murdered in 2005 as a result of struggles over land.[78]

According to the Catholic Church's Pastoral Land Commision (PLC), Pará, a rural state in the isolated Amazon region, has long been at the epicenter of land disputes between peasants, farmers, and land speculators. Some 40% of the 1,237 land-related killings in Brazil between 1985 and 2001 took place there. The February 2005 murder in Pará of U.S. missionary and landless activist, Dorothy Stang, brought increasing national and international attention to Brazil's land distribution problem.[79] The conviction of three suspects in connection with Sister Stang's death has led some observers to hope that more perpetrators of land-related crimes in Pará may finally be brought to justice. Some 750 land activists have died there in the last 30 years, but only nine killers have been convicted for those deaths.[80] Some assert that Sister Stang's death prompted the Brazilian government to enact several aggressive measures that resulted in recent reductions in Amazon deforestation in Brazil. International environmental groups and human rights organizations have increased scrutiny on the Lula government's handling of the related problems of promoting sustainable development in the Amazon and providing land to the country's thousands of landless peasants.

Source: Map Resources. Adapted by CRS. (K.Yancey 11/28/05).

Figure 1. Map of Brazil.

REFERENCES

[1] Brazil has never had a large indigenous population. Today Brazil's indigenous population consists of roughly 400,000 persons (0.9% of the country's population), many of whom reside in the Amazon. U.S. Department of State, *Country Reports on Human Rights Practices 2005: Brazil*, February 2006.

[2] Lincoln Gordon, *Brazil's Second Change En Route Toward the First World*, Washington, D.C.: The Century Foundation, 2001; Iêda Siqueira Wiarda, "Brazil: The

Politics of A New Order and Progress," in *Latin American Politics and Development*, Howard J. Wiarda and Harvey F. Kline, eds., Boulder, CO: Westview Press, 2000.

[3]   For a historical overview of Brazil's political development, see Bolivar Lamounier, "Brazil: Inequality Against Democracy," in Larry Diamond, Jonathan Hughes, Juan J. Linz, and Seymour Martin Lipset, eds., *Democracy in Developing Countries: Latin America,* Boulder, CO: Lynne Reiner, 1999.

[4]   Mercosul is the Portuguese variation of the more widely seen Spanish acronym, Mercosur. It is a common market composed of Brazil, Argentina, Paraguay, and Uruguay that was established in 1991.

[5]   Susan Kaufman Purcell and Riordan Roett, eds., *Brazil Under Cardoso*, Boulder, CO: Lynne Reiner Publishers, 1997; Mauricio A. Font and Anthony Peter Spanakos, *Reforming Brazil*, New York: Lexington Books, 2004;

[6]   Wendy Hunter and Timothy J. Power, "The Lula Government at Mid-Term: Shaping a Third Decade of Democracy in Brazil," *Journal of Democracy*, July 2005.

[7]   Anthony Hall, "From *Fome Zero* to *Bolsa Familia*: Social Policies and Poverty Alleviation Under Lula," *Journal of Latin American Studies*, vol. 38, November 2006.

[8]   Jeffrey Cason, "Hopes Dashed? Lula's Brazil," *Current History*, February 2006.

[9]   Barry Ames, *The Deadlock of Democracy in Brazil*, Ann Arbor, MI: University of Michigan Press, 2001.

[10]   Wendy Hunter, "The Normalization of An Anomaly: The Worker's Party in Brazil," Paper Presented at the Latin American Studies Association Conference, San Juan, Puerto Rico, March 2006.

[11]   "Leadership Contests Cast Doubt on New Legislature," *Latin American Brazil and Southern Cone Report*, January 2007.

[12]   "Voters Rebuff of Lula Shows Impact of Scandals," *Miami Herald*, October 3, 2006.

[13]   Matt Moffett and Geraldo Samor, "In Brazil Campaign, A Barroom Brawl and a Class War," *Wall Street Journal*, October 27, 2006; Wendy Hunter and Timothy J. Power, "Rewarding Lula: Executive Power, Social Policy, and the Brazilian Elections of 2006," *Latin American Politics and Society*, (forthcoming)

[14]   "Country Report: Brazil," *Economist Intelligence Unit*, January 2007; "Brazil Tones Down Leadership Ambitions," *Latin News Weekly Report*, November 7, 2006.

[15]   "Brazil Foreign Debt at $168.9 Billion End-2006," *Latin America News Digest*, January 26, 2007.

[16]   Sources: Brazilian Ministry of Development, Industry, and Foreign Trade, U.S. Department of Agriculture's Foreign Agriculture Service, United Nation's Food and Agriculture Organization. Sources elaborated by Marcos Jank, Institute for International Trade Negotiations, São Paulo, Brazil.

[17]   "Preliminary Overview of the Economies of Latin America and the Caribbean 2006," U.N. Economic Commission for Latin America and the Caribbean, December 2006.

[18]   "Brazil: Expansive Mood," *EIU Business Latin America,* January 29, 2007; "Stirred, But Not Shaken Up," *Economist*, January 25, 2007; Jonathan Wheatley and Richard Lapper, "Left Turn Ahead? How Lula's Plan Could Condemn Brazil to Mediocrity," *Financial Times*, February 21, 2007.

[19]   David De Ferranti et al., *Inequality in Latin America: Breaking with History?* Washington, DC: The World Bank, 2004.

[20] "Special Report: Land Report Dilemma," *Latin America Regional Report*, December 21, 2004.

[21] Ricard Henriques, "Desigualdade racial no Brasil," Brasilia: *Instituto de Pesquisa Econômica Aplicada (IPEA)*, 2001.

[22] "Economic Survey of Brazil 2005,"*Organization for Economic Cooperation and Development*, March 2005.

[23] Hall, "From *Fome Zero* to *Bolsa Familia,"* November 2006.

[24] Georges D. Landau, "The Decisionmaking Process in Foreign Policy: The Case of Brazil," *Center for Strategic and International Studies*: Washington, DC: March 2003.

[25] See CRS Report RL33620, *Mercosur: Evolution and Implications for U.S. Trade Policy*, by J.F. Hornbeck; "Disappointing Summit Fails to Address Mercosur Schism," *Latin American Brazil and Southern Cone Report*, January 2007.

[26] Ibid.

[27] Andres Oppenheimer, "Powerful Brazil is Becoming an Encircled Giant," *Miami Herald*, May 14, 2006; "Bolivia's Populism Steps on Brazil," *Christian Science Monitor*, May 8, 2006; "Brazil May Pay a Price for Generous Deal on Gas," *Financial Times*, February 22, 2007.

[28] See CRS Report RL33258, *Brazilian Trade Policy and the United States*, by J.F. Hornbeck.

[29] Otávio Cabral, "Nem na Ditadura,"*Veja*, February 7, 2007.

[30] Peter Hakim, "The Reluctant Partner," *Foreign Affairs*, Jan/Feb 2004; Carlos Eduardo Lins, "La Casa Blanca y El Planalto: Respeto y Solidaridad," *Foreign Affairs En Español*, January-March 2003.

[31] See "President Bush Meets with President Lula of Brazil" and "Joint Statement on the Visit by President George W. Bush to Brazil," November 6, 2005, on the White House website.

[32] For more information on ASPA sanctions, see CRS Report RL33337, *Article 98 Agreements and Sanctions on U.S. Foreign Aid to Latin America*, by Clare M. Ribando.

[33] "Bush Cites 20 Nations as Major Drug-Transit/Producer Countries," September 15, 2005, U.S. Department of State, Washington File, [http://usinfo.state.gov].

[34] U.S. Department of State, *International Narcotics Control Strategy Report*, March 2006.

[35] For more information, see CRS Report RS21049, *Latin America: Terrorism Issues,* by Mark P. Sullivan.

[36] "Treasury Targets Hezbollah Fundraising Network in the Tri-Border Region," December 6, 2006, [http://www.ustreas.gov/press/releases/hp190.htm]; "Brazil: America's Triple Border Area Under Constant Watch," *Dow Jones Commodity Service*, February 8, 2007.

[37] See David Sandalow, "Ethanol: Lessons from Brazil," *Brookings Institution*, May 2006; "Brazil: Racing Cars," *EIU - Business Latin America*, January 22, 2007.

[38] "With Big Boost From Sugar Cane, Brazil is Satisfying Its Fuel Needs,"*New York Times*, April 10, 2006.

[39] "Commodities Corner: The Rush for Ethanol," *Barron's*, May 1, 2006.

[40] For more information, see CRS Report RS21930, *Ethanol Imports and the Caribbean Basin Initiative*, by Brent D. Yacobucci.

[41] Andres Oppenheimer, "Some Success Predicted in U.S. Courting of Brazil," *Miami Herald*, February 22, 2007; Monte Reel, "U.S. Seeks Partnership with Brazil on Ethanol; Countering Oil-Rich Venezuela is Part of Aim," *Washington Post*, February 8, 2007; "U.S.-Brazil Ethanol Diplomacy Seen Aiding U.S. Influence in Latin America," *Dow Jones Commodities Service*, February 9, 2007.

[42] "Brazil Nearly Built Bomb in 1990s, Scientist Says," *Associated Press*, August 30, 2005.

[43] "Brazil, South Africa Boost India's Quest for Civilian Energy," *Organization of Asia-Pacific News Agencies*, September 14, 2006.

[44] "New Round of Nuclear Enrichment Scare Stories," *Latin American Weekly Report*, February 12, 2006.

[45] "Brazil's Enrichment Program Overshadowed by Iran's: Could Produce Nuclear Weapons," *Montreal Gazette*, April 24, 2006.

[46] Bernard Aronson, "Brazil's Chance to Lead on Nuclear Containment," *Wall Street Journal*, March 18, 2005; Sharon Squassoni and David Fite, "Brazil as Litmus Test: Resende and Restrictions on Uranium Enrichment," *Arms Control Today*, October 2005.

[47] For more information, see CRS Report RL32060, *World Trade Organization Negotiations: The Doha Development Agenda*, by Ian. F. Fergusson.

[48] See "WTO Ministerial Agrees on Setting Course for Final Stage of Talks; Some Disappointed," *International Trade Reporter*, December 22, 2005.

[49] For more information, see CRS Report RS20864, *A Free Trade Area of the Americas: Major Policy Issues and Status of Negotiations*, by J.F. Hornbeck.

[50] See "USDA Calls for Repeal of Cotton Subsidy to Achieve WTO Compliance," *Inside U.S. Trade*, July 8, 2005. For more information, see CRS Report RL32571, *Background on the U.S.-Brazil WTO Cotton Subsidy Dispute*, by Randy Schnepf.

[51] William C. Prillaman, "Crime, Democracy, and Development in Latin America," *Center for Strategic and International Studies*, June 2003.

[52] Brazilian authorities report that, partially in response to violent gang attacks, São Paulo state police killed 533 alleged criminals in 2006 compared to 300 in 2005. See "Police Killings of Suspects Up in Brazil," *Associated Press*, February 1, 2007. President Lula has taken some steps to combat police brutality in Brazil.

[53] U.S. Department of State, *Country Reports on Human Rights Practices 2005: Brazil*, February 2006.

[54] Stephen Hanson, "Brazil's Powerful Prison Gang," *Council on Foreign Relations*, September 26, 2006.

[55] "Brazil: Battle of São Paulo Leaves a Disquieting Balance," *Latin American Weekly Report*, May 23, 2006; "Police are Criticized in Wave of Gang Violence in Brazil," *New York Times*, May 30, 2006; "Attacks in São Paulo Prompt Fears of Renewed Gang Offensive," *EFE*, February 7. 2007.

[56] "Troops Alone Will Not Solve State of Violence," *Latin American Brazil and Southern Cone Report*, January 2007; "Brazilian Slums Face a New Problem: Vigilante Militias," *Christian Science Monitor*, February 8, 2007.

[57] "Troops Alone Will Not Solve State of Violence," *Latin American Brazil and Southern Cone Report*, January 2007; "Brazil: Child's Violent Death Spurs Congress Into Action," *Latin News Weekly Report*, February 15, 2007.

[58] For more information, see CRS Report RL32713, *Afro-Latinos in Latin America and Considerations for U.S. Policy*, by Clare Ribando.

[59] Ricard Henriques, "Desigualdade racial no Brasil," Brasilia: Instituto de Pesquisa Econômica Aplicada (IPEA), 2001

[60] Racial democracy attributes the different conditions under which blacks and whites or mestizos live in Latin America to class differences, not racial discrimination. See Robert J. Cottrol, "The Long Lingering Shadow," *Tulane Law Review*, 2001.

[61] Livio Sansone, "Anti-Racism in Brazil," *NACLA Report on the Americas*, September 1, 2004.

[62] Dayanne Mikevis and Matthew Flynn, "Brazil's Civil Rights Activists Achieving Overdue Policy Reform," *Citizen Action in the Americas*, No. 17, April 2005.

[63] For more information, see CRS Report RL33200, *Trafficking in Persons in Latin America and the Caribbean*, by Clare M. Ribando.

[64] U.S. Department of State, *Trafficking in Persons Report, 2006,* June 5, 2006, [http://www.state.gov/g/tip/rls/tiprpt/2006/65983.htm]. Trafficking in Persons Interim Assessment, [http://www.state.gov/g/tip/rls/rpt/78948.htm].

[65] TIP Report, 2006, [http://www.state.gov/g/tip/rls/tiprpt/2006/].

[66] "A Global Alliance Against Forced Labor," ILO, 2005; Michael Smith and David Voreacos, "The Secret World of Modern Slavery," *Bloomberg Markets*, December 2006.

[67] Daniel R. Hogan and Joshua A. Salomon, "Prevention and Treatment of HIV/AIDS in Resource-Limited Settings," *World Health Organization*, February 2005.

[68] Mary Anastasia O'Grady*, Wall Street Journal*, December 16, 2005.

[69] "Drug Costs Imperil AIDS Fight," *Boston Globe*, January 3, 2007; "World Looking to Brazil for Answers," *Toronto Star*, August 5, 2006.

[70] Monte Reel, "Where Prostitutes Also Fight AIDS," *Washington Post*, March 2, 2006.

[71] David Kaimowitz, "Amazon Deforestation Revisited," *Latin American Research Review*, 2002: 37, 2.

[72] Some have suggested that access to pristine tracts of rainforests through roads is the primary driver of deforestation in the Amazon. Regional roads constructed by the government, as well as local roads created by logging operations, provide access to forested areas. Using these roads, farmers clear remaining forests and practice slash and burn agriculture until the land loses much of its soil fertility and it becomes more profitable to move to other forested tracts rather than resuscitate their existing lands. After agriculture, pastures grasses are generally planted and cattle are raised. Eventually, cattle grazing and cyclical burning (either accidental or induced) will alter the ecosystem sufficiently that forests cannot regenerate.

[73] "Brazil Gambles on Amazon Logging," *Chicago Tribune*, January 15, 2007.

[74] Soares-Filho et al., "Modelling Conservation in the Amazon Basin," *Nature*, March 2006.

[75] See [http://www.usaid.gov/locations/latin_america_caribbean/ environment/ abci.html] for more information, accessed February 20, 2007.

[76] "Special Report: Land Report Dillemma," *Latin America Regional Report*, December 21, 2004.

[77] Miguel Carter, "The Landless Workers' Movement (MST) and Democracy in Brazil," *Center for Brazilian Studies, University of Oxford*, 2005.

[78] "Brazilians Wonder: Where's the Reform?" *Christian Science Monitor*, March 22, 2006; "Brazil: Official Statistics at Odds with Landless Figures," *Latinnews Daily*, February 1, 2007; "Waiting for Land on the Fringes," *Fort-Worth Star-Telegram*, December 10, 2006; "Rural Violence at Record Levels in Brazil," *BBC Monitoring Americas*, April 20, 2006.

[79] "Brazil: A Nun's Murder Triggers Action Against Landgrabbers," *Latin News Weekly Report*, February 22, 2005; "Human Rights Violations in the Amazon: Conflict and Violence in the State of Pará," *CommisSão Pastoral da Terra, Global Justice, and Terra de Direitos*, November 2005.

[80] "Third Man Jailed for U.S. Nun Death," *BBC News Online*, April 27, 2006.

In: Brazil in Focus: Economic, Political and Social Issues   ISBN: 978-1-60456-165-4
Editor: Jorge T. Almeida, pp. 27-44   © 2008 Nova Science Publishers, Inc.

Chapter 2

BACKGROUND ON THE U.S.-BRAZIL WTO COTTON SUBSIDY DISPUTE[*]

Randy Schnepf

ABSTRACT

In late 2002, Brazil initiated a World Trade Organization (WTO) dispute settlement case (DS267) against specific provisions of the U.S. cotton program. On September 8, 2004, a WTO dispute settlement (DS) panel ruled against the United States on several key issues in case DS267. On October 18, 2004, the United States appealed the case to the WTO's Appellate Body (AB) which, on March 3, 2005, confirmed the earlier DS panel findings against U.S. cotton programs.

Key findings include the following: (1) U.S. domestic cotton subsidies have exceeded WTO commitments of the 1992 benchmark year, thereby losing the protection afforded by the "Peace Clause," which shielded them from substantive challenges; (2) the two major types of direct payments made under U.S. farm programs — Production Flexibility Contract payments of the 1996 Farm Act and the Direct Payments of the 2002 Farm Act — do not qualify for WTO exemptions from reduction commitments as fully decoupled income support and should therefore count against the "Peace Clause" limits; (3) Step-2 program payments are prohibited subsidies; (4) U.S. export credit guarantees are effectively export subsidies, making them subject to previously notified export subsidy commitments; and (5) U.S. domestic support measures that are "contingent on market prices" have resulted in excess cotton production and exports that, in turn, have caused low international prices and have resulted in "serious prejudice" to Brazil.

What happens next? On March 21, 2005, the AB and panel reports were adopted by the WTO membership, initiating a sequence of events, under WTO dispute settlement rules, whereby the United States will bring its policies into line with the panel's recommendations or negotiate a mutually acceptable settlement with Brazil. First, the panel recommended that all "prohibited" U.S. export subsidies (i.e., Step 2 payments and exports of unscheduled commodities — including cotton —made with GSM export credit guarantees) must be withdrawn by July 1, 2005. Second, as concerns a ruling on "actionable" subsidies under a finding of serious prejudice caused by "price contingent" subsidies (e.g., loan deficiency payments, marketing loss assistance payments, counter-

---

[*] Excerpted from CRS Report RL32571, dated July 11, 2005.

cyclical payments, and Step-2 payments), the United States is under an obligation to "take appropriate steps to remove the adverse effects or withdraw the subsidy."

It is noteworthy that the panel finding that U.S. direct payments do not qualify for WTO exemptions from reduction commitments as fully decoupled income support (i.e., they are not green box compliant) appears to have no further consequences within the context of this case and does not involve any compliance measures. This is because direct payments were deemed "non-price contingent" and were evaluated strictly in terms of the Peace Clause violation.

BACKGROUND ON THE U.S. COTTON SECTOR

The cotton industry is a major component of the U.S. agricultural sector. From 1997 to 2002, U.S. cash receipts from cotton production averaged $4.6 billion per year, while export sales averaged over $2.1 billion. Cotton is grown across the southern tier of states stretching from Virginia down through the Carolinas and into Georgia, then westward through a belt of contiguous states stretching to California. Texas is the largest cotton-producing state, accounting for an average of 26% of U.S. production since 1993. In 2002, 17 states reported cotton production valued at over $10 million.

Cotton is one of the principal U.S. program crops, along with wheat, rice, feed grains, soybeans, and peanuts. Qualifying U.S. cotton producers are eligible for direct payments, counter-cyclical payments, loan deficiency payments, Step-2 payments, and other program benefits.[1] From FY1991 to FY2004, U.S. farm subsidies for cotton production averaged $1.7 billion per year. (See table 1.)

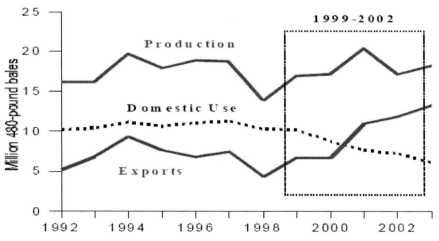

Source: USDA, ERS, *Cotton Yearbook*, November 2003.

Figure 1. U.S. Cotton Production, Use, and Exports.

The United States is the second-largest producer of cotton in the world. In recent years, the United States has been exporting an increasing share of its annual production, due in large part to a decline in domestic mill use. (See figure 1.) U.S. exports as a share of production have averaged 59% since 2001, up from a 42% average during the early 1990s.

The United States is the world's largest cotton exporter. During the 2001-03 period, U.S. exports accounted for 40% of world trade, on average. Large U.S. subsidy levels coupled with U.S. prominence in global markets have directed much international attention to U.S. cotton program outlays in recent years.

Table 1. U.S. Upland Cotton Program Outlays, FY1991-FY2005[a]

Fiscal year[b]	Total Outlays ($ million)[c]
1991	382
1992	1,443
1993	2,239
1994	1,539
1995	99
1996	685
1997	561
1998	1,132
1999	1,882
2000	3,809
2001	1,868
2002	3,307
2003	2,889
2004	1,372
2005[d]	4,721
Sum: 1991-2004	23,026
Average: 1991-2004	1,658
Average: 2000-2003	2,968

Source: USDA, Farm Service Agency, Budget Division, History of Budgetary *Expenditures of the Commodity Credit Corporation*, Books 3 (April 9, 2001) and 4 (July 15, 2003), and table 35 — CCC Net Outlays by Commodity and Function, available at [http://www.fsa.usda.gov/dam/bud/bud1.htm]. [a] Data are for outlays within the reported fiscal year. Payments may be specific to cotton from several different crop or marketing years. [b] The fiscal year starts Oct. 1 and ends Sept. 30 of the following year. Fiscal year identification is with the second year. For example, FY1993 starts Oct. 1, 1992, and runs through Sept. 30, 1993. [c] Includes deficiency payments, production flexibility contract payments, loan deficiency payments, user market payments (Step 2), marketing loss assistance payments, outlays from general loan operations, and other miscellaneous payments. Payments exclude loan repayment write-offs (otherwise referred to as producer marketing loan gains) and certificate sales proceeds/losses, both of which are treated as non-cash transactions. [d] USDA estimate, table 35, "CCC Net Outlays by Commodity and Function," downloaded on March 4, 2005, available at [http://www.fsa.usda.gov/dam/bud/bud1.htm].

SEQUENCE OF EVENTS IN WTO CASE DS267

In 2002, Brazil — a major cotton export competitor — expressed its growing concerns about U.S. cotton subsidies by initiating a WTO dispute settlement case (DS267) against certain features of the U.S. cotton program.[2] Once initiated, a dispute settlement case follows a sequence of events designed to produce resolution of the dispute within a 12-15 month time frame. (See table 2 for a timeline of the dispute settlement case.)

Table 2. Timeline: U.S.-Brazil WTO Dispute Settlement Case 267

Date	Event
Sept. 27, 2002	Brazil made a formal "request for consultations" with the United States.
Oct. 2002 to Jan. 2003	Brazil and the United States held three consultations to discuss the dispute over U.S. cotton subsidies. The consultations were unsuccessful.
Feb. 7, 2003	Brazil's first request for the establishment of a dispute panel to rule on its complaint is vetoed by the United States.
Mar. 18, 2003	Upon Brazil's second request, the WTO's Dispute Settlement Body (DSB) established a panel at its meeting on March 18, 2003.
May 19, 2003	Appointment of the panelists by the WTO Director-General. Once formed, a panel normally has six months to hold hearings and gather testimony before issuing its final report to both parties.
July 22-24, 2003	First meeting with the DSB panel. The panel decides to review the peace clause issue and Brazil's challenge to U.S. cotton subsidies separately.
Sept. 2003	The panel reversed an earlier procedural decision and stated that it would decide both the peace clause issue and Brazil's challenge to U.S. cotton subsidies together.
Nov. 17, 2003	The panel chairman informed the DSB that the panel would not be able to complete its work in six months due to the complexity of the matter. An extension was announced.
April 26, 2004	The panel's interim report is released confidentially to the two parties. Both parties review the interim report and submit written comments by May 10, at which time they have three additional weeks to review each other's comments and respond. Although the report was released confidentially, news reports suggested at least a partial finding against the United States on each of the five major claims.[3]
June 18, 2004	The panel's final report is released confidentially to the two parties. News reports suggested that the final ruling varied little from the interim ruling against the United States.[4]
Sept. 8, 2004	After translation into English, French, and Portuguese, the final report is delivered to the WTO Dispute Settlement Body (DSB), as well as to the public.[5]
Oct. 18, 2004	The United States notified its intention to appeal 14 specific points of the final report to the Appellate Body. The 14 points identify certain issues of law covered in the panel's final report and certain legal interpretations developed by the panel in the dispute.[6] An appeal cannot reexamine existing evidence or examine new evidence.
Nov. 16, 2004	Several additional countries filed a third participant's submission, while others notified their intention to appear at the oral hearing.
Dec. 10, 2004	Due to the extent and complexity of issues under review, both the United States and Brazil agreed to an extension to March 3, 2005, for circulation of the Appellate Body's (AB's) final report.
Mar. 3, 2005	The Appellate Body issued its report upholding most of the panel's rulings.[7]
Mar. 21, 2005	The DSB adopted the AB and panel reports, thus initiating a sequence of compliance deadlines.

Compliance procedures are discussed in a later section. For information on U.S. compliance actions and their implications for the U.S. cotton sector, see CRS Report RS22187, *U.S. Agricultural Policy Response to WTO Cotton Decision.*

ARGUMENTS IN THE U.S.-BRAZIL WTO COTTON CASE

Brazil's case was broadly written and touched on almost every aspect of U.S. commodity programs, although the focus has been on six principal claims (see below).[8] Each of Brazil's main claims is presented here along with the WTO

Claim 1: Peace Clause Violation

Brazil claimed that the United States is no longer exempt from WTO dispute proceedings under the so-called "peace clause" (Article 13) of the WTO's Agreement on Agriculture (AA) because U.S. domestic and export subsidies to its cotton sector are in excess of its WTO commitments.[9] Article 13 exempts domestic support measures that comply with the AA's requirements from being challenged as illegal subsidies through dispute settlement proceedings, as long as the level of support for a commodity remains at or below the benchmark 1992 marketing year (MY) levels. Brazil argued that U.S. cotton subsidies were about $2 billion in MY1992 compared with over $4 billion in MY2001.[10] Therefore, Brazil argued that the United States was no longer in compliance with the requisite conditions and could no longer seek protection under the WTO's peace clause rule.

In response, U.S. trade officials argued that WTO members agreed to the peace clause recognizing that agricultural subsidies could not be eliminated immediately and needed, under certain conditions, to be exempted from the Subsidies and Countervailing Measures (SCM) Agreement and GATT 1994 subsidies disciplines. As a result, U.S. officials argued that the words "exempt from actions" as used in Article 13 of the AA are of overarching importance and precluded not only the "taking of legal steps to ... obtain a remedy," as Brazil has argued, but also the "taking of legal steps to establish a claim."[11] Furthermore, U.S. trade officials argued that the immunity granted by the peace clause was still important, since even if a country was no longer in compliance with the peace clause, it was incumbent on the complaining party to prove there has been injury. (See "Claim 5," below.)

Finding 1
The panel found (and was upheld by the AB) that Brazil had successfully discharged its burden to show that U.S. domestic cotton support measures during MY1999-MY2002 (which averaged $3.28 billion) were in excess of WTO commitments (of $2.0 billion) during MY1992. (See table 3.) As a result, U.S. domestic cotton support measures lose the protection afforded by the "Peace Clause" which has shielded them from substantive challenges in the past. This occurs in part because, under Finding 2, Production Flexibility Contract and Direct Payment outlays are included with other commodity program outlays and evaluated against "peace clause" limits.

Table 3. Comparison of U.S. Domestic Cotton Support in Accordance with Article 13(b)(ii)

$ million	MY1992	MY1999	MY2000	MY2001	MY2002
Total	$ 2,012.7	$ 3,404.4	$ 2,429.3	$ 4,144.2	$ 3,140.3

Source: *United States — Subsidies on Upland Cotton*, "Report of the Panel," WTO, WT/DS267/R, Sept. 8, 2004; p. 157.

Claim 2: U.S. Direct Payments Do Not Qualify for Exemption from Reduction Commitments as Decoupled Income Support

Brazil claimed that two types of U.S. payments — Production Flexibility Contract (PFC) payments made under the 1996 farm bill and Direct Payments (DP) made under the 2002 farm bill — fail to fully meet the conditions for decoupled income support in Annex 2 of the Agreement on Agriculture and should therefore count against the U.S. "Peace Clause" domestic support benchmark limit.

The United States considers both PFC and DP programs to be consistent with WTO language for exempt domestic support that has "no, or at most minimal, trade-distorting effects or effects on production."[12] As a result, the United States notifies both the PFC and DP outlays as "green box" where they are not subject to any limits. Furthermore, the United States argued strongly against including such "minimally distorting, non-commodity specific" payments in evaluating whether the United States has met or exceeded its "peace clause" limits.

Finding 2

The panel found (and was upheld by the AB) that U.S. payments made under the PFC and DP programs, because of the prohibition on planting fruits, vegetables, and wild rice on covered program acreage,[13] do not qualify for the WTO's green box category of domestic spending. (The green box contains only non-distorting program payments and is not subject to any limit). Instead, they should be counted as domestic subsidies directly affecting cotton production (i.e., distorting) and be included with other commodity program outlays to evaluate whether the United States has met or exceeded its "peace clause" limits.

Claim 3: The Step-2 Program Functions as an Export Subsidy

Brazil argued that Step-2 payments made under the U.S. cotton program function as export subsidies and are inconsistent with U.S. WTO obligations regarding export subsidies as specified under the SCM Agreement.

Step-2 payments are part of special cotton marketing provisions authorized under U.S. farm program legislation to keep U.S. upland cotton competitive on the world market. Step-2 payments are made to exporters and domestic mill users to compensate them for their purchase of higher priced U.S. upland cotton. Under the 2002 Farm Act, the Step-2 payment rate for the 2002-2005 marketing years is calculated as the difference between the price of U.S. upland cotton, delivered c.i.f. (cost, insurance, freight) in Northern Europe and the average of the five lowest prices of upland cotton delivered c.i.f. Northern Europe from any source.[14]

The United States argued that Step-2 payments are part of its domestic support program since they are targeted to domestic cotton users as well as exporters. As a result, Step-2 payments are notified to the WTO as "amber" box (trade-distorting) domestic support payments and not as export subsidies. Consequently, U.S. trade officials contend that Step-2 payments are not subject to any limitations placed on export subsidies.

Finding 3

In its finding, the panel considered Step-2 program payments to eligible exporters separately from payments to domestic users.

- Payments to exporters were found to be "contingent upon export performance" and therefore qualified as prohibited export subsidies in violation of WTO commitments.
- Payments to domestic users were found to be "contingent on the use of domestic over imported goods" and therefore qualified as prohibited import substitution subsidies.

The DS panel finding was upheld by the Appellate Body.

Claim 4: U.S. Export Credit Guarantees Function as Export Subsidies

Brazil claimed that the favorable terms (i.e., the interest rate and time period that countries have to pay back the financing) provided under U.S. export credit guarantee programs — GSM102, GSM103, and the Supplier Credit Guarantee Program (SCGP)[15] — are effectively export subsidies inconsistent with the WTO's AA and SCM Agreements. Further, the subsidy effects of export credit guarantees apply not only to cotton, but to other eligible commodities.[16]

U.S. trade officials argued that the U.S. export credit guarantee programs are consistent with WTO obligations. Furthermore, the United States asserted that Article 10.2 of the AA reflected the deferral of disciplines on export credit guarantee programs contemplated by WTO members to the next WTO multilateral negotiating round — the Doha Round.

Finding 4

The panel found (and was upheld by the AB) that U.S. export credit guarantees effectively functioned as export subsidies because the financial benefits returned by these programs failed to cover their long-run operating cost.[17] Furthermore, the panel found that this applies, not just to cotton, but to all commodities that benefit from U.S. commodity support programs and receive export credit guarantees. As a result, export credit guarantees for any recipient commodity are subject to previously scheduled export subsidy commitments for that commodity. This refers to those U.S. export subsidies under the Export Enhancement Program (EEP).[18] Under these criteria, export credit guarantees benefits extended to cotton and other "unscheduled" commodities (that are supported under U.S. agricultural programs) are found to be in violation of previous WTO commitments. With respect to "scheduled" commodities, export credit guarantees extended to U.S. rice exports were found to be in violation of previous EEP volume commitments.

The panel found (and was upheld by the AB) that "unscheduled" commodities not supported under U.S. agricultural programs, as well as scheduled agricultural products that remain within WTO commitments are exempt from actions under this dispute settlement case.

Claim 5: U.S. Subsidies Have Caused "Serious Prejudice"

Brazil argued that the subsidies provided to U.S. cotton growers contributed to significant overproduction and resulted in a surge in U.S. cotton exports, particularly during the 1999-2002 marketing years, when unusually large outlays were made under provisions of the U.S. cotton program (see table 1 and figure 1). Brazil claimed that the resultant rise in U.S. exports led to three market conditions, each of which contributed to serious injury to Brazilian cotton exporters: (i) by increasing the U.S. share of the world upland cotton market; (ii) by displacing or impeding Brazilian upland cotton sales in third-country markets; and (iii) by contributing to a steep decline in world cotton prices (see figure 2).[19] In particular, Brazil claims that injury to its economy due to low cotton prices, measured as the sum of individual negative impacts on income, foreign trade revenue, fiscal revenues, related services (transportation and ginning), and employment, exceeded $600 million in 2001 alone. Brazil asserts that injury under each of these three circumstances are in violation of the SCM Agreement.[20] In addition, Brazil argued that these same programs would be harmful (i.e., threatened serious prejudice) in future years.

U.S. trade officials argued that the subsidies provided to U.S. cotton growers have been within the allowable WTO limits and are consistent with U.S. WTO obligations. Furthermore, they argued that the decline in U.S. domestic use (due to declining U.S. competitiveness in textile and apparel production), rather than government support program outlays, contributed to larger U.S. raw cotton exports. In addition, they contended that international market forces — including weakness in world demand for cotton due to competing, low-priced synthetic fibers, and weak world economic growth — have played a larger role in determining the generally weak price level during the period in question, rather than U.S. export levels. For example, see figure 3 for a visibly strong correlation between China cotton imports and the international cotton "A-index."

In evaluating this particular claim, the DS panel separated U.S. cotton support programs into two groups: those that are directly contingent on market price levels (loan deficiency payments, marketing loss assistance payments, counter-cyclical payments, and Step-2 payments), and those that are not (PFC and Direct Payments, and the federal crop insurance program).

Finding 5

The panel found (and was upheld by the AB) that U.S. domestic support measures that are directly contingent on market price levels caused serious prejudice in terms of market price suppression for the period 1999 to 2002. However, U.S. domestic support measures that are not contingent on market price levels were not included in this finding. The panel also did not find in favor of Brazil's alleged serious prejudice in terms of an effect on international market share. Article 6.3 of the SCM lists several factors indicating serious prejudice; the panel only had to find one of the factors in violation to rule in Brazil's favor on the claim of serious prejudice during the 1999 to 2002 period.

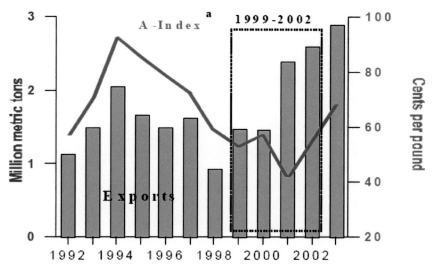

[a] The A-index is an average of the five lowest priced types of 1-3/32 in chstaple length cotton offered on the European market.

Source : USDA, ERS, *Cotton Yearbook* , November 2003; and USDA, PSD online database.

Figure 2. U.S. Cotton Exports and International Cotton Price Index.

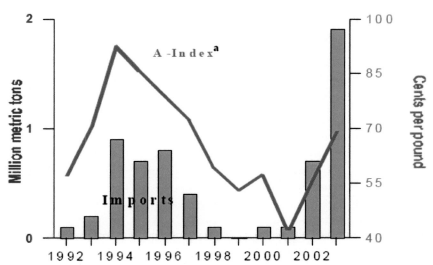

[a] The A-index is an average of the five lowest priced types of 1-3/32 in chstaple length cotton offered on the European market.

Source: USDA, ERS, *Cotton Yearbook*, November 2003; and USDA, PSD online database.

Figure 3. China Cotton Imports and International Cotton Price Index.

With respect to Brazil's claim of a threat of serious prejudice going forward (i.e., 2003 to 2007 — the remaining life of the 2002 farm act), the panel stated in its final report that those "prohibited" subsidies that cause the serious prejudice during the 1999-to-2002 period — namely, user marketing (Step-2) payments to exporters and domestic users; and export credit guarantees in respect of certain products under the GSM 102, GSM 103, and SCGP programs — must be withdrawn "without delay" pursuant to Article 4.7 of the SCM Agreement.[21] According to the panel, required withdrawal of the prohibited subsidies, within the time frame set by the panel, would curtail the future threat posed by U.S. cotton support programs. As a result, the panel stated that "...it is not necessary or appropriate to address Brazil's claims of threat of serious prejudice..."[22]

Claim 6: FSC-ETI Act of 2000 Acts as an Export Subsidy to Upland Cotton

Brazil claimed that the Foreign Sales Corporation Repeal and Extraterritorial Income Act of 2000 (ETI Act of 2000), by eliminating tax liabilities for U.S. upland cotton exporters who sell to foreign markets, constitutes an export subsidy and is inconsistent with U.S. export subsidy commitments for cotton.

The United States asserted throughout the proceedings that Brazil failed to make any specific case with respect to the ETI Act of 2000 and U.S. upland cotton exports.

Finding 6

The panel concurred with the United States (and was upheld by the AB) in stating that Brazil failed to present any new arguments or evidence concerning effects upon upland cotton, but instead simply repeated the arguments that the European Union made in its WTO dispute settlement case with the United States (DS108).[23] As a result, the panel declined to further examine Brazil's claims on this particular issue.

PANEL RECOMMENDATIONS

Prohibited Subsidies

In its final report, the panel recommends that the United States withdraw those support programs identified as prohibited subsidies within six months of the date of adoption of the panel report by the Dispute Settlement Body (DSB) or by July 1, 2005 (whichever is earlier).[24] Since the DSB adopted the AB and panel reports on March 21, 2005, the relevant deadline for withdrawal of prohibited subsidies is July 1, 2005. The list of prohibited subsidies subject to withdrawal "without delay" includes:

Prohibited Export Subsidies
- export credit guarantees under GSM 102, GSM 103, and SCGP that assist exports of upland cotton and other unscheduled agricultural products that are supported under government agricultural support programs;
- export credit guarantees under GSM 102, GSM 103, and SCGP that assist exports of one scheduled agricultural product (rice), but in excess of the scheduled volume; and
- Step-2 program payments to exporters of upland cotton.

Prohibited Import Substitution Subsidy
•   Step-2 payments to domestic users of upland cotton.

In contrast, the panel ruled that unscheduled agricultural products not supported under government agricultural support programs and scheduled agricultural product exports that remain within their schedules do not circumvent U.S. export commitments and are not subject to trade remedy actions in this case.

Actionable Subsidies
The panel also issued recommendations concerning the "actionable" subsidies identified as contributing to serious prejudice to the interests of Brazil during the marketing years 1999-2002. Specifically, this involves those U.S. subsidy measures singled out as price-contingent — marketing loan provisions, Step-2 payments, and CCP payments. The panel recommended that, upon adoption of its final report, the United States take appropriate steps to remove the adverse effects or to withdraw the subsidies.

However, it is noteworthy that the actionable subsidies remedy is dealing with serious prejudice and injury that occurred during a historical time period and not future prejudice or injury. In support of this concept, the panel stated (in its original ruling on the "threat of serious prejudice" by actionable subsidies) that U.S. compliance with recommendations on prohibited subsidies — i.e., the Step-2 provisions and export credit guarantees — could so significantly transform the basket of measures currently in question that it is not necessary or appropriate to address Brazil's claims of threat of serious prejudice.[25] This appears to leave open the possibility that removal of the prohibited subsidies may resolve the dispute under the actionable subsidies recommendation.

Implementation Phase[26]

Following is a discussion of how the implementation phase could potentially unfold in accordance with WTO dispute settlement rules. However, this report does not discuss how the implementation phase unfolded and the nature and effects of U.S. compliance decisions. Eventual U.S. compliance actions and their implications for the U.S. cotton sector are covered in CRS Report RS22187, *U.S. Agricultural Policy Response to WTO Cotton Decision.*

The evolution of the implementation phase depends on how both parties choose to respond to the different sequence of events as they unfold. In addition to the potential time tracks described below, the implementation phase also provides opportunities for the disputing parties to mutually resolve the dispute. Furthermore, if the complaining country does not want to press ahead full force with imposing sanctions, there is considerable opportunity to delay compliance steps.

From this point forward, the time track may diverge depending on whether the United States chooses to respond separately to the rulings on prohibited subsidies and actionable subsidies. This is because prohibited subsidies are given expedited treatment under SCM, Article 4.12, which states that, "except for time-periods specifically prescribed in [SCM, Article 4], time-periods applicable under the DSU for the conduct of such disputes shall be half the time prescribed therein."

Prohibited Subsidies Potential Time Track

The panel has recommended that the United States remove the prohibited export subsidies listed above by July 1, 2005. If the United States fails to comply, Brazil could (upon visible evidence of noncompliance) request negotiations with the United States to determine mutually acceptable compensation (e.g., tariff reductions in areas of particular interest). The first scheduled event was scheduled to occur within 15 days after the AB and panel reports were adopted by the DSB (done on March 21, 2005).[27] During this period the United States is expected to present an implementation plan to the DSB, although precedence suggests that such a plan could be as minimal as stating intentions to work with Congress to bring U.S. policies into compliance. This was indeed the case when, on April 20, the U.S. representative to the WTO announced that the United States intended to implement the recommendations and rulings of the DSB in a manner that respected U.S. WTO obligations.[28] The representative noted, however, that determining acceptable options would take a reasonable period of time and requested that Brazil be willing to consult on the potential timetable.

If, 10 days after the designated period (July 1, 2005) expires, no satisfactory compensation is agreed to, the complaining side (Brazil) may ask the DSB for permission to impose limited trade sanctions against the United States.[29] The trade sanctions are limited to a value equivalent to no more than the level of nullification or impairment of benefits. The DSB must grant this authorization within 15 days of expiry of the "reasonable" time period unless a consensus exists against the request.[30]

If the United States objects to the amount proposed by Brazil, the level of suspension would be arbitrated (by the original panel if available). Arbitration shall be completed within 30 days after the date of expiry of the designated period (July 1, 2005).[31] No trade sanctions are to be imposed during the arbitration period.

Once armed with the authority to impose trade sanctions, Brazil could still choose to wait. A precedent for this occurred under the WTO Dispute Settlement case (DS108) involving the U.S. Foreign Sales Corporation Statute. Under DS108, the European Communities (EC) requested and received authorization to impose retaliatory measures against the United States on May 7, 2003.[32] However, the EC refrained from immediate action, stating that it would review U.S. actions for a period of time before proceeding. The EC eventually began imposing additional duties on U.S. products in March 2004.

Actionable Subsidies Potential Time Track

The panel recommends that, upon adoption of its final report, the United States take appropriate steps to remove the adverse effects or to withdraw those subsidies identified as contributing to serious prejudice to the interests of Brazil — marketing loan provisions, Step-2 payments, and CCP payments. In contrast to the July 1, 2005 deadline, the removal of actionable subsidies is subject to a six-month period starting on the date of adoption of the AB and panel reports (March 21, 2005) — i.e., September 21, 2005.[33] At that point, in the absence of mutual agreement on compensation and if the United States has not fully complied with the recommendation, then the timetable for actionable subsidies would follow the same sequence of events listed above for prohibited subsidies, but subject to the full time allotment for each event as described in the preceding footnotes rather than the "halved" time periods.

Preliminary U.S. Government and Industry Response

A spokesperson for the Office of the U.S. Trade Representative (USTR) expressed disappointment in the AB ruling, but also said that USTR would study the AB report carefully and work closely with Congress and U.S. farmers on its next steps.[34] However, U.S. officials have said that they prefer to resolve the cotton case through trade negotiations in the WTO Doha Round rather than a separate settlement.[35]

The National Cotton Council (NCC) of America — the principal national organization representing the interests of U.S. producers, ginners, warehousers, merchants, cottonseed processors/dealers, cooperatives and textile manufacturers —also expressed disappointment in the AB ruling, but has stated that it would work with USTR and USDA to coordinate a response to the decision.[36]

POTENTIAL IMPLICATIONS OF WTO PANEL RULING

Trade experts have expressed concern that the panel findings could extend beyond cotton to other major field crops, particularly as concerns the potential limits on export credit guarantees. Some trade and market analysts, as well as legislators, have expressed concern that a broad finding against program provisions of the U.S. cotton program such as the mandatory Step-2 provisions could necessitate legislative changes to bring existing program operations into compliance; and that such potential program changes could necessitate that the U.S. farm bill be reopened well before its scheduled expiration in 2007. The July 1, 2005, deadline for removal of prohibited export subsidies including Step 2 payments and export credit guarantees appears to increase the likelihood of that possibility.

Concerns have also been expressed regarding the reclassification of PFC and Direct Payments away from non-trade-distorting green box support.[37] However, the panel finding that U.S. direct payments do not qualify for WTO exemptions from reduction commitments as fully decoupled income support (i.e., they are not green box compliant) appears to have no further consequences within the context of this case and does not involve any compliance measures. This is because direct payments were deemed "non-price contingent" and were evaluated strictly in terms of the Peace Clause violation.

The panel did not specifically reclassify U.S. PFC and DP payments as "amber box," nor did the panel recommend that the United States should notify such future payments as "amber box." This is a subtle but critical distinction because of the enormity of PFC and DP payments. During FY2000 to FY2003, PFC and DP payments averaged nearly $5 billion per year and accounted for 32% of total U.S. agricultural program outlays. Shifting this amount to amber box could have important implications for future dispute settlement cases, as well as for the United States' ability to meet its WTO amber box commitments.

U.S. cotton industry and government officials are concerned that the specific finding on the apparent failure of U.S. "decoupled" payments to meet WTO green box criteria leaves such programs open to future charges, and that third countries may feel emboldened by knowing how a WTO panel is likely to rule on such matters. The European Union (EU) is also likely to be concerned about this finding since the EU's agricultural program (following agricultural policy reforms of June 2003) relies heavily on "decoupled" payments similar to the those of the U.S. program.

OTHER COTTON-RELATED TRADE ISSUES

Besides Brazil's WTO-initiated dispute settlement case (DS267), U.S. cotton subsidies are being challenged at the WTO on two additional fronts.

- First, the Doha Development Agenda negotiating round has substantial reductions in trade-distorting domestic program support as one of its principal modalities.[38] If realized, a new round of domestic spending limitations could potentially represent a "real" ceiling on U.S. commodity spending and could result in lower program outlays.
- Second, a consortium of four African cotton-producing countries —Benin, Burkina Faso, Chad, and Mali — has submitted a WTO proposal calling for a global agreement to end all production-related support for cotton growers of all WTO-member cotton producing nations.[39] In acknowledgment of the concerns of African cotton-producing countries, the United States — while not agreeing with the African proposal — worked with the African countries on a formulation in the recently completed agriculture framework (July 31, 2004) of the WTO's ongoing Doha Round.[40] Although no specific cotton program concessions were mentioned in the framework, the United States committed "to achieve ambitious results expeditiously" under the framework. Further, it is notable that cotton is the only commodity singled out for special mention in the framework.

ROLE OF CONGRESS

Given the importance of cotton in the U.S. agricultural economy and the potential for WTO-imposed limitations on U.S. cotton program operations, Congress likely will be closely monitoring developments as the U.S. seeks to bring its programs into compliance with the WTO Appellate Body ruling and recommendations. The July 1, 2005, deadline for removal of prohibited export subsidies including Step 2 payments and export credit guarantees appears to increase the likelihood of that some sort of legislative change may be needed to bring existing program operations into compliance.

The House Committee on Agriculture regularly holds hearings on agricultural trade negotiations.[41] Last year two such hearings were held (April 28 and May 19, 2004). Among the trade issues discussed during these hearings, both U.S. Trade Representative Zoellick and Woody Anderson, chairman of the National Cotton Council, provided testimony on and responded to questions regarding the U.S.-Brazil WTO cotton case.

In his testimony to the House Committee on Agriculture, May 19, 2004, Mr. Anderson expressed his support for the WTO negotiations stating that "[a] rational, rules-based international trading system is superior to the alternative. We will do our part, working with this committee and the administration, to maintain an effective U.S. cotton program that complies with WTO rules."[42] However, he also expressed his concern that U.S. programs such as the export credit guarantees and decoupled direct payments — programs that he felt were clearly exempted from reduction commitments under the Uruguay Round Agreement — might fail to withstand challenges under the WTO dispute settlement process.

In addition to congressional hearings, under fast track or Trade Promotion Authority (TPA) legislation, Congress will be engaged in consultations with the Administration on negotiations of the Free Trade Agreement for the Americas (FTAA) and the agriculture negotiations in the WTO. Such consultations will be a major vehicle for Members to express their views on this dispute and on the negotiating issues it raises. Ultimately Congress is responsible for passing farm program legislation that complies with U.S. commitments in international trade agreements.

REFERENCES

[1]   For more details on U.S. cotton program operations, see CRS Report RL32442, *Cotton Production and Support in the United States*, June 24, 2004.

[2]   *United States — Subsidies on Upland Cotton*, WT/DS267 (WTO Dispute Settlement Case 267). Documentation is available at [http://www.wto.org/english/tratop_e/dispu_e/ dispu_e. htm].

[3]   "Brazil Wins Key Points in Interim WTO Panel on U.S. Cotton Subsidies," *Inside U.S. Trade*, April 30, 2004; "WTO Panel Backs Brazil in Complaint Against U.S. Over Cotton Subsidies," *International Trade Reporter*, Vol. 21, No. 18, April 29, 2004; and "WTO Panel Reportedly Rules Direct Payments are Trade Distorting and Thus 'Amber Box,'" AgWeb.com, April 30, 2004.

[4]   "WTO Ruling Against U.S. Cotton Subsidies is Not Limited to Cotton," AgWeb.com, June 29, 2004; and "WTO Issues Final Ruling Condemning U.S. Cotton Subsidies; U.S. Plans Appeal," *International Trade Reporter*, Vol. 21, No. 26, June 24, 2004.

[5]   *United States — Subsidies on Upland Cotton*, "Report of the Panel," WTO, WT/DS267/R, Sept. 8, 2004; available at [http://www.wto.org/english/tratop_e/dispu_e/ 267r_a_e.pdf].

[6]   The U.S. appeal notification may be obtained by searching for WT/DS267/17 using the WTO online documents search engine at [http://docsonline.wto.org/ gen_home.asp? language=1 and _=1].

[7]   *United States — Subsidies on Upland Cotton*, AB-2004-5, "Report of the Appellate Body," WTO, WT/DS267/AB/R, March 3, 2005; available at [http://www.wto.org/ english/tratop_e/ dispu_e/267abr_e.doc].

[8]   Ministry of Foreign Affairs [Ministério das Relações Exteriores], Brasilia; "Brazil-U.S.A. Dispute on Subsidies on Upland Cotton," translation from the original in Portuguese, Nota n° 248-18/06/2004; Distribuição 22 e 23.

[9]   WTO, *The Legal Texts: The Results of the Uruguay Round of Multilateral Trade Negotiations*, Cambridge Univ. Press, ©World Trade Organization 1999; hereafter referred to as *WTO Legal Texts*. Text of the Agreement on Agriculture is available online at [http://www.wto.org/english/docs_e/legal_e/14-ag.pdf].

[10]   USDA reports commodity program outlays on a fiscal year (FY) basis. (See table 1.) However, marketing year data, not fiscal year, must be used in the WTO case. The U.S. cotton marketing year starts Aug. 1 and ends July 31 of the following year, but identifies with the first year, such that MY1992 starts Aug. 1, 1992, and ends July 31,

1993. The principal period in question, MY1999-MY2002, corresponds roughly with FY2000-FY2003.

[11]   *United States — Subsidies on Upland Cotton*, WT/DS267, "Initial Brief of the United States of America on the Question Posed by the Panel," June 13, 2003; available from the USTR website at [http://www.ustr.gov/assets/Trade_Agreements/ Monitoring_ Enforcement/Dispute_Settlement/WTO/Dispute_Settlement_Listings/asset_ upload_file376_5598.pdf].

[12]   WTO, "Annex 2 — Domestic Support: The Basis for Exemption from the Reduction Commitments," Agreement on Agriculture, *WTO Legal Texts*, p. 48.

[13]   For more information on these restrictions see USDA, Farm Service Agency, Fact Sheet, *Direct and Counter-Cyclical Payment Program Wild Rice, Fruit, and Vegetable Provisions*, February 2003, at [http://www.fsa.usda.gov/pas/publications/facts/html/ fav03.htm].

[14]   Only prices for Middling (M) 1-3/32-inch upland cotton are used in the calculation. Also, certain price triggers must be met and held for a specified period of time before payments can be made. For information on the Step-2 program and other U.S. cotton program features, see USDA, ERS, "Cotton Briefing Room,"at [http://www.ers.usda.gov/ Briefing/Cotton/].

[15]   For information on U.S. export credit programs, see USDA, Foreign Agricultural Service (FAS), "Export Credit Guarantee Programs," at [http://www.fas.usda.gov/ excredits/default.htm].

[16]   For a list of commodities eligible for export credit guarantees see USDA, Foreign Agricultural Service, *USDA Amends Commodity Eligibility under Credit Guarantee Programs*, News Release, Sept. 24, 2002; available at [http://www.fas.usda.gov/ scriptsw/PressRelease/pressrel_dout.asp?Entry=valid&PrNum=0346-02].

[17]   Found to violate Annex I(j) of the SCM, *WTO Legal Texts*, p. 267, which identifies as an export subsidy, "The provision by governments (or special institutions controlled by governments) of export credit guarantee or insurance programmes, of insurance or guarantee programmes against increases in the cost of exported products or of exchange risk programmes, at premium rates which are inadequate to cover the long-term operating costs and losses of the programmes."

[18]   The United States has scheduled export subsidy reduction commitments for the following thirteen commodities: wheat, coarse grains, rice, vegetable oils, butter and butter oil, skim milk powder, cheese, other milk products, bovine meat, pigmeat, poultry meat, live dairy cattle, and eggs. For more information on the EEP program, see CRS Issue Brief IB98006, *Agricultural Export and Food Aid Programs*, Foreign Agricultural Service, USDA, at [http://www.fas.usda.gov/ excredits/eep.html].

[19]   Articles 5(c) and 6.3(b) of the Agreement on Subsidies and Countervailing Measures (SCM) deal with subsidies that result in adverse effects in other WTO-member countries. Brazil specifically identified Argentina, Bangladesh, Colombia, Germany, India, Indonesia, Italy, Portugal, Philippines, Slovenia, South Africa, South Korea, Switzerland, Thailand, and Turkey as the relevant third-country markets. WTO "Communication from Brazil," WT/DS267/9, March 21, 2003.

[20] Text of the Agreement on SCM is available online at [http://www.wto.org/english/docs_e/legal_e/24-scm.pdf].

[21] *Report of the Panel*, "United States — Subsidies on Upland Cotton," WTO, WT/DS267/R, para 7.1503, Sept. 8, 2004, p. 345.

[22] Ibid.

[23] For more information on DS108, see CRS Report RL32014, *WTO Dispute Settlement: Status of U.S. Compliance in Pending Cases* by Jeanne Grimmett.

[24] Done in accordance with SCM, Article 4.7.

[25] *Report of the Panel*, "United States — Subsidies on Upland Cotton," WTO, WT/DS267/R, para. 7.1503, p. 354.

[26] For details, see *Understanding the WTO: Settling Disputes*, "The Case Has Been Decided, What Next?" at [http://www.wto.org/english/thewto_e/whatis_e/ tif_e/ disp1_e.htm].

[27] Normally a 30-day period is given to respond (DSU, Article 21.3); however, this is halved under SCM, Article 4.12.

[28] U.S. Mission to the United Nations in Geneva, Press Release, "Statements by the U.S. Representative at the meeting of the WTO Dispute Settlement Body," April 20, 2005.

[29] Normally a 20-day period is given (DSU, Article 22.2); however, for disputes involving prohibited subsidies the prescribed time is halved (SCM, Article 4.12).

[30] Normally a 30-day period is given for authorization (DSU, Article 22.6); however, for disputes involving prohibited subsidies the prescribed time is halved (SCM, Article 4.12).

[31] Normally a 60-day period is given for arbitration (DSU, Article 22.6); however, for disputes involving prohibited subsidies the prescribed time is halved (SCM, Article 4.12).

[32] For more information, see CRS Report RL32014, *WTO Dispute Settlement: Status of U.S. Compliance in Pending Cases*, by Jeanne Grimmett.

[33] In accordance with SCM, Article 7.9.

[34] *Inside U.S. Trade*, "Appellate Body Favors Brazil in Cotton Subsidies Challenge," Vol. 23, No.9, March 4, 2005.

[35] *Congressional Daily*, "Comply Quickly With WTO Ruling, Brazil Urges U.S." March 15, 2005.

[36] NCC, "NCC Statement on WTP Appellate Ruling," March 3, 2005; available at [http://www.cotton.org/news/releases/2005/wtostatement.cfm].

[37] "Brazil Wins Key Points in Interim WTO Panel on U.S. Cotton Subsidies," *Inside U.S. Trade*, April 30, 2004.

[38] WTO, Doha Ministerial Declaration, WT/MIN(01)/DEC/1, Nov. 20, 2001.

[39] For more information, see CRS Report RS21712, *The African Cotton Initiative and WTO Agriculture Negotiations*.

[40] For more information, see CRS Report RS21905, *Agriculture in the WTO Doha Round: The Framework Agreement and Next Steps*.

[41] House of Representatives, 108th Congress, Committee on Agriculture, *Agricultural Trade Negotiations*, Serial No. 108-29; available at [http://agriculture.house.gov/hearings/108/ 10829.pdf].

[42] Statement of Woody Anderson, chairman, National Cotton Council, before the Committee on Agriculture, U.S. House of Representatives, May 19, 2004; available at [http:// agriculture.house.gov/hearings/108/10829.pdf].

In: Brazil in Focus: Economic, Political and Social Issues ISBN: 978-1-60456-165-4
Editor: Jorge T. Almeida, pp. 45-60 © 2008 Nova Science Publishers, Inc.

Chapter 3

BRAZIL'S AGRICULTURAL PRODUCTION AND EXPORTS: SELECTED DATA[*]

Logan Rishard Council and Charles E. Hanrahan

ABSTRACT

Brazil is a major world producer and exporter of agricultural products. In 2004, Brazil exported $30.9 billion worth of agricultural and food products, making it the world's third-largest exporter of agricultural products after the United States and the European Union. Brazil's major agricultural exports include soybeans, poultry, beef, pork, orange juice, and coffee.

Highlights of Brazil's agricultural production and exports include:

- Soybeans: In 2005, Brazil, the world's second largest producer, became the world's leading exporter, with 39% of global export market share. The United States, the world's leading producer of soybeans, had a 37% share of the world soybean market, although forecasts are for the United States to return to its leading position in 2006.
- Poultry (Broilers): Brazil, the world's third largest producer of broilers, was the leading exporter in 2005, with 41% of the world's export market. The United States, the world's leading producer, was the second largest exporter, with 35% of the world's export market.
- Beef and Veal: Brazil was the world's second largest producer and the leading exporter of beef and veal in 2005. In 2005, the United States, the top global producer of beef and veal, fell to eighth place in terms of exports, due to the discovery of a cow with BSE in late 2003.
- Orange Juice: Brazil is the world's leading producer (59% share) and exporter (83% share) of orange juice.
- Coffee: Brazil is the world's leading producer and exporter of coffee. Its share of world coffee production in 2005 was 32%, while its share of world coffee exports was 28%.
- Sugar: Brazil is the world's leading producer and exporter of sugar. The United States is a major producer, but a minor exporter of sugar.

---

[*] Excerpted from CRS Report RL33699, dated October 16, 2006.

- Cotton: Brazil is the world's fifth largest producer and exporter of cotton. The United States, the world's second largest producer, is the world's leading exporter of cotton, with 41% of world exports.

BRAZIL'S POSITION IN GLOBAL AGRICULTURE[1]

Global agricultural gross domestic product (GDP) totaled $1.65 trillion in 2004, about 4% of global total GDP. Brazil's agricultural gross domestic product (GDP) was $60.4 billion in 2004, 10% of its total GDP. In the United States, agricultural GDP equaled $117.1 billion in 2004, 1% of its total GDP.

Table 1. Agricultural GDP: Global, Brazil, and United States

Country	2004 Agricultural GDP ($ millions)	% of Country's GDP	% of Global Agricultural GDP
Brazil	60,397	10	3.7
United States	117,118	1	7.1
World	1,650,000	4	100

Source: The World Bank Group. 2006 World Development Indicators.

Global agricultural and food exports totaled $823 billion in 2004, 9% of total global merchandise exports. In Brazil, agricultural and food exports totaled $30.9 billion in 2004, 32% of its total merchandise exports. In the United States, agricultural and food exports totaled $73.7 billion in 2004, 9% of total U.S. merchandise exports.

Table 2. Agricultural Exports: Global, Brazil, and United States

Country	2004 Agricultural and Food Exports ($ millions)	% of Country's Total Merchandise Exports	% of Global Total Merchandise Exports
Brazil	30,872	32	3.8
United States	73,689	9	9
World	823,052	9	100

Source: The World Bank Group. 2006 World Development Indicators.

BRAZIL'S COMMODITY PRODUCTION AND EXPORTS

Brazil is the world's largest producer of orange juice and coffee, and the second largest producer of soybeans, beef, and poultry. For many of these products, such as orange juice, soybeans, beef, and poultry, the United States and Brazil compete with each other in world markets. In 2005, Brazil was the world's leading exporter of soybeans, poultry (broilers), beef, orange juice, coffee, and sugar. It was also the world's fourth largest exporter of pork.

Soybeans

Production

Global soybean production rose to 220 million metric tons (mt) in 2005, from the previous year's total of 192 million mt. Production in Brazil also rose from 47.8 million mt in 2004 to 55.7 million mt in 2005. Brazil's share of world soybean production was 25% in 2005. The United States continued to be the world's top producer of soybeans, increasing production from 76.1 million mt in 2004 to 84 million mt in 2005. The U.S. share of global soybean production in 2005 was 39%. Argentina remained the world's third largest soybean producer with 40.5 million mt, up from 30 million mt in 2004. Argentina produced 18% of the world's soybeans in 2005.

Table 3. Soybean Production, 2005

Country	Production (1000 mt)	World Share (%)	Rank
Brazil	55,700	25	2
United States	84,000	39	1
Argentina	40,500	18	3
China	17,200	8	4
India	6,300	3	5
Rest of World	15,630	7	N/A
World Total	220,190	100	N/A

Source: U.S. Dept. of Agriculture (USDA) Foreign Agriculture Service (FAS). June 2006 Oilseeds Circular. Table 4.

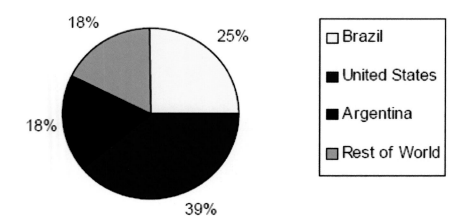

Figure 1. Soybean Production, 2005.

Exports

Brazil's soybean exports increased in 2005 as well. Brazil exported 25.9 million mt of soybeans in 2005, up from 20.1 million mt in 2004. Brazil's share of world soybean exports was 40% in 2005. The United States exported 24.5 million mt in 2005, down from 30 million mt in 2004, just slightly below Brazil's total exports. The U.S. share of soybean exports in 2005 was 37%. U.S. Department of Agriculture (USDA) forecasters expect that the United States will become the leading exporter again in 2006. Argentina, the world's third largest exporter of soybeans, exported 10.5 million mt in 2005, up from 9.3 million mt exported in

2004. Argentina's share of world soybean exports was 16% in 2005. These three countries accounted for almost 93% of world soybean exports in 2005.

Table 4. Soybean Exports, 2005

Countries	Exports (1000 metric tons)	Market Share (%)	Rank
Brazil	25,991	39	1
United States	24,494	37	2
Rest of World	4,743	8	N/A
World Total	65,727	100	N/A

Source: USDA-FAS. June 2006 Oilseeds Circular. Table 8.

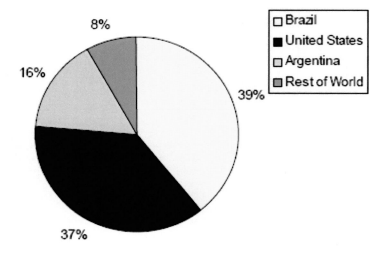

Figure 2. Soybean Exports, 2005.

Poultry (Broilers)

Production

Global broiler production increased in 2005, totaling 58.7 million mt, up from 56 million mt in 2004. Brazil followed the trend and was third in production behind the United States and China with 9.4 million mt, up from 8.4 million mt in 2004. Brazil's share of world poultry production was 16% in 2005. The United States produced 15.9 million mt of broilers in 2005, up from the 15.3 million produced in 2004. The United States is the world's leading producer of poultry with 27% of world production. China produced 10.2 million mt after producing 10 million mt in 2004. China, the world's second largest producer of poultry meat, accounts for 17% of world production. The European Union produced about 7.6 million mt in both 2004 and 2005, about 13% of world production.

Table 5. Broiler Production, 2005

Countries	Production (1000 metric tons)	World Share (%)	Rank
Brazil	9,360	16	3
United States	15,870	27	1
China	10,200	17	2
European Union	7,625	13	4
Mexico	2,510	4	5
Rest of World	13,156	22	N/A
World Total	58,721	100	N/A

Source: USDA-FAS. Production, Supply, and Distribution Tables. Broiler Summary Selected Countries. March 2006.

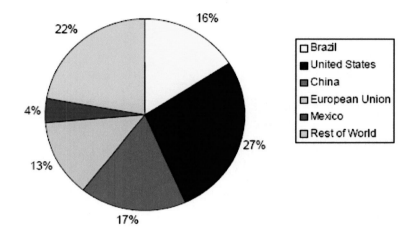

Figure 3. Broiler Production, 2005.

Exports

Global broiler exports increased significantly in 2005 to 6.7 million mt from 6 million in 2004. Brazil led the world in broiler exports in 2005 at 2.7 million mt (41% of global poultry exports) after exporting 2.4 million mt in 2004. The United States exported 2.3 million mt in 2005, up from 2.2 million mt in 2004. The U.S. share of world broiler exports was 35% in 2005. The two countries accounted for some 76% of global exports in 2005.

Table 6. Broiler Exports, 2005

Country	Exports (1000 metric tons)	Market Share (%)	Rank
Brazil	2,739	41	1
United States	2,335	35	2
European Union	740	11	3
China	331	5	4
Thailand	240	3	5
Rest of World	295	4	N/A
World Total	6,680	100	N/A

Source: USDA-FAS. Production, Supply, and Distribution Tables. Broiler Summary Selected Countries. March 2006.

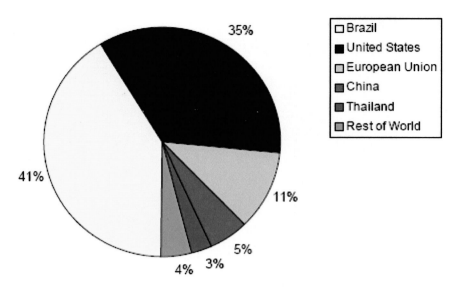

Figure 4. Broiler Exports, 2005.

Beef and Veal

Production

Global beef and veal production increased in 2005 to 52.2 million mt from 51.3 million mt the previous year. Brazil produced 8.6 million mt in 2005, up from 8 million mt in 2004. Brazil accounts for 16% of world beef production. The United States led the world in beef and veal production with 11.3 million metric tons, slightly above the 11.2 million mt produced in 2004. The U.S. share of global beef production was 22% in 2005. The European Union and China were the next largest producers of beef and veal in 2005. The European Union produced 7.8 million mt in 2005, or 15% of the world's beef production, down from 8 million mt in 2004, while China produced 7.1 million mt, 14% of global beef production, and slightly above the 6.8 million mt it produced in 2004.

Table 7. Beef Production, 2005

Country	Production (1000 metric tons)	World Share (%)	Rank
Brazil	8,592	16	2
United States	11,317	22	1
European Union	7,770	15	3
China	7,140	14	4
Argentina	3,200	6	5
Rest of World	14,228	27	N/A
World Total	52,247	100	N/A

Source: USDA-FAS. Production, Supply, and Distribution Tables. Beef and Veal Summary Selected Countries. March 2006.

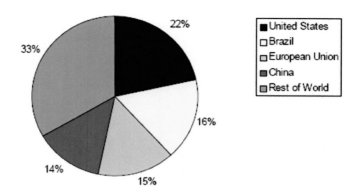

Figure 5. Beef Production, 2005.

Exports

Globally, beef and veal exports increased from 6.5 million mt in 2004 to 7 million mt in 2005. Brazil led the way, increasing from 1.6 million mt in 2004 to 1.9 million mt in 2005. Brazil's world export market share for beef was 26% in 2005. Australia was next with 1.4 million metric tons (20% of the world export market share), nearly equaling its beef exports from the previous year. Argentina was third with 759,000 mt exported (11% of export market share) up from 623,000 the year before. The United States exported 313,000 mt in 2005(4.4% of world beef exports), an increase from the 209,000 mt exported in 2004, but still low compared to exports of 1.142 million mt in 2003, the year in which a case of Bovine Spongiform Encephalopathy (BSE) or "mad cow" disease was discovered in the United States.

Table 8. Beef Exports, 2005

Country	Exports (1000 metric tons)	Market Share (%)	Rank
Brazil	1,867	26	1
Australia	1,413	20	2
Argentina	759	11	3
Rest of World	2,729	38	N/A
World Total	7,043	100	N/A

Source: USDA-FAS. Production, Supply, and Distribution Tables. Beef and Veal Summary Selected Countries. March 2006.

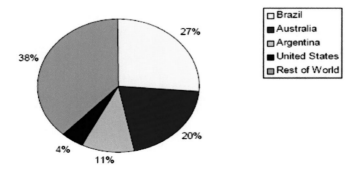

Figure 6. Beef Exports, 2005.

Pork

Production

Global pork production increased in 2005 from 91.4 million mt in 2004 to 94.2 million mt in 2005. The People's Republic of China led the world with 49.7 million mt produced in 2005, up from 47 million mt produced in 2004. China accounted for more than half (53%) of global pork production. The European Union produced about 21.2 million mt in both 2004 and 2005, 23% of world production. The United States produced nearly 9.4 million mt of pork in 2005, slightly more than the 9.3 million mt produced in 2004. The U.S. share of global pork production in 2005 was 10%. Brazil produced 2.8 million mt in 2005 (3% of global production) up from 2.6 million in 2004.

Table 9. Pork Production, 2005

Country	Production (1000 metric tons)	World Share (%)	Rank
Brazil	2,800	3	4
United States	9,392	10	3
China	49,685	52	1
European Union	21,200	23	2
Canada	1,915	2	5
Rest of World	9,210	10	N/A
World Total	94,202	100	N/A

Source: USDA-FAS. Production, Supply, and Distribution Tables. Pork Summary Selected Countries. March 2006.

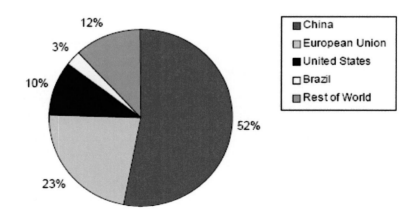

Figure 7. Pork Production, 2005.

Exports

Pork exports increased from 4.6 million mt in 2004 to 5 million mt in 2005. The European Union was the world's largest exporter of pork with 1.3 million mt (28% of world exports of pork), a decrease from the nearly 1.5 million mt exported in 2004. The United States exported 1.2 million mt of pork in 2005, a substantial jump from the 989,000 mt exported in 2004. The U.S. share of world pork exports was 24% in 2005. Canada exported 1.1 million mt in 2005 (22%), up from 972,000 mt in 2004. Brazil was the world's fourth largest pork exporter in 2005, exporting more than 760,000 mt, 15% of world pork exports.

Table 10. Pork Exports, 2005

Country	Exports (1000 metric tons)	Market Share (%)	Rank
Brazil	761	15	4
United States	1,207	24	2
European Union	1,380	27	1
Canada	1,083	22	3
China	331	7	5
Rest of World	255	5	N/A
World Total	5,017	100	N/A

Source: USDA-FAS. Production, Supply, and Distribution Tables. Pork Summary Selected Countries. March 2006.

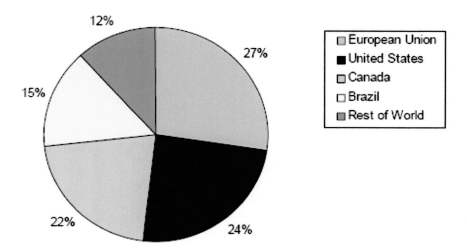

Figure 8. Pork Exports, 2005.

Orange Juice

Production

Global orange juice production was nearly 2.4 million mt in 2005, up from the 2.3 million mt produced in 2004. Brazil produced 1.4 million mt, up from 1.3 million mt in 2004. Brazil's share of world orange juice production was 59% in 2005. The United States produced 709,000 mt, up from the 693,000 mt in 2004, but substantially lower than its 1 million mt production in 2003. The U.S. share of global orange juice production was 30% in 2005.

Table 11. Orange Juice Production, 2005

Country	Production (1000 metric tons)	World Share (%)	Rank
Brazil	1,402	59	1
United States	709	30	2
Italy	48	2	3
Spain	46	2	4
Mexico	42	2	5
Israel	42	2	5
Rest of World	78	3	N/A
World Total	2,367	100	N/A

Source: USDA-FAS. Production, Supply, and Distribution Tables. Orange Juice: Production, Supply, and Demand in Selected Countries. March 2006.

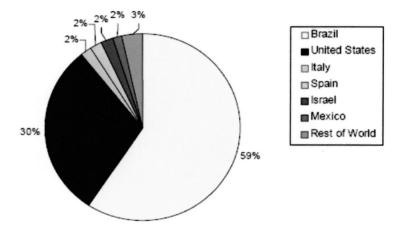

Figure 9. Orange Juice Production, 2005.

Exports

Global exports of orange juice in 2005 were 1.65 million mt, down slightly from the 1.7 million mt exported in 2004. Brazil continued its dominance of world orange juice trade with nearly 1.4 million mt of exports, 83% of the global total, up from 1.33 million in 2004. The next largest exporter was Spain with 102,000 metric tons (6% of global exports), down from a high of 110,000 in 2004. U.S. exports (5% of the total) were also down from nearly 85,000 mt in 2004 to 75,000 mt in 2005.

Table 12. Orange Juice Exports, 2005

Country	Exports (1000 metric tons)	Market Share (%)	Rank
Brazil	1,367	83	1
United States	75	5	3
Spain	102	6	2
Mexico	38	2	4
Israel	33	2	5
Rest of World	39	2	N/A
World Total	1,654	100	N/A

Source: USDA-FAS. Production, Supply, and Distribution Tables. Orange Juice: Production, Supply, and Demand in Selected Countries. March 2006.

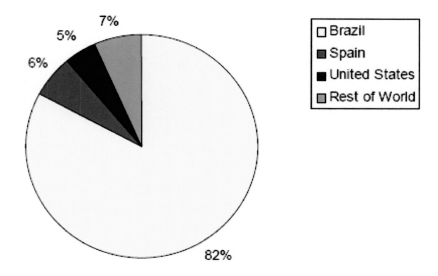

Figure 10. Orange Juice Exports, 2005.

Coffee

Production

Globally, coffee production totaled 112.7 million 60-kilogram (kg) bags in 2005, down from 120.7 million bags in 2004. Coffee production in Brazil decreased in 2005 to 36.1 million bags, down from 43.6 million bags in 2004. Brazil's share of world coffee production is 32%. The United States produced 161,000 bags in 2005, an increase from the 146,000 produced in 2004. Coffee is produced in the United States in only Hawaii and Puerto Rico. Vietnam produced 12.3 million bags in 2005, the second largest amount that year, but a decrease from the 14.5 million bags it produced in 2004. Vietnam's share of world coffee production was 11% in 2005. Colombia followed closely behind with 11.6 million bags in 2005 (10.2%), a slight increase from the 11.4 million produced in 2004.

Table 13. Coffee Production, 2005

Country	Production (1000 60-kilogram bags)	World Share (%)	Rank
Brazil	36,100	32	1
United States	161	.001	—
Vietnam	12,333	11	2
Colombia	11,550	10	3
Indonesia	6,750	6	4
Ethiopia	6,000	5	5
Rest of World	39,799	35	N/A
World Total	112,693	100	N/A

Source: USDA-FAS. Production, Supply, and Distribution Tables. Coffee: Production, Supply, and Demand in Selected Countries. June 2006.

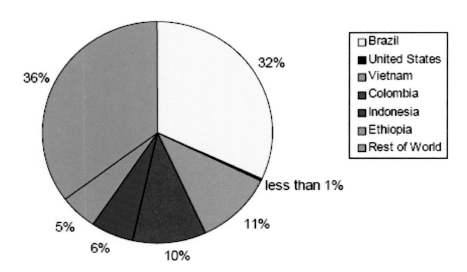

Figure 11. Coffee Production, 2005.

Exports

Globally, coffee exports were down in 2005 at 85.6 million 60-kg bags, from 91.2 million bags in 2004. Brazil led the world in coffee exports in 2005 with 24 million bags, a decrease from 27.9 million bags exported in 2004. Brazil's share of world coffee exports in 2005 was 28%. The United States did not export any coffee in 2005, consuming all its limited production domestically, as it did in 2004. Vietnam exported 11.7 million bags (14% of the world's total) in 2005, a decrease from 14 million bags in 2004. Colombia was third in exports with 10.8 million bags in 2005 (13% of global coffee exports), down from 11 million bags in 2004.

Table 14. Coffee Exports, 2005

Country	Exports (1000 60-kilogram bags)	Market Share (%)	Rank
Brazil	24,050	28	1
United States	161	.002	—
Vietnam	11,709	14	2
Colombia	10,840	13	3
Indonesia	5,070	6	4
Guatemala	3,300	4	5
Rest of World	30,441	35	N/A
Total	85,571	100	N/A

Source: USDA-FAS. Production, Supply, and Distribution Tables. Coffee: Production, Supply, and Demand in Selected Countries. June 2006.

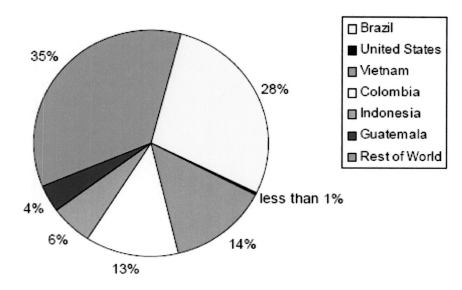

Figure 12. Coffee Exports, 2005.

Sugar

Production

Global sugar production decreased from 142.5 million mt in 2003/2004 to 140.7 million mt in 2004/2005. Brazil produced 28.2 million mt equal to 20% of total world sugar production. The European Union was the world's second largest producer of sugar with 21.6 million mt of production or 15.4% of the world's total. India, the third largest producer of sugar, produced 14.2 million mt in 2004/2005, giving it a 10% share of total world production.

Table 15. Sugar Production, 2004/2005

Country	Production (1000 metric tons, raw value)	World Share (%)	Rank
Brazil	28,175	20	1
United States	7,146	5	5
European Union	21,648	15	2
India	14,210	10	3
China	9,826	7	4
Mexico	6,149	4	6
Rest of World	53,522	38	N/A
World Total	140,676	100	N/A

Source: USDA-FAS. Production, Supply, and Distribution Tables. Sugar: World Markets and Trade. May 2006.

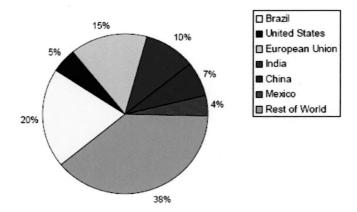

Figure 13. Sugar Production, 2004/2005.

Exports

Brazil is the world's leading exporter of sugar, accounting for 38% of global sugar exports. The United States with only 235,000 mt of sugar exports in 2004/2005 is a minor exporter. The European Union is the second largest exporter of sugar with more than 6 million mt of exports or 12.6% of total world exports. Australia, Thailand, and Guatemala are the world's third, fourth, and fifth largest sugar exporters, respectively.

Table 16. Sugar Exports, 2004/2005

Country	Exports (1000 metric tons, raw value)	Market Share (%)	Rank
Brazil	18,020	38	1
United States	235	0.5	—
European Union	6,028	13	2
Australia	4,447	9	3
Thailand	3,115	7	4
Guatemala	1,497	3	5
Rest of World	14,409	30	N/A
World Total	47,751	100	N/A

Source: USDA-FAS. Production, Supply, and Distribution Tables. Sugar: World Markets and Trade. May 2006.

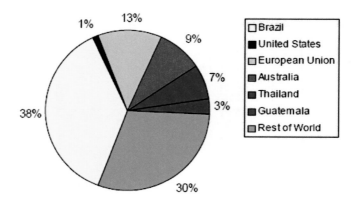

Figure 14. Sugar Exports, 2004/2005.

Cotton

Production

Global cotton production in 2004/2005 was 26.2 million mt, an increase of almost 5.5 million mt over 2003/2004. China, the world's leading producer of cotton, produced 6.3 million mt, almost a quarter of total world production in 2004/2005. The United States is the world's second largest producer of cotton with production amounting to 5 million mt in 2004/2005 or 19% of total world production. India and Pakistan are the world's third and fourth largest producers, while Brazil with production of 1.3 million mt in 2004/2005 is the world's fifth largest producer. Its production accounts for 5% of the world's total.

Table 17. Cotton Production, 2004/2005

Country	Production (1,000 metric tons)	World Share (%)	Rank
Brazil	1,285	5	5
United States	5,062	19	2
China	6,314	24	1
India	4,317	17	3
Pakistan	2,426	9	4
Rest of World	6,796	26	N/A
Total	26,200	100	N/A

Source: USDA-FAS, Cotton: World Markets and Trade Circular, September 13, 2006.

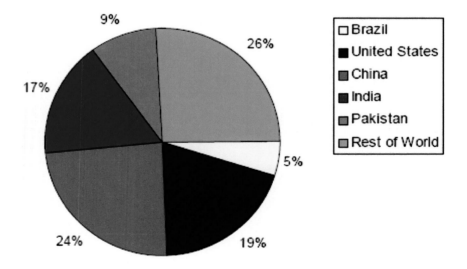

Figure 15. Cotton Production, 2004/2005.

Exports

The United States is the world's leading exporter of cotton with exports in 2004/2005 of 3.1 million mt, amounting to 41% of world cotton exports. Uzbekistan, Australia, and Greece were the world's second, third, and fourth largest exporters in 2004/2005, while Brazil with exports of 339,000 mt ranked fifth in world cotton exports.

Table 18. Cotton Exports, 2004/2005

Country	Exports (1,000 metric tons)	Market Share (%)	Rank
Brazil	339	4	5
United States	3,143	41	1
Uzbekistan	860	11	2
Australia	435	6	3
Greece	255	3	4
Rest of World	2,588	34	N/A
Total	7,620	100	N/A

Source: USDA-FAS, Cotton: World Markets and Trade Circular, September 13, 2006.

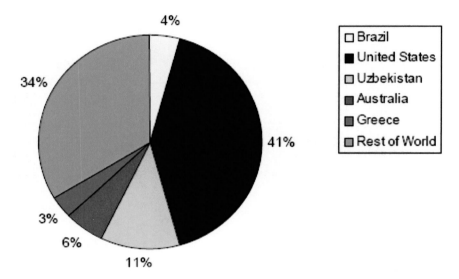

Figure 16. Cotton Exports, 2004/2005.

REFERENCE

[1] Carol Canada, Knowledge Services Group, Resources, Science and Industry Division, contributed to the preparation of this report.

In: Brazil in Focus: Economic, Political and Social Issues   ISBN: 978-1-60456-165-4
Editor: Jorge T. Almeida, pp. 61-77   © 2008 Nova Science Publishers, Inc.

Chapter 4

REACTION OF THE BRAZILIAN STOCK MARKET TO POSITIVE AND NEGATIVE SHOCKS

*Otavio Ribeiro de Medeiros**

Graduate Program in Administration, Graduate Program in Accounting
University of Brasilia, Campus Universitário Darcy Ribeiro,
FACE – salas 200/204, Brasilia – DF - Brazil

ABSTRACT

The paper makes use of an event study to test the Efficient Market Hypothesis and its variant, the Uncertain Information Hypothesis, for the Brazilian stock market. Previous literature has associated inefficiencies generated by thin markets with investor overreaction or underreaction, thereby refuting the Efficient Market Hypothesis. However, the arrival of new information introduces a period of increased risk and uncertainty to the rational agents. The Uncertain Information Hypothesis was devised to be a more realistic variation of the efficiency theory, since it accounts for investor reactions to unexpected surprises. The evidence found here indicates that neither the Efficient Market nor the Uncertain Information Hypotheses are supported by the Brazilian data. Actually, we found evidence that the Brazilian stock market overreacts to positive shocks and underreacts to negative shocks, which suggests the prevalence of institutional inefficiency.

1. INTRODUCTION

Many empirical attempts to consistently encounter the Efficient Market Hypothesis (EMH) in different markets have failed. Faced with the arrival of unexpected information, agents do not adjust prices immediately in accordance with the news. The implications of new

* MSc (Coppead), MSc (Birkbeck/London), PhD (Southampton), Professor of Finance, Graduate Program in Administration, Graduate Program in Accounting, University of Brasilia, Campus Universitário Darcy Ribeiro,FACE – salas 200/204, Brasilia – DF – Brazil, Phone: 55 61 3273 8538. Fax: 55 61 3349 7388. e-mail: otavio@unb.br

information on financial assets are often exaggerated and therefore, time for adjustment is required to equate the price level with the mean rate of return. Attempts to cope with violations of the EMH led to the conception of hypotheses such as overreaction and underreaction. However, an alternative version to the EMH has been pointed out to be more realistic and capable of explaining some apparent anomalies without actually violating market efficiency.

This paper studies the behavior of the Brazilian stock market, in order to find support for the presence of efficiency. Although there has been intense investigation on American, Asian, and European stock markets, Latin American emerging markets have often been disregarded[1]. This is especially applicable to Latin American markets such as the Brazilian. Its relatively small size, in terms of both the number of securities listed and investors, implies a lack of efficiency and could explain the lack of interest. However, the increasing trend of financial globalization might change this picture. Improvements in the Brazilian regulations and monitoring have improved the Brazilian stock exchange operating efficiency and increased its importance in the domestic financial sector. Our study uses market indexes as a benchmark in order to eliminate stock specific anomalies and to examine market behavior. The paper's main purpose is to verify the consistency of the Brazilian stock market with respect to the Efficient Market Hypothesis (EMH) and its variant, the Uncertain Information Hypothesis (UIH). The Overreaction (OH) and Underreaction (UH) Hypotheses are also tested as alternatives. Making use of an event study, the examination traces the effects of the passage of time on stock returns following favorable and unfavorable news. The benchmark adopted for generating abnormal returns for the Brazilian stock exchange is the Dow Jones Stock Index, which is associated to the New York Stock Exchange (NYSE). The return of the Brazilian market index is then regressed on the return of the Dow Jones Index to generate events.

The remainder of the paper is organized as follows. Section 2 provides some information on the Brazilian stock exchange; Section 3 explains the underlying theoretical background; Section 4 presents previous empirical work; Section 5 describes the methodology and the data; Section 6 documents the empirical results; and Section 7 concludes.

2. THE BRAZILIAN STOCK MARKET

The Brazilian stock market is virtually represented by a single stock exchange – Bovespa (Sao Paulo Stock Exchange) – which was founded on August 23, 1890. Up to the mid sixties, Bovespa and other Brazilian exchanges were official entities linked to finance departments of state governments, and brokers were appointed by the public sector. After the enactment of the Securities Act in 1965, the Brazilian financial system and capital market underwent a series of reforms, which provided the institutional character the Brazilian stock exchanges still have today. The Brazilian stock exchanges became non-profit self-regulating institutions, with administrative and financial autonomy. Brokerage firms replaced the traditional

---

[1] For the American market see for example DeBondt and Thaler (1985, 1987, 1990); Howe (1986); Brown and Harlow (1988); Brown, Harlow, and Tinic (1988, 1993); Zarowin (1989, 1990); and Conrad and Kaul (1993); for other foreign markets see Hogholm (2000); Ratner and Leal (1999); Gunaratne and Yonesawa (1997); and Shachmurove (2002).

individual government securities brokers, and firms established as joint stock companies or private limited liability companies. Located in the City of Sao Paulo, Bovespa is a self-regulating entity operating under the supervision of CVM – Comissao de Valores Mobiliarios, the Brazilian equivalent to the SEC - Securities and Exchange Commission in the US. In 1972, Bovespa implemented automated trading sessions with information displayed on-line and in real-time via a computer terminal network and in the late 70s, Bovespa introduced the options market in Brazil. By using electronic technology, Bovespa has expanded the potential information processing volume and has consolidated its position as the most important trading center in the Latin American market.

The Bovespa Index (Ibovespa) is the oldest and most traditional indicator of the average stock-price behavior in Brazil. In terms of liquidity, the stocks that integrate Ibovespa's theoretical portfolio represent more than 80% of the number of trades and the financial value registered on Bovespa's cash market and in terms of market cap. Firms with stocks included in the Ibovespa are responsible, in average, for approximately 70% of the sum of all Bovespa's firms' cap. To ensure the representativeness of Bovespa's indexes over time, the stock exchanges indexes portfolios are recalculated at the end of each four months. At the rebalancings, the changes in the relative participation of each stock in the index are identified, as well as their maintenance or exclusion, and possible inclusions of new papers are defined. Thus, Ibovespa's theoretical portfolio is valid for four months, for the periods of January to April, May to August and September to December. Table 1 provides some data on Bovespa and compares its size with the Brazilian GNP.

3. THEORETICAL BACKGROUND

This paper uses the event study methodology in order to investigate the Brazilian market's reaction to positive and negative shocks. The event study methodology is well documented in the literature and detailed descriptions of it can be found, for example, in MacKinlay (1997) and Cuthbertson and Nitzsche (2004).

Table 1. Bovespa and the Brazilian Economy

	Firms listed	Daily trading (US$ x 10^6)	Mkt. Cap. (US$ x 10^9)	Brazilian GNP (US$ x 10^9)	Mkt. Cap./GNP (%)
1994	582	360	189.1	543.1	34.8
1995	577	283	147.6	705.5	20.9
1996	589	394	216.9	775.5	28.0
1997	595	767	255.4	807.8	31.6
1998	599	569	160.9	787.9	20.4
1999	534	347	228.5	536.6	42.6
2000	495	410	225.5	602.2	37.5
2001	468	265	185.4	509.8	36.4
2002	436	197	124.0	459.4	27.0
2003	410	271	234.2	493.3	47.5
2004	390	419	340.9	604.9	56.4

Source: Bovespa (www.bovespa.com.br) and IPEA (www.ipeadata.gov.br).

Figure 1 depicts the expected market reaction of the EMH, the OH, the UH and the UIH with respect to positive (favorable) and negative (unfavorable) events. According to the conventional paradigm, financial agents interact with each other in a rational and efficient manner. A competitive environment, such as the one governing financial markets, fosters efficiency. New information is constantly being absorbed by investors and reflected in security returns. The instantaneous processing of data means that future rates of return cannot be predicted by past returns. These postulations have been put together under the Efficient Market Hypothesis (EMH).

The Uncertain Information Hypothesis (UIH) models this rational behavior of agents in an uncertain environment. According to Shachmurove (2002), the theory predicts that return volatilities will increase following an announcement. Specifically, post-negative disclosure volatilities are greater than positive volatilities. The latter is a rational consequence of risk-averse agents attempting to err on the side of caution. Brown, Harlow and Tiniç (1988) initially proposed the UIH with the purpose of providing a more flexible and realistic version of the EMH based on quite general and completely rational decision rules for investors. The model begins with the assumption that investors often set stock prices before the full implications of a dramatic financial event are known. The UIH then predicts that in the aftermath of new information, both the risk and the expected return of the affected firms increase in a systematic way. The authors claim that in addition to increasing measurable risk, a noisy bit of favorable or unfavorable news immediately causes a market containing risk-averse investors to set stock prices significantly below their conditional expected values. As the uncertainty over the eventual outcome is resolved, subsequent price changes tend to be positive on average, regardless of the nature of the catalyzed event. Further, if investors' preferences exhibit decreasing absolute risk aversion, the UIH predicts that the average price change will be larger following bad news than good ones.

The Overreaction Hypothesis (OH) states that stock prices react too sensitively on new information. Favorable disclosures are foreseen to influence the market to establish equity prices above the average rate of return. However, after some time has elapsed, investors realize that stock prices were set too high and so they are brought back to more realistic levels. On the other side, when unfavorable events arrive, overreaction makes prices to be set too low, but after a while these will rise and eventually find their new fundamental values.

The Underreaction Hypothesis (UH) states that stock prices incorporate information slowly. Stock price underreaction is the outcome of insufficient investor reaction due to conservatism behavior and slow diffusion of information, respectively. Conservatism means that investors react insufficiently, pushing prices up too little. Barberis et al's (1998) version of underreaction hypothesis implies that investors exhibit conservatism and underreact to information that has a high weight when adjusting their beliefs. In particular, this view claims that investors do not update their expectations adequately based on the strength and weight of new information. In contrast with the stock price underreaction explanation of Hong et al. (1999), which stems from the slow diffusion of firm-specific information (low analyst coverage), momentum is the result of systematic errors that investors make when they use publicly available information to form expectations about future cash flows (Barberis et al, 1998). Namely, investors exhibit conservatism and underreact to information that has high weight when they adjust their beliefs in forming cash flow expectations (Doukas and Phillip, 2003).

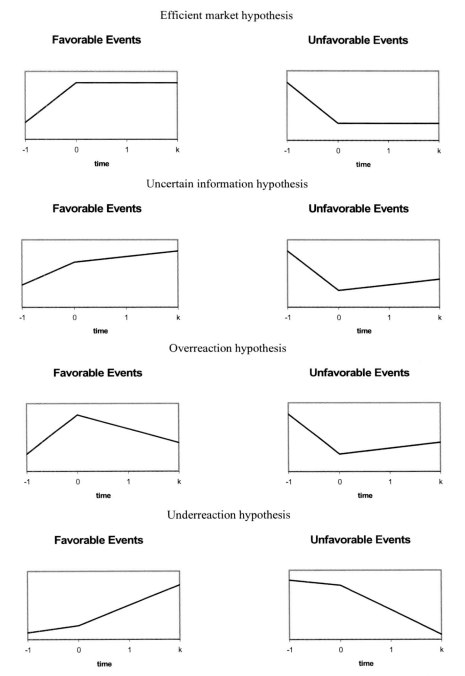

$t = 0$ = event date; p = initial price; p^e = equilibrium price; p^o = overreaction price; p^{ui} = uncertain information price; p^u = underreaction price

Figure 1. Stock price reactions according to EMH, OH, UIH, and UH[2].

---

[2] Based on Brown, Harlow and Tiniç (1988) and Shachmurove (2002).

4. EMPIRICAL EVIDENCE

Using data on an equally weighted CRSP index and the 200 largest individual stocks in the SandP 500, Brown, Harlow and Tiniç (1998) found evidence that the average post-event returns following both favorable and unfavorable events tend to be significantly positive. However, they also find that the correlations between the immediate price changes caused by the events and the direction of the subsequent price changes are extremely low, even in the very large samples of major favorable and unfavorable surprises tested. The authors argue that these findings are consistent with the UIH, which implies that the responses following individual events are random. They also report evidence that these increases in expected returns are directly linked to increases in stock variability induced by the events themselves.

Shachmurove (2002) studied the behavior of thirteen small European stock markets, searching to find international support for the presence of the EMH or the UIH in financial markets. The thirteen bourses are located in Belgium, Denmark, Finland, Greece, Ireland, Luxembourg, Netherlands, Norway, Portugal, Spain, Sweden, Switzerland, and Turkey. He then reports evidence that the European investors operating in the small continental stock exchanges generally react to uncertain information in an efficient and rational behavior. He argues that the investors initially set stock prices below their market value. Despite the prevalence of institutional inefficiency, the markets subsequently experience increased or non-negative returns. Moreover, he claims that the random patterns predicted by the EMH are evident as well. Therefore, he believes that by adhering to the paradigm of the UIH and the random course typical of the EMH, the majority of the surveyed stock exchanges are efficient.

Stock market overreaction and underreaction to public news events have been documented by several authors with respect to several kinds of event, such as stock splits (Grinblatt et al, 1984; Desai and Jain, 1997), tender offer and open market repurchases (Lakonishok and Vermaelen, 1990), analyst recommendations (Groth et al, 1979), Womacck (1996), dividend initiations and omissions (Michaely et al, 1995), seasoned issues of common stock (Loughran and Ritter, 1995; Spiess and Affleck-Graves, 1995), earnings surprises (Bernard and Thomas 1989, 1990; Brown and Pope, 1996), quarterly earnings announcements (Arbanell, 1991; Arbanell and Bernard, 1992), among others.

5. DATA AND METHODOLOGY

The methodology, introduced by Brown, Harlow and Tiniç (1988) and reproduced by Shachmurove (2002), is used here to test for efficiency over sixty days after an unexpected disruption in the Brazilian stock index, relative to the Dow Jones Stock Index, which can be interpreted as a proxy for the World Stock Market Index. Therefore, the data refers to the closing daily stock market index for the Brazilian stock market (Ibovespa) and for the Dow Jones stock index. The Brazilian stock market is considered a relatively small market taking into account the number of companies listed, securities traded and low market capitalization. However, the Brazilian stock market is open to foreign investment, despite its unfavorable liquidity and size. The question remains whether this transparency is sufficient to produce an efficient market. The period spans from 01/04/1994 to 11/10/2005 and the total number of daily observations for the study is 2016. The two relevant indexes were obtained from Economatica^{TM} (www.economatica.com). The stock-market index data series are then converted into daily return data series. The methodology focuses on the measures of post-event volatility and the cumulative abnormal returns. The Dow Jones Stock Index – used here as a proxy for the World Stock Index – is used as the benchmark to generate the positive and negative excess returns for the Brazilian stock market. The rate of return of the Brazilian stock market is regressed on the Dow Jones Index's rate of return, with the residual identified as an event if it is found to be greater than or equal to +2.5 percent in deviation (positive events) or lesser than or equal to –2.5% in deviation (negative events). This regression is expressed as:

$$R_t = \alpha + \beta R_t^{DJ} + u_t \qquad (1)$$

where R_t is the Brazilian stock market return, R_t^{DJ} is the Dow Jones stock market return, α and β are the regression coefficients, and u_t is a Gaussian white-noise error term. The returns are computed on a continuous-time capitalization basis:

$$R_t = \log\frac{I_t}{I_{t-1}} \quad \text{and} \quad R_t^{DJ} = \log\frac{I_t^{DJ}}{I_{t-1}^{DJ}}, \qquad (2)$$

where log is the natural logarithm operator, whereas I_t and I_t^{DJ} are the Brazilian and the Dow Jones stock market indexes, respectively. The fitted values of the Brazilian stock return are given by

$$\hat{R}_t = \hat{\alpha} + \hat{\beta} R_t^{DJ} \qquad (3)$$

where $\hat{\alpha}$ and $\hat{\beta}$ are the regressions parameters estimated by OLS. It will be seen on Section 6 that after finding that the data series of the logs on I_t and I_t^{DJ} are cointegrated, equation (1) had to be modified to include an error correction term. The regression residuals from (1) $\hat{u}_t$ are expressed as

$$\hat{u}_t = R_t - \hat{R}_t \qquad (4)$$

where R_t is the actual return and $\hat{R}_t$ is the fitted market return. The residual is identified as a positive (negative) event if it is found to be greater (lesser) than or equal to +2.5 (–2.5) percent in deviation. Hence, by definition, a positive event occurs on time t if

$$\hat{u}_t > 0.025 \qquad (5)$$

whereas a negative event occurs on time t if

$$\hat{u}_t < 0.025 \tag{6}$$

The event day is considered Day 0 and the relevant observations are obtained by examining subsequent Day 1 through Day 60. The variances of the residuals are computed as

$$Var(\hat{u}_t) = \frac{\hat{u}'\hat{u}}{N_j - 2} \tag{7}$$

where N_j denotes the number of post-event days ($N_j = 60$), while j = 1, 2, 3 stand for positive, negative and non-events, respectively, and $\hat{u}$ is the vector of residuals. The estimated residuals $\hat{u}_t$ are squared, added together and divided by the number of post-event days minus 2, which gives an unbiased estimate of the residuals' variance. Two F-statistics are then calculated to find out a significant difference between positive or negative events and non-event returns. Daily post-event abnormal returns for the two sets of events are computed and averaged in the cross-sectional dimension over the 60-day period following favorable and unfavorable observations. These 60-Day returns are then added to obtain the cumulative abnormal returns (CARs) for each type of news. Formally, this implies that the abnormal return for the stock market index on day t ($t = +1, +2...+60$) following the unexpected event d (AR_{td}) is calculated by subtracting the mean stock market return ($\overline{R}_3$) from the daily stock market return:

$$AR_{td} = R_{td} - \overline{R}_3 \tag{8}$$

where $d = 1, ..., n$, denotes the number of favorable or unfavorable events. R_{td} is the stock market return on day t for event d, and R_3 equals the mean return of the stock market for non-event days. The mean abnormal return (AR_t) on day t is obtained as follows:

$$\overline{AR_t} = \frac{1}{n}\sum_{d=1}^{n} AR_{td}, \ t = +1, +2, ..., +60. \tag{9}$$

The abnormal return for every event (AR_t) is added together and divided by the number of such events (n). The Cumulative Abnormal Return (CAR_t) is calculated by adding the mean abnormal returns over t days (AR_t), such that

$$CAR_t = CAR_{t-1} + \overline{AR_t} \tag{10}$$

The statistical significance of the CARs is determined through the application of a t test (MacKinlay, 1997):

$$t = \frac{CAR_{pt}}{[Var(CAR_{pt})]^{1/2}} \tag{11}$$

6. EMPIRICAL RESULTS

The current section summarizes the statistical results and is divided into three parts. The first one compares post-event and non-event variances, as documented in table 3. This is followed by an analysis of the cumulative abnormal returns and an evaluation of the adherence of the Brazilian stock market to the EMH or the UIH. Table 4 helps explaining this discussion. The final part addresses the implications of the statistics. As seen on the previous section, the determination of positive and negative events is achieved by regressing the return of the Brazilian sock market index (Ibovespa) on the return of the Dow Jones Index. However, by applying Johansen's cointegration test with $\log(I_t)$ and $\log(I_t^{DJ})$, we found that there is a cointegration relationship at the 5% level, with a likelihood ratio of 5.48 against a critical value of 9.24, which means that the null of cointegration cannot be rejected. Then we used the Engle-Granger estimation technique in order to estimate the parameters of a cointegrated relationship. By regressing $\log(I_t)$ on $\log(I_t^{DJ})$, we found the following cointegrating equation:

$$\log(I_t) = -6.0924 + 1.7060 \log(I_t^{DJ}) + \hat{u}_t. \tag{12}$$

After saving the residuals $\hat{u}_t$ obtained in equation (12), we regressed the return of the Brazilian stock market on the Dow Jones return, including the error correction term ($\hat{u}_{t-1}$). The result is expressed by equation (13):

$$\Delta\log(I_t) = \underset{(0.0005)}{0.0011} + \underset{(0.0483)}{1.049}\Delta\log I_t^{DJ} - \underset{(0.0020)}{0.0041}\hat{u}_{t-1} \qquad R^2 = 0.1918; DW = 2.0101 \tag{13}$$

However, it is very unlikely that this result is valid for the whole sample period. Structural changes might have occurred which imply different regressions with different parameters for sub-sample periods defined by the structural breaks. To check for structural breaks we used the Chow test (Chow, 1960). We found one structural break only, which occurred on 09/11/1998. Therefore, we divided the sample in two sub-sample periods: from 01/04/1994 to 09/11/1998 and from 09/12/1999 to 11/10/2005. The regressions obtained for these two sub-sample periods are:

$$\Delta\log(I_t) = \underset{(0.0009)}{0.0024} + \underset{(0.1168)}{1.2407}\Delta\log I_t^{DJ} - \underset{(0.0027)}{0.0118}\hat{u}_{t-1} \qquad R^2 = 0.1287; DW = 1.7838 \tag{14}$$

$$\Delta\log(I_t) = \underset{(0.0006)}{0.0014} + \underset{(0.0492)}{0.9455}\Delta\log I_t^{DJ} - \underset{(0.0018)}{0.0037}\hat{u}_{t-1} \qquad R^2 = 0.2201; DW = 2.0205 \tag{15}$$

Considering equations (14) and (15), the positive and negative events are then determined by finding out the outliers, i.e. the dates where $\hat{u}_t > 0.025$ or $\hat{u}_t < 0.025$, respectively.

Table 3. Variance of Returns after Events

	Variance
Positive events	0.00122912
Negative events	0.00064352
No events	0.00023502

Table 4. Test for Equality of Variances between Series

Sample: 1 2016					
Included observations: 2016					
1) H0: Variance positive events = Variance no events					
Method	df	Value	Probability		
F-test	(1665, 160)	5.229792	0.000000		
Bartlett	1	310.2851	0.000000		
Levene	(1, 1825)	66.13109	7.71E-16		
Brown-Forsythe	(1, 1825)	43.43846	5.71E-11		
Category Statistics					
			Mean Abs.	Mean Abs.	MeanTukey-
Variable	Count	Std. Dev.	Mean Diff.	Median Diff.	Siegel Rank
Positive	161	0.035059	0.020425	0.019079	337.3478
No shock	1666	0.015330	0.012250	0.012250	969.7269
All	1827	0.021152	0.012970	0.012851	914.0000
Bartlett weighted standard deviation: 0.017949					
2) H0: Variance negative events = Variance no events					
Method	df	Value	Probability		
F-test	(1665, 188)	2.738147	5.86E-16		
Bartlett	1	111.3848	0.000000		
Levene	(1, 1853)	48.16592	5.40E-12		
Brown-Forsythe	(1, 1853)	37.46399	1.13E-09		
Category Statistics					
			Mean Abs.	Mean Abs.	MeanTukey-
Variable	Count	Std. Dev.	Mean Diff.	Median Diff.	Siegel Rank
Negative	189	0.025368	0.017816	0.017272	322.5212
No shock	1666	0.015330	0.012250	0.012250	996.6888
All	1855	0.020822	0.012817	0.012761	928.0000
Bartlett weighted standard deviation: 0.016627					
3) H0: Variance positive events = Variance negative events					
Method	df	Value	Probability		
F-test	(188, 160)	1.909975	3.01E-05		
Bartlett	1	18.04446	2.16E-05		
Levene	(1, 348)	1.081647	0.299051		
Brown-Forsythe	(1, 348)	0.455662	0.500107		
Category Statistics					
			Mean Abs.	Mean Abs.	MeanTukey-
Variable	Count	Std. Dev.	Mean Diff.	Median Diff.	Siegel Rank
Positive	161	0.035059	0.020425	0.019079	162.2547
Negative	189	0.025368	0.017816	0.017272	186.7831
All	350	0.050419	0.019016	0.018103	175.5000
Bartlett weighted standard deviation: 0.030212					

6.1. Impact of Events on Return Volatilities

The variances of the return volatilities following unexpected shocks represent an important test for the EMH and the UIH. Ajayi and Mehdian (1995), Brown, Harlow and Tiniç (1988), Dissanaike (1996), and Fleming and Remolona (1999) find that unexpected announcements produce enhanced volatility statistics. Furthermore, variance volatilities following unfavorable disclosures should be greater than volatilities following positive news (Kaul and Nimalendran, 1990; Ketcher, 1994; Veronesi, 1999). Table 3 shows the variances obtained for post-positive, post-negative negative and no-events, respectively. Table 4 depicts the result of tests of equality of variances between these three categories, using F, Bartlett, Levene, and Brown-Forsythe tests.

The summary shown in tables 3 and 4 does not exhibit statistical support for the EMH. Both post-positive and post-negative shock variances are significantly different from the no-shock variance. Besides, the post-positive shock variance is significantly greater than the post-negative shock variance, which contradicts the UIH.

The results also show that, contrary to the Uncertain Information Hypothesis, the results document greater variances following favorable rather than unfavorable news.

Actually, greater return variances than normal may in fact indicate a rational response to uncertain announcements. Specifically, return variances should be larger following negative rather than positive reports, which would sustain the UIH (Shachmurove, 2002). However, Brazil deviates from the aforementioned rule and display characteristics similar to the OH and the UH. The arrival of unexpected information translates into increased volatilities on the Brazilian market. This also leads to the rejection of the EMH.

6.2. Cumulative Abnormal Returns

The cumulative abnormal return (CAR) data are more straightforward than the variance volatility statistics, since it constitutes the main test of market efficiency. Table 5, which in the Appendix at the end of the paper, shows the values of CARs after positive and negative events, whereas figure 2 below plots the CAR response the events events. From the CAR behavior shown, it can be seen that when a favorable event occurs, stock prices jumps to a higher level, corresponding to a CAR of around +0.0405, significant at the 1% level. Subsequent CARs show that stock prices oscillate around this new level up to day +30, when they start falling until they reach the vicinity of the pre-event level or even lower. If we examine the stock price response up to day +30, we would say that the EMH would have applied, since after the positive events, stock prices seem to stabilize around a new threshold. However, extending the analysis up to day +60, it becomes clear that an overreaction occurred on day 0, since prices keep falling until the end of the post-event window. Hence, the observed evidence supports the OH in the favorable scenario. It should be mentioned that Lasfer, Melnik and Thomas (2003) found CARs of 0.66% and 1.54% subsequent to positive events over 5 days for developed and emerging markets respectively, whereas we found a much higher CAR, around 3%, for the same period.

Examining the market reaction to negative events, we can see that stock prices fall sharply on days 0 and +1, producing a CAR of –0.054 (significant at the 1% level). Subsequently, a reversion seem to occur between days +1 and +5, with the CAR reaching –

0.034. From day +5 onwards, the CARs fall more or less steadily, reaching around –7% after 60 days. Summing up, upon the arrival of negative events, stock prices fall immediately, but subsequently, rather than remaining stable as expected by the EMH or moving up as postulated by the OH, they keep falling, implying that the initial adjustment was insufficient. This points out toward the UH. Therefore, with respect to negative events the Brazilian stock market must be classified as supporting the UH. Incidentally, Lasfer, Melnik and Thomas (2003) found CARs of –0.14% and –0.50% after negative events for developed and emerging markets respectively, whereas we found –3.4%.

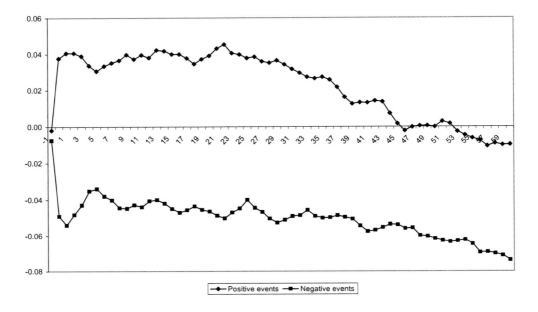

Figure 2. CARs after positive and negative events.

CONCLUSION

In this study, we found evidence that the Brazilian stock market overreacts to positive events and underreacts to negative events. The volatility response to both positive and negative events refutes the EMH. Besides, the propensity for positive post-event variances to be more volatile than the variances following negative events also contradicts the UIH. This outcome might be related to the nature of the Brazilian stock exchange surveyed. One possible explanation is that the Brazilian market is small as measured by the number of securities listed, quantity of investors, and market capitalization. Usually, such small exchanges are dominated by a small number of professionals who respond to long-run rather than short-run market fluctuations (Loughran and Ritter, 1996; Shachmurove, 2002).

We can think of another perhaps more plausible explanation in which the Brazilian market would be prone to be manipulated by informed traders. On the favorable events side, the informed traders would pull up stock prices attracting noisy traders. After some time, the informed traders would sell their positions to make profits and bring prices down, leaving "lemons" to the noisy traders. On the downward side, the informed traders would let prices fall to a certain level in order to attract noisy traders that would assume that this might be a good opportunity to purchase cheap stock. The informed traders would then sell their shares to minimize their losses, making stock prices to fall still further.

A secondary finding of our study is that the Brazilian market presents, after positive and negative shocks, much larger CARs in absolute value than those documented for example by Lasfer, Melnik and Thomas (2003), although this is according to their finding that the CARs are larger for less liquid (emerging) markets.

Economists assume that individuals behave rationally. Consequently, investors set stock prices to reflect all available information. However, the existence of efficiency in global security exchanges has been questioned. The critics point to the fact that the arrival of unexpected announcements leads investors to deviate from the efficiency paradigm. Market disturbances induce financial agents to overvalue stocks after positive events and undervalue securities following negative events. The Overreaction and the Underreaction Hypotheses rejects the canons of the Efficient Market Hypothesis. Besides, smaller markets should be more susceptible to this sort of irrational behavior. Yet, some authors argue that the anomalies can be attributed to institutional factors.

An altered version of the EMH has been acclaimed as offering an accurate explanation of financial markets. The Uncertain Information Hypothesis states that when faced with the arrival of unexpected information, anticipating increased insecurity and risk, investors protect their investment positions by initially undervaluing equity prices. In the following periods, the market experiences increasing or non-negative returns. This price adjustment should be accompanied by increased return variances. This paper shows that Brazilian investors operating in a relatively small stock exchange do not generally react to uncertain information in an efficient and rational manner. At the arrival of positive events, the agents immediately increase stock prices, but these prices start falling to their previous levels after about 30 days, which indicates that overreaction has occurred. On the downward side, investors facing negative events immediately lower stock prices, but after a brief recovery, prices begin to fall even further, evidencing that underreaction has taken place. Therefore, the random patterns predicted either by the Efficient Market or the Uncertain Information Hypotheses are not evident in our study. Contrary to the findings of Shachmurove (2002) in connection with small European markets, we have found that the Brazilian market behaves neither according to the Efficient Market nor the Uncertain Information Hypotheses, but presents instead strong signs of overreaction and underreaction.

REFERENCES

Ajayi, R. A. and S. Mehdian. 1995. Global Reaction of Security Prices to Major US-Induced Surprises: An Empirical Investigation, *Journal of Applied Financial Economy*, 5, pp. 203-218.

Brown, K. C. and W. V. Harlow. 1988. Market Overreaction: Magnitude and Intensity, *Journal of Portfolio Management*, 14:2, Winter, pp. 6-13.

Brown, K. C.; W. V. Harlow, and S. M. Tiniç. 1988. Risk Aversion, Uncertain Information, and Market Efficiency, *Journal of Financial Economics*, 22, pp. 355-85.

Brown, K. C.; W. V. Harlow, and S. M. Tiniç. 1993. The Risk and Required Return of Common Stock Following Major Price Innovations, *Journal Financial and Quantitative Analysis*, 28:1, pp. 101-16.

Chow, G.C. 1960. Tests of Equality between Sets of Coefficients in Two Linear Regressions, *Econometrica*, 28, 591-605.

Conrad, J. and G. Kaul. 1993. Long-Term Market Overreaction or Biases in Computed Returns? *Journal of Finance*, 48:1, March, pp. 39-63.

Cuthbertson, K. and Nitzsche, D. 2004. *Quantitative Financial Economics*, 2nd Ed., Chichester, West Sussex (UK): Wiley.

DeBondt, W. F. and R. H. Thaler. 1985. Does the Stock Market Overreact? *Journal of Finance*, 40, pp. 793-805.

DeBondt, W. F. and R. H. Thaler. 1987. Further Evidence on Investor Overreaction and Stock Market Seasonality, *Journal of Finance*, 42, pp. 557-581.

DeBondt, W. F. and R. H. Thaler. 1990. Do Security Analysts Overreact? *American Economic Review*, 80, pp. 52-57.

Dissanaike, G. 1996. Are Stock Price Reversals Really Asymmetric? A Note, *Journal of Banking and Finance*, 20:1, January, pp. 189-201.

Doukas, J.A. and McKnight, P.J. 2003. European Momentum Strategies, Information Diffusion, and Investor Conservatism, Research paper, Inquire Europe - Institute for Quantitative Investment Research, http://www.inquire-europe.org/. February 12, 2003 accessed on November 28, 2005.]

Fleming, M. J. and E. M. Remolona. 1999. What Moves Bond Prices? *Journal of Portfolio Management*, 25:4, pp. 28-38.

Gunaratne, P. S. M. and Y. Yonesawa. 1997. Return Reversals in the Tokyo Stock Exchange: A Test of Stock Market Overreaction, *Japan World Economy*, 9:3, August, pp. 363-84.

Howe, J. S. 1986. Evidence on Stock Market Overreaction: Size and Seasonality Effects, *Finan. Analysts Journal,* 42, pp. 74-77.

Kaul, G. and M. Nimalendran. 1990. Price Reversals: Bid-Ask Errors or Market Overreaction? *Journal of Financial Economics,* 28:1-2, November-December, pp. 67-93.

Ketcher, D. N. and B. D. Jordan. 1994. Short-Term Price Reversals Following Major Price Innovations: Additional Evidence on Market Overreaction, *Journal of Economics and Business*, 46:4, October, pp. 307-23.

Kocagil, A. E. and Y. Shachmurove. 1998. Return-Volume Dynamics in Futures Markets, *Journal of Futures Markets,* 18:4, June, pp. 399-426. Lo, A. W. and A. C.

Lasfer, M.A., Melnik, A. and Thomas, D.C. 2003. Short-term Reaction of Stock Markets in Stressful Circumstances, *Journal of Banking and Finance*, 27. 1959-1977.

Lo, A. W. and A. C. MacKinlay. 1997. When Are Contrarian Profits Due to Stock Market Overreaction? in *Market Efficiency: Stock Market Behavior in Theory and Practice*, 2, Andrew W. Lo, ed., *Elgar Reference Collection. International Library of Critical Writings in Financial Economics*, 3, Cheltenham, U.K. and Lyme, N.H.: Elgar, distributed by American International Distribution Corporation, Williston, Vt., Previously Published: 1990, pp. 429-59.

Lo, A. W. and A. C. MacKinlay. 1999. *A Non-Random Walk Down Wall Street*. Princeton: Princeton University Press.

Loughran, T. and J. R. Ritter. 1996. "Long-Term Market Overreaction: The Effect of Low-Priced Stocks," *Journal of Finance*, 51:5, December, pp. 1959-70.

MacKinlay. 1990. When Are Contrarian Profits Due to Stock Market Overreaction? *Review of Financial Studies*, 3:2, pp. 175-205.

Organization For Economic Cooperation and Development (OECD) Economic Surveys 1994-1995: Greece. Paris and Washington, D.C.: 1995.

Ratner, M., and R. P. C. Leal. 1999. Evidence of Overreaction in the Emerging Equity Markets of Latin America and Asia, *Journal of Emerging Markets*, 4:3, Fall-Winter, pp. 5-24.

Ruback, R. S. 1982. The Effect of Discretionary Price Control Decisions on Equity Values, *Journal of Financial Economics,* 10, pp. 83-105.

Shachmurove, Y. 1996. Dynamic Linkages Among Latin American and Other Major World Stock Markets, in *Research in International Business and Finance: International Stock Market Interactions and Financial Issues in Emerging Markets*, 10, John Dukas and Larry Lang, eds. Greenwich, Conn. and London: JAI Press Inc., pp. 3-33.

Shachmurove, Y. 1999. The Premium in Black Foreign Exchange Markets: Evidence From Developing Economies, *Journal of Policy Modeling,* 21:1, January, pp. 1-39.

Shachmurove, Y. 2002. The Behavior of Secondary European Stock Markets to Positive and Negative Shocks. *International Journal of Business*, 7(2).

Veronesi, P. 1999. Stock Market Overreaction to Bad News in Good Times: A Rational Expectations Equilibrium Model, *Review of Financial Studies*, 12:5, Winter, pp. 975-1007.

Zarowin, P. 1989. Short-run Market Overreaction: Size and Seasonality Effects, *Journal Portfolio Management*, 15:3, Spring, pp. 26-29.

Zarowin, P. 1990. Size, Seasonality, and Stock Market Overreaction, *Journal Financial and Quantitative Analysis*, 25:1, March, pp. 113-25.

APPENDIX

Table 5. Market reaction to positive and negative shocks

Date	Market reaction to positive events			Market reaction to negative events		
	Index	AR	CAR	Index	AR	CAR
-1	100,00	-0,00190	-0,00190	100,00	-0,00742	-0,00742 *
0	104,23	0,03958	0,03768 *	96,64	-0,04162	-0,04904 *
1	100,48	0,00288	0,04056 *	100,24	-0,00501	-0,05404 *
2	100,20	0,00007	0,04062 *	101,33	0,00583	-0,04821 *
3	100,02	-0,00168	0,03894 *	101,28	0,00531	-0,04290 *
4	99,66	-0,00527	0,03367 *	101,52	0,00768	-0,03521 *
5	99,88	-0,00306	0,03062 *	100,87	0,00126	-0,03395 *
6	100,47	0,00282	0,03343 *	100,33	-0,00410	-0,03805 *
7	100,36	0,00173	0,03517 *	100,52	-0,00218	-0,04023 *
8	100,32	0,00135	0,03651 *	100,32	-0,00420	-0,04444 *
9	100,51	0,00318	0,03969 *	100,71	-0,00031	-0,04475 *
10	99,94	-0,00247	0,03722 *	100,94	0,00192	-0,04283 *
11	100,42	0,00227	0,03949 *	100,63	-0,00110	-0,04392 *
12	100,04	-0,00149	0,03799 *	101,07	0,00327	-0,04065 *
13	100,62	0,00425	0,04224 *	100,81	0,00062	-0,04003 *
14	100,14	-0,00053	0,04171 *	100,55	-0,00197	-0,04201 *
15	100,01	-0,00178	0,03993 *	100,45	-0,00297	-0,04497 *
16	100,19	-0,00001	0,03992 *	100,53	-0,00209	-0,04706 *
17	99,97	-0,00219	0,03773 *	100,89	0,00144	-0,04563 *
18	99,87	-0,00316	0,03457 *	100,96	0,00209	-0,04353 *
19	100,46	0,00267	0,03725 *	100,55	-0,00197	-0,04551 *
20	100,37	0,00184	0,03909 *	100,65	-0,00092	-0,04643 *
21	100,59	0,00399	0,04308 *	100,51	-0,00231	-0,04874 *
22	100,41	0,00221	0,04529 *	100,59	-0,00155	-0,05029 *
23	99,72	-0,00474	0,04055 *	101,08	0,00332	-0,04697 *
24	100,11	-0,00082	0,03974 *	100,97	0,00220	-0,04477 *
25	99,99	-0,00196	0,03778 *	101,22	0,00471	-0,04006 *
26	100,26	0,00070	0,03848 *	100,31	-0,00433	-0,04439 *
27	99,93	-0,00256	0,03592 *	100,51	-0,00237	-0,04676 *
28	100,11	-0,00075	0,03517 *	100,38	-0,00365	-0,05042 *
29	100,32	0,00130	0,03648 *	100,51	-0,00229	-0,05271 *
30	99,96	-0,00225	0,03423 **	100,91	0,00161	-0,05110 *
31	99,94	-0,00254	0,03168 **	100,95	0,00199	-0,04910 *
32	99,98	-0,00208	0,02961 **	100,80	0,00051	-0,04860 *
33	99,96	-0,00227	0,02733	101,04	0,00289	-0,04570 *
34	100,11	-0,00083	0,02651	100,41	0,00333	-0,04903 *
35	100,27	0,00082	0,02733	100,64	0,00107	-0,05010 *
36	100,04	-0,00152	0,02581	100,77	0,00028	-0,04982 *
37	99,78	-0,00411	0,02170	100,86	0,00116	-0,04865 *
38	99,63	-0,00556	0,01614	100,64	0,00099	-0,04965 *
39	99,82	-0,00365	0,01249	100,64	0,00100	-0,05065 *

Table 5. (Continued).

Date	Market reaction to positive events			Market reaction to negative events		
	Index	AR	CAR	Index	AR	CAR
40	100,26	0,00072	0,01321	100,37	0,00374	-0,05439 *
41	100,18	-0,00012	0,01310	100,42	0,00320	-0,05758 *
42	100,29	0,00101	0,01411	100,82	0,00073	-0,05686 *
43	100,14	-0,00050	0,01361	100,90	0,00149	-0,05536 *
44	99,55	-0,00637	0,00724	100,92	0,00178	-0,05358 *
45	99,63	-0,00561	0,00164	100,71	0,00031	-0,05389 *
46	99,81	-0,00383	-0,00219	100,54	0,00207	-0,05596 *
47	100,39	0,00198	-0,00021	100,78	0,00039	-0,05557 *
48	100,26	0,00066	0,00045	100,31	0,00435	-0,05992 *
49	100,20	0,00010	0,00055	100,70	0,00048	-0,06040 *
50	100,13	-0,00060	-0,00006	100,62	0,00129	-0,06169 *
51	100,49	0,00294	0,00289	100,64	0,00108	-0,06276 *
52	100,07	-0,00115	0,00173	100,67	0,00070	-0,06347 *
53	99,76	-0,00432	-0,00258	100,79	0,00050	-0,06297 *
54	99,98	-0,00206	-0,00464	100,81	0,00060	-0,06237 *
55	100,03	-0,00160	-0,00624	100,51	0,00229	-0,06466 *
56	100,07	-0,00119	-0,00743	100,26	0,00483	-0,06949 *
57	99,87	-0,00320	-0,01063	100,77	0,00023	-0,06925 *
58	100,34	0,00148	-0,00916	100,66	0,00085	-0,07011 *
59	100,10	-0,00086	-0,01002	100,63	0,00110	-0,07121 *
60	100,21	0,00023	-0,00978	100,49	0,00257	-0,07378 *

* Significant at the 1% level; ** Significant at the 5% level.

In: Brazil in Focus: Economic, Political and Social Issues   ISBN: 978-1-60456-165-4
Editor: Jorge T. Almeida, pp. 79-98   © 2008 Nova Science Publishers, Inc.

Chapter 5

STATE AND REGIME IN POST-64 BRAZIL: BUREAUCRATIC AUTHORITARIANISM OR MILITARY DICTATORSHIP?[1]

João Roberto Martins Filho

Department of Political Science at Universidade Federal de São Carlos, Brazil

INTRODUCTION

What are the dynamics of the political crisis of the post-64 Brazilian dictatorship? What place do intra-military processes have in the configuration of these broader dynamics? What types of divisions took shape within the military field during the dictatorship? These are the questions that guided my research on the political processes of the Brazilian dictatorship in the period of its consolidation (1964-69). The approach that I propose here focuses specifically on the political dynamics of the regime. The relationship between these two terms – political dynamics and regime form – both defines the field where my general concerns lay and calls for a review of the most relevant literature about the Southern Cone military regimes of the 1960s and 1970s. In this regard I will suggest that the dominant theses on those military governments lead to a series of difficulties in our understanding of the political process of the dictatorships, insofar as they underestimate the role that military processes played within them.

---

[1] This chapter is an abridged version of the first chapter of my book *O Palácio e a Caserna: a Dinâmica Militar das Crises Políticas da Ditadura, 1964-1969*, published in Brazil in 1995. My research was supported by the Fulbright Foundation, as well as the Brazilian CNPq and CAPES. As a Fulbright scholar I benefited from a stay at the University of California, Riverside, in 1991, where I was hosted by my then advisor and now close friend Ronald Chilcote. A different version was published in *Revista de Sociologia e Política*, v. 2 , p. 7-23, june 1994. Translated by Meryl Adelman.

PERSPECTIVES FROM POLITICAL SCIENCE

I suggest to start from one of the fundamental models of Comparative Politics, and more specifically, from the well-known dichotomy that it establishes between "civic" and "praetorian" societies. According to the master of such explanations, in contrast to civic systems, with their high correlation between institutionalization and participation, praetorian systems correspond to societies "with low levels of institutionalization and high levels of participation ... where social forces, using their own methods act directly in the political sphere". (Huntington, 1968, p. 80) In the context of the polemic that began, in the mid-1960s, on the relationship between processes of economic and political modernization in developing societies, these authors went on to argue that within them, processes of economic change would not necessarily lead to the perfecting of political institutions. Concerned with the pressing problem of stability and order in societies "undergoing rapid and disruptive social and economic change" (Huntington, 1968, vii), they argued that within them, "the rates of social mobilization and the expansion of political participation are high; the rates of political organization and institutionalization are low. The result is political instability and disorder". (Huntington, 1968, p. 5) Brazil in the sixties then becomes one of the most notable examples of their notion of praetorian mass societies or political societies reminiscent of the perverse constitutions and degenerated states mentioned by the classics of political theory. These theses influenced an entire generation of experts on Latin America that produced particular resonance within the US inspired current of Brazilian Political Science.

My interest here lies in identifying how these writings dealt with the issue of political crisis in praetorian societies. Legitimate heir to the long-standing concern of elitist theorists regarding popular political participation, this current states that mass societies, given their inability to reconcile high levels of mobilization with strong institutions were characterized by endemic political crisis. "In a praetorian system social forces confront each other nakedly. ... Each group employs means which reflect its peculiar nature and capabilities. ... The absence of effective political institutions in a praetorian society means that power is fragmented: it comes in many forms and in small quantities" (Huntington, 1968, p.196-197). The fragility and transitory nature of all forms of authority are their trademark and military "are seen as only one specific manifestation of a broader phenomenon in underdeveloped societies: the general politicization of social forces and institutions". (Huntington, 1968, p. 81 e 194)

As some analysts have realized, this approach was deeply rooted in the methodological emphasis that this school explicitly placed on the degree, rather than the on forms or on the nature of power. Within the field of Comparative Politics, as one critic of such positions has already argued, this leads to the conclusion that "the accumulation of power is the alpha and omega of 'political development'", and to a strong tendency to legitimate all forms of power upon emphasizing "any consolidation of political power which is capable of exercising effective control" (O'Donnell, 1977, p. 52). This is said explicitly in the opening paragraph of Huntington's *Political Order in Changing Societies*:

> "The most important political distinction among countries concerns not their form of government but their degree of government. The differences between democracy and dictatorship are less than the differences between those countries whose politics

embodies consensus, community, legitimacy, organization, effectiveness, stability, and those countries whose politics is deficient in these qualities". (Huntington, 1968, p. 1)

What we see clearly manifested there is a tendency to analyze political processes at a very high level of generality which does not seem to leave any room for the topic of the relationship between political crises and different types of power. In this regard, and moving on to another current of analysis that has heavily influenced the study of the dictatorships under consideration here, the theory of authoritarianism can be seen as an attempt to overcome such limitations. One of its most important characteristics is its effort to perfect the traditional dualism of Political Science, centered on an opposition between democratic and totalitarian systems. For the authors belonging to this school, the situation of a whole group of contemporary societies calls for the definition of an intermediate type of regime, with a life and features of it own, that can neither be considered democratic nor totalitarian (Linz, 1970). However, in terms of what interests us here, a more attentive examination reveals the limitations of such an effort to analyze forms of domination, as part of the task of understanding political crises. Its central tenet seems precisely to be the refusal of any form of structural determinism; its cornerstone, the methodological precedence of elite political action for the comprehension of processes of crisis. This is the case for Juan Linz' model for deciphering the crises of democratic regimes and the consideration of their alleged inevitability.

Regarding the problems of political crises in dictatorial regimes, we should still recognize that within the limits of the Political Science mainstream, certain authors explore possibilities that distinguish them from the authors discussed above. In this regard, it has remained up to a variety of corporatist approaches, concerned with the critique of the culturalist tradition of this school, to bring to the debate on the authoritarian regimes a particular topic that was uncommon in the American literature: the relevance of historical and structural factors for the differentiation of forms of political domination. These theoreticians set out to build an elaborate typology of modern arrangements for "interest representation" that would be able to go beyond the classic pluralist paradigm. In this effort, representatives of this current of thought show a rare sensitivity for issues of political and social structure.

Alongside other types of modern arrangements, such as pluralism, monism, and trade unionism, corporatism is seen as one of the possible institutional forms for the linking of the socially organized interests of civil society to the decision-making structures of the State. Sharing a basic structural similarity, the set of contemporary arrangements for the corporatist system of interest representation were seen to hold within different subtypes that were a product of highly varied "social, political and economic processes". It is precisely in this effort to define the contrasts between "societal" and "statist" sub-types that authors such as Philippe Schmitter (1974, p.105) introduce the subject of historical and structural factors. In his view, it is a matter of considering the constraints, opportunities and contradictions that the operation of the economic system creates for political actors, which means that the basic institutions of capitalism and the class structure of power and property that it generates must be examined. (Schmitter, 1974, p. 107)

The diverse origins of corporatist modes are seen as related to certain basic needs of capitalist reproduction in different phases of its international context. The societal subtype is seen as a component of post-liberal advanced capitalism and it statist variant as an element, if not a structural need of the late capitalist, anti-liberal, authoritarian and Neo-mercantilist State. (Schmitter, 1974, p.105)

This dislocation of the field of analysis from action to structure was all the clearer in the works of the Argentine political scientist Guillermo O'Donnell. In proposing a revision of corporatist perspectives, he draws attention to the "exclusion of the historical-structural factors" as their main limitation, as well as their inability to understand corporatism as "a set of structures which link society with the state". (O'Donnell, 1977, p. 49, 47). The path that O'Donnell took can be seen as an exemplary case of the tendency to reconcile concepts of mainstream Political Science with Marxist theories of the State.[2] Although this feature was hardly noted, his work can be divided in two periods: an initial analysis focused on a "genetic explanation of certain fundamental characteristics of contemporary South American political systems" and later attempts to define bureaucratic authoritarianism – a notion to which I will return further on – as "a type of capitalist state (that) should ... be understood in light of the distinctive features of capitalist states in general". (O'Donnell, 1973, p. 53 and 1988, p. 2). In this vein, the author goes on to develop a historical-structural approach that involves investigating "the temporal relations between a system of forces and social relationships – capitalism – and its mutually consonant patterns of political domination". (O'Donnell, 1980).

Having carried out this evaluation of the hegemonic views within the debate on military dictatorships, we can then move on to the issue of the obstacles that its categories create for understanding the issue that interests us here. Once again, I suggest starting from Huntington. His theses on the endemic political crises and endemic militarism of societies that are undergoing modernization processes seem to neglect the particular power structures that were implemented as of the 60s in a variety of Latin American countries. In this sense, it is worth noting that the authors who belong to this current are so preoccupied with the question of the viability of the role of the military as institution builder that they seem to have forgotten the real changes in the State apparatus that were made in the aftermath of the military coups, as was the case for post-64 Brazil. It is no coincidence that many of the analyses made by so-called Brazilianists took on a normative tone, positively evaluating gains in terms of economic development, order and stability, while at the same time expressing reservations for what they saw as the negative side of the phenomenon: its inability to create true political institutions, in the shape of the political party system of civic societies.[3] In other words, in focusing their attention on political institutions that did not emerge, these scholars turn their eyes away from the whole dictatorial structure that was thus built "behind their backs." Whether stable or not, regimes like the Brazilian one created effective power structures. In my opinion, it is to the study of the latter that we must turn.

Furthermore, elitist approaches' neglect for the forms of power became a specific obstacle to the analyses of crisis dynamics. It is no coincidence that representatives of this perspective that turned to the specific case of post-1964 Brazil were unable to make progress in their understanding of the concrete content of the conflicts that structured the political crises of the military regime. Within the context of neglect for structural determinations, their emphasis on projects, discourse and ideologies ran up against the need for constant

---

[2] This move toward Marxist theory was denied by commentators of O'Donnell's work. In David Collier's words (1982, p. 31), there was not more than a simple "change in terminology: the substitution of the concept of political system for that of the State.

[3] This is the case of Schneider (1971), Roett (1973), Perlmutter (1969), Feit (1973) and Rowe (1966).

reconstruction of predictions on the direction of leaderships' actions; they were frequently lost in the precarious visibility of analyses that had been carried out in the "heat of the moment". (Mendes, 1966 and 1967). Following another route, attempts to define the post-1964 regime through research on selection criteria, attitudes and values of the power elite contributed little regarding the specific dynamic of the political conflicts, which marked the crisis of the period. (Druckman and Vario, 1983). Lastly, in their analysis of the Brazilian case, the corporatist perspectives discussed above seem, although remaining within the interest representation paradigm, to go beyond some of the most visible limitations of the debate on "incomplete institutionalization", making it possible to consider actual modifications of power structures post-1964. For example, in posing the question, "What did the military do to alter the type of authoritarian domination developed under Getúlio Vargas?", authors such as Philippe Schmitter make progress in the study of power arrangements.

From this vantage point, institutionalization comes to be seen in terms of effective processes rather than absent processes. Nonetheless, Schmitter's propositions on the corporatism of the Brazilian state, although not blocking analysis of the structural modifications that mark the processes of political crisis, do present some limitations to deepening our understanding of these processes. The idea that corporatism is compatible with several types of regime does not lead to greater exploration of the specific nature of the power arrangements that were gradually implanted after 1964. Symptomatically, in analyzing the processes of power centralization and control over the political system periphery – with emphasis on the National Information Service (Serviço Nacional de Informações, SNI) this author also seems to be unable to resist the "sirens' call" of institutionalization.

POLITICAL CRISIS AND STATE FORMS

We may perhaps define the argument presented here in a single statement: the study of processes of political crisis requires analysis of the structural forms of political power. In the field of Marxist theory of the State, this means returning to the classic concern with the variation of bourgeois power: the different "forms of government", as brought out in Marx, Trotsky and Gramsci's writings on Bonapartism, fascism and Caesarism. On other occasions, it should be added, this topic reappears in the Marxist analysis of "typical" and "atypical", "complete" and "incomplete" forms of bourgeois power. (Guimarães, 1988). Later, Nicos Poulantzas' work took up the Marxist theory of the State and politics again, seeking to systematize and develop it through his new propositions on regime and State types. Through a particular reading of Poulantzas' work (1977, 1978, 1978a), I attempt to present a proposal for the analysis of the critical processes of military dictatorships.

Through his pioneering attempt that develops the idea of the political as a regional level of the capitalist mode of production and an analysis of the bourgeois State as a specific form of juridical and political apparatus, Poulantzas' work produces several decisive ruptures. This however is not the appropriate place to discuss the development of his work; rather, I shall limit myself to his reflections on "exceptional" forms of State and regime. In looking at those latter, he sought to demonstrate that the variation in those forms of the State are the result of specific political crises. Bonapartism, fascism and military dictatorship can be considered to be *critical forms of the State.*

In this sense, the focus of my work here is not the study of the political crises that are at the root of transition from one form of State to another. Rather, the processes of crisis occurring after the implantation of the military dictatorships turn our attention to the concept of "forms of exceptional regimes" which means *critical forms of regimes.* Thus, the brief examination of the issue of forms of State that I will engage in here has the aim of introducing the question of the relationship between regime forms and political crisis.

From the start, one essential aspect of this issue must be kept in mind: exceptional forms of the State regard a situation of rupture in the State apparatus – a crucial reorganization of State apparatuses. In this sense, students of the post-1964 Brazilian political process will certainly recognize the pertinence of Poulantzas' characterization of the basic features that underlie the changes taking place in those arrangements. For our purposes here, it should be enough to enunciate the following: a tendency to control the entirety of State and non-State apparatuses, by one apparatus alone; the workings of the sub-ideology of this dominant apparatus in legitimating repression and obtaining the submission of other apparatuses; the "dislocation of dominance" from within the State as a whole to the site of a specific apparatus within which a previously secondary aspect – the ideological – becomes primordial; significant changes in the juridical system (public law no longer exercising a role in regulating and establishing limits); modification of the principle of suffrage, with the crisis of political party representation and the curtailment of voting rights; higher rates of bureaucratization; parallel chains of power, meaning the end of discrete spheres of competence, with the dislocation of contradictions to the interior of State apparatuses themselves. (Poulantzas, 1978a, p. 335-353)

Poulantzas' scholars will certainly note that here the concept of the ideological apparatuses of the State is missing. Actually I do not consider all the political parties, the educational system and the Church as *State* apparatuses. So, I have concentrated on Poulantzas' analysis of the apparatuses and branches of the State per se[4]. My focuses of attention are the exceptional forms of regime. Thus, although in *Fascism and Dictatorship* the criteria for distinguishing between fascist, Bonapartist and military dictatorship regimes lies mainly in the relationship between repressive and ideological apparatuses – "the dominance of one or the other specifying the forms that regimes or States of exception take on" – I will restrict myself to the notion that the dominance of a fascist party, civil administration or the Army, *as branches of the State,* and that the relationship between these branches and non-State apparatuses is what distinguishes these forms.

A more in-depth analysis of the problem of the specificity of regime forms requires a return to some of the observations that Poulantzas put forth in his book, *Political Power and Social Classes,* in which he seems to be suggesting a different approach. State forms, he argues, can only be studied in conjunction with *regime forms,* which are related to the political scenario and to periodization. From my perspective, it is here where a more

---

[4] In my opinion, Poulantzas' book, *Political Power and Social Classes* does away with the distinction between the 'repressive' and 'ideological' State apparatuses. This distinction, which appears in the famous Poulantzas-Miliband debate and in *Fascism and Dictatorship,* sets forth two problems which I will only mention here: if in *Political Power and Social Classes* the definition of the capitalist State is based on its specific dual function in isolating and representing unity, then why are the school system, leftist parties and the State considered "State apparatuses"? Do they really carry out this dual function, and if so, how?

interesting possibility for the study of regime forms can be found. I suggest that it is possible to make progress in the understanding of the military dictatorial regime through the analysis of the dynamics of its political crises. This perspective should become clearer through the following evaluation of analyses that have been made on the nature of the regimes that emerged from Latin American military coups of the sixties and seventies.

To do this, I will return to the debate on the autocratic form of the State and on the regimes that were the result of military coups in Latin America in the sixties and seventies. To remain within Brazil, the definition of the military dictatorship as fascist was, for a time, well accepted (Jaguaribe, 1968). In order to refute this perspective, it should be enough to take a look at the distinctive characteristics of fascism according to Poulantzas, or to turn to the Latin American literature that criticized that type of interpretation.[5]

But the problem seems to be more complex in the case of Bonapartism. Even if we were able to return to the specific nature of the political crisis that leads to this type of State, Marxist analyses seeking to understand the post-64 regime in terms of this framework bring out a crucial point in our approach to the political dynamics of dictatorship (Antunes, 1988, p. 112-26) I refer to the issue of the bureaucratization of the State and the autonomy that bureaucracy obtains, as fundamental characteristics of regimes like the one established in post-1964 Brazil. In effect, even the quickest examination of the literature on "military authoritarianism" reveals that one of the dominant perspectives is the one that gives salience to bureaucratic elements in defining the characteristics of this type of regime.

CRITIQUE OF BUREAUCRATIC AUTHORITARIANISM

Actually, at least within academic discussion, the work of Guillermo O'Donnell has long been regarded as a point of reference for studies on the new type of military regimes that emerged in Latin America. In his earlier writing – works published originally in 1972 – he attempted to construct an explanation of this type of "political system" in terms of David Apter's analyses of modernization processes and Samuel Huntington's thesis on the "political gap" of praetorian societies (O'Donnell, 1973 and 1986a). Later, as we already have seen, this author modified his perspective, first in the sense of incorporating a Marxist variety of corporatism (O'Donnell, 1974) and then, a historical and structural view of the capitalist State. At this point I would like to examine his work in terms of another key issue: why should the Brazilian and Argentine regimes be characterized as bureaucratic rather than military? Why the emphasis on processes of bureaucratization rather than militarization?

In this regard, even the slightest look at the writings of this Argentine political scientist is enough to reveal that the shifts in his general perspective coexist alongside strong elements of continuity. The basis for that analytical continuity can be found, in my opinion, in the notion of *bureaucratization*. It is no coincidence that the cornerstone of his first important study, in which he proposes a genetic explanation of the political systems of countries such as Argentina and Brazil, was the hypothesis of the "penetration of technocratic roles" in societies with high levels of modernization. It is within this context that he offers the concept

---

[5] To mention just a few examples, we have Quartim's work (1971) on the role of the army in political dictatorships as the political party of the bourgeoisie and the analyses of the lack, in such regimes, of a party capable of mobilizing the masses, in Borón (1977) and Cardoso (1982).

of bureaucratic authoritarianism, through the twin borrowing of notions from Juan Linz (autocratic regime) and David Apter (bureaucratic system). In his own words,

> this awkward term [is used] because it facilitates the use of the term "authoritarian" as a genus that includes other types of non-democratic South American political systems associated with lower levels of modernization. The term "bureaucratic" suggests the crucial features that are specific to authoritarian systems of high modernization: the growth of organizational power of many social sectors, the government attempts to control by "encapsulation", the career patterns and the power bases of most incumbents of technocratic roles, and the pivotal role played by large (public and private) bureaucracies. (O'Donnell, 1973, p.95).[6]

In my opinion, the later shifts in O'Donnell's work do not change this analytical hardcore of his work.

Summarizing then in this way the most consistent attempt that was made to provide a definition of the regimes that are at issue here as "bureaucratic", the following question remains: does such a definition adequately cope with the nature and dynamic of the dictatorships like the Brazilian and the Argentine in the 60s? The answer, which I will attempt to develop below, can initially be responded to as follows: the "bureaucratic" approach leaves out a key element of this type of political arrangement: its military-dictatorial nature. That is, the military nature of such dictatorships can be lost if they are defined primarily in terms of their aspects of bureaucratic rationalization. In this way, comprehension not only of their nature but their political dynamics is blocked.

In order to develop this critique, we need to return to Poulantzas' analyses. It is there that the distinction between "bureaucracy" and "bureaucratism" emerges clearly. The first term refers to a social category that has the responsibility for managing the State; the second, to a "specific system of organization and internal functioning of the State apparatus". (Poulantzas, 1977, p. 328) Along these lines, when O'Donnell refers to the bureaucratization that characterizes the deepening of modernization processes in countries such as Brazil and Argentina, he is able to account for a real process, visibly intensified in the mentioned countries after the military coups: we are dealing here with "bureaucratism" as a constitutive feature of capitalism (Weber) or of the capitalist State apparatus (Marx). In Poulantzian terms, bureaucratism makes up part of the juridical and political structure of the bourgeois State (Saes, 1982). Thus, to see the political arrangements under consideration here as "bureaucratic" does not contribute to our understanding of the specific form of State that characterizes the Argentine and Brazilian situations. The specificity of the State form that is consolidated in these two cases does not lie in the advance of bureaucratization, which is a general characteristic of capitalist societies, but in the further militarization of the State, and in the special place that the Armed Forces come to occupy within the new power structures.

Nonetheless, this matter alone does not in itself exhaust the authoritarian-bureaucratic hypothesis. The latter is also founded on the idea that the regimes under consideration here are defined by the central role of bureaucracy, as a social category. It is on this point that the bureaucratic thesis has several variations (which in turn, serves to show how well received it

---

[6] With this I explain my option for not using the term "bureaucratic-authoritarian State" that was predominant in the Spanish and Portuguese language versions of O'Donnell's work. In effect, in the author's own words, this concept sought to define a "bureaucratic" variety of the "authoritarian" type of political system.

has been in studies on these dictatorships.) For some of these authors, among which O'Donnell himself stands out, the undeniable preponderance of the military in the new technocratic arrangement does not stop us from defining these forms of power as bureaucratic, to the extent that they take the Armed Forces primarily as a bureaucratic organization; for others, heirs of the theory of the elites, regimes such as the Argentine and the Brazilian can be defined through their alliance between civil (technocratic) and military bureaucracies. (Mendes, 1967) A Marxist variation based on the concept of Bonapartism sees the governmental counter-revolutionary elite that came to power with the coups that took place in the 1960s as military and techno-bureaucratic currents. (Martins, 1977). All of these variations have a point in common: insofar as political representation is concerned, the bureaucratic nature of these regimes subordinates their military aspects.

In order to perform a more in-depth critique of such a view, I would like to take a closer look at the work of an author whom, although still working within the bureaucratic hypothesis, also considers elements that in my opinion permit an alternative approach to the study of the regimes examined here. I refer to Fernando Henrique Cardoso and his work on the "Brazilian political model" (1979). In that piece, he offers an analysis of the post-1964 regime that emphasizes its "hybrid aspects" or its "contradictory duality", referring to the special autonomy that economic policy maintains in relation to specifically political aspects. According to Cardoso, in Latin America, regardless of the type of State that prevails, countries with similar levels of industrialization present evident similarities in the content of their economic policies. Thus, in "bureaucratic-authoritarian" regimes, economic dynamics would maintain significant autonomy in relation to specifically political aspects. "In this regard, the militarization of power played a lesser role than we would have expected", Cardoso concludes, while at the same time affirming: the military "is in command. They control the State. But this command and control do not determine the central policies of government." (1984, p.48)[7] This seems to be the basis of Cardoso's approach to bureaucratization, which follows closely along the lines established by O'Donnell's analyses. And this is also the framework within which he introduces his famous concept of "bureaucratic rings" which cut horizontally across the two bureaucratic structures that are present on the Brazilian political scenario: the large private firm and the public bureaucracy (1975a).

Up to this point, Cardoso's argument fits within the boundaries of the bureaucratic paradigm for the analysis of political regimes. Nonetheless, in his own analyses, elements can be found that point toward the centrality of the military aspect of political arrangements. Thus, in criticizing the elitist bias of authors such as Cândido Mendes, who have taken the projects and ideology of political actors themselves all too seriously, Cardoso suggests to "rescue the nerve of politics, in other words, conflict", which means to pay attention to "opposition between groups within the system of power and between them and those who are outside of it." The analyst's task thus becomes the "identification of existing political forces, demarcating the area in which they operate and evaluating the results of their action". Furthermore, it becomes necessary to recognize the "zigzags" of politics that "create a margin

---

[7] In this same sense, Cardoso proposes that these arrangements be understood in terms of a contradictory duality, "the creation of two guidelines for decision-making, one that is political/administrative/repressive and the other that it political/economic", with the military president as arbiter. (1975, p. 209)

for the formation of power structures that, although neither foreseen nor intended by political actors, must bear some relation to existing political forces."(1979, p. 72-74)

Such observations seem fundamental for the analysis of the military regimes and their political dynamics. Let us begin with the issue of power structures. In my view, Cardoso himself does not give adequate consideration to the central characteristics of the transformation of political arrangements in post-1964 Brazil. In the period that follows the military coup, the new form of political representation that is a result of the ensuing crisis of bourgeois hegemony seems to point less to a process of bureaucratization than one of militarization of the State apparatus. In other words, the role that the Armed Forces come to play as the "political party of the bourgeoisie" upon the withdrawal of properly political representatives has as its institutional expression the emergence and consolidation of seats of military power – the presidency and its organs of military advisory, the three military ministries, as well as the Army commanders, the chiefs of staffs, and, after 1967 the High Command of the Armed Forces – that, in their political dimensions, are marked by a sharp "structural inequality" in relation to other branches and apparatuses of the State. In this regard, the preponderance of the military bureaucracy within the whole of the bureaucratic structure leads the analyst to emphasize, above all, the specific characteristics of this sector, insofar as it is the dominant branch of the repressive apparatus amongst all the branches that make up this form of dictatorial State. Thus, the concept that is most pertinent for our understanding of these regimes is that of military dictatorship, rather than bureaucratic autocracy.

Furthermore, Cardoso seems to pointing in this very direction himself, in his attempt to answer the question "What regime is this?", posed in relation to the election of General Medici (1969). On that occasion, he states that the "fundamental decision ... had the following characteristics: a) it was taken by the upper strata of the military bureaucracy (four star generals); it followed bureaucratic criteria of hierarchy and corporate representation; c) it put a damper on the greatest risk that the Army as dominant bureaucratic force had to face: a disunion produced by the proliferation of tendencies and factions; d) it thus led to conciliation among groups within the Army (1979, p. 78).

On this issue, a critique of dominant hypotheses will demand that we consider the consequences they imply for the analysis of the dynamics of political crises in dictatorial regimes. For such purposes, I propose focusing attention on the way in which this issue appears in analyses of the post-1964 Brazilian military dictatorship.

BUREAUCRATIC ELITISM AND POLITICAL DYNAMICS

From my point of view, examining the dynamics of political crises is a privileged resource for the study of certain characteristics of the Brazilian military dictatorship. My central hypothesis is that an underestimation of its fundamentally military nature will lead to particular difficulties in understanding the political processes of the dictatorial regime. This is the context in which I will return to the critique of the elitist bureaucratic paradigm.

In his first book, O'Donnell has tried to take up the issue of the evolution of bureaucratic authoritarian regimes focusing his attention on the political interplay of domestic social

actors, that is, on the values and the actions of the "technocratic elite". (1973, p. 106-109)[8]
His analysis of the viability of the coalition that led the coup is thus based on the criteria
according to which those who were "in pivotal technocratic roles" evaluated governmental
performance. In his hypothesis, the government's "success" or "failure" in suppressing
resistance from the social sectors t hurt by the authoritarian economic policy creates two
possible routes of political evolution. In the "successful cases", support for the technocratic
elite would be reinforced, at the cost of isolation from the affected social strata; government
policies are employed in the sense that was previously noted and chances of dissidence are
minimal. The process only looses intensity when technocratic criteria themselves are no
longer able to sustain growth. At that point, however, the system has already been implanted
and a new type of "political game" has been initiated.

On the other hand, in the case of "unsuccessful systems" (incapable of applying coercion
efficiently) a wide range of consequences emerges. The search for technocratic goals
generates effective social resistance but the government has no choice but to reinforce
technocratic policies. New measures of this sort increase resistance and repression, which in
turn make inevitable the reappearance of mass praetorianism and of political instability within
the authoritarian context. This process also tends to split the dominant coalition in two: one
sub-coalition that seeks to maintain continuity and a second one open to external alliances. If
the former prevails and the process is thus continued along earlier lines, this will occur only
until a new impasse is reached. On the other hand, the possibility of return to a democratic
system means the return to the well-known conditions of mass praetorianism.

This framework of analysis refers explicitly to the case of the "successful" Brazilian
dictatorship and the "failure" of the 1966 Argentine military regime. Nonetheless, this is not
the place to go into greater detail on this hypothesis of comparative politics. The point to be
made is that in this light, the Brazilian and Argentine military dictatorships appear to be
voided of any specifically military dynamic. Such effects of the elitist bureaucratic approach
appear clearly in other analyses. One example should be enough: Cândido Mendes' work on
the dynamics of the post-64 Brazilian political system, whose cornerstone is the technocracy
as a sort of classic sub-species of the power elite. The characteristics that define these groups
are then relative social neutrality, ideological homogeneity, rationalist ideologies and
ideologies of salvation. (Mendes, 1966). It is not quite surprising that authors that conceive of
the new type of military regime as "authoritarian and bureaucratic" or that define them as
"systems of the power elite" do not emphasize military processes in the general dynamics of
these regimes. Less evident is why the elitist-bureaucratic paradigm is so strong in some of
the main studies of the political role of the Armed Forces in Brazil and Argentina during the
sixties. In this regard the most significant case is that of Alfred Stepan, whose views on the
changing role of the military in countries with high levels of modernization, have been
heavily incorporated by Guillermo O'Donnell (1986a).

Since its first edition in 1971, *The Military in Politics: Changing Patterns in Brazil,* the
book that brought Stepan his fame, was welcomed as an undeniable step beyond the reigning
theses on the military in modernizing countries. In opposition to ideas that until then had been

---

[8] Within the framework of "game theory", the author proposes understanding political action as "action in a
situation (policy issues, type of political system and rules of competition, and set of players) that must be taken
into account at least by 'players' trying to achieve goals." (O'Donnell, 1973, p. 106) In a later text, he would
see this approach as indispensable for "an adequate analysis of the dynamic, evolution and impact" of such
arrangements. (O'Donnell, 1982, p. 41)

widely accepted regarding the unity and self-isolation of the military corporation, Stepan suggested focusing research not on the institutional characteristics of the Armed Forces but on the interaction between the "military subsystem" and the wider political system. This was the framework within which he carried out his discussion on the changing political role of the military in Brazil. It thus seems natural that both critics and fans of Stepan's ideas have focused on his thesis on the "moderating pattern" of civil-military relations. Nonetheless, in emphasizing this aspect they have left the issue that interests us more specifically here on a lesser level: the consequences of Stepan's methodological approach for the analysis of the post 1964 Brazilian military regime.

In order to make progress in this direction, let us start from a first notion that can seem provocative: the hypothesis that the moderating pattern is not the most original aspect of Stepan's work.[9] Actually, the object of this research seems to lead us less to the moderating model than to the processes that were at the origin of its break-up and the implantation of a new "pattern" or "model" of civil-military relations. More precisely, it locates here – in the hypothesis of the emergence of a military ideology marked by a "new professionalism" – not only Stepan's most original contribution but also the key to understanding the limitations of his approach to post-1964 military processes in Brazil. In order to move ahead in this regard, I propose a reading of that author's propositions that focuses attention not only on his explicit theses but also in what the latter actually keep hidden.

In *The Military in Politics,* Stepan argues that the key element to understanding the role of the military lies in the examination of their interaction with the civil elite or, to use his own terminology, the relationship between the military subsystem and the global political system (54-55). The Armed Forces in his approach thus constitute "more of a dependent than an independent variable"(p.80). In building his moderating model, Stepan sought to attribute to the civilian elite a major role in the configuration of military behavior, through his hypothesis of the role of civil legitimacy in the success of Armed Forces intervention (66). Within this general context, the idea that the institutional characteristics of the military, although not "politically irrelevant", are subordinate to the interaction of the civil sphere in defining the behavior of the Armed Forces, seems coherent with his analytical framework (54-55). This is so to the point that, upon a first reading, Stepan's approach cannot be seen as "organizational". It is no coincidence that, upon examining the literature on the Brazilian military as it can be classified into "instrumental" and "organizational" approaches, some analysts have associated his moderating model with the first category, insofar as he suggests "that the arbitration of conflicts between classes and groups is carried out in consonance with the prevalent currents in public opinion." (Coelho, 1976, p. 19)

My approach here contests such a vision. In my hypothesis, although Stepan has sought to distinguish his studies through the emphasis given to the civil-military interaction, we can detect -in the very way in which he conceives of the two subsequent patterns of civil-military relationship – the need for a particular concept of military institution. In order to explain this point, it is necessary to go back to the issue of the "changing patterns" in military behavior.

---

[9] The author himself in the preface to his work recognizes his indebtedness to two Brazilian analysts: Fernando Pedreira and Cândido Mendes. In fact, as early as the mid sixties the two of them were widely advocating the notion of the moderating pattern. Perhaps it is enough to remember the text of the latter of these two authors published in 1966 in the Brazilian journal *Dados,* in which the Costa e Silva candidacy was considered to be major evidence of a "change in the role of the Armed Forces, from a moderating and arbitrating function to the open assuming of responsibilities in national political decision-making." (1966, p. 16)

As is known, Stepan's point of departure was Samuel Huntington's thesis on the "professional" model of civil-military relations (Stepan,1973ᵃ) Stepan has presented his reasoning as an effort to break with that model on basically two accounts. To begin with, his critique of the Huntington model of civilian control over the military through professionalization is an important part of the building of the moderating model and is the basis of the idea that in praetorian societies the military is politicized and that civilians concede a "partial legitimacy" to military participation in politics (1974, p. 49) At a following moment, the Huntington model becomes a reference for his construction of the concept of a "new professionalism" of the military. Thus, a change in military ideology is identified as being at the roots of the erosion of the moderating pattern and the emergence of a "new attitude" toward politics on the part of the military. (1973, p. 50)

The emphasis that Stepan places on this divergence can distract us from the convergence of the various models that we have analyzed. In effect, belying the definition of moderating, professional and leadership (or "new professionalism") patterns is a conception of the Armed Forces as a bureaucratic elite, in the terms of a systemic analysis of the military apparatus. Huntington's model seems to dispense with further explanations in this regard.[10] Regarding the moderating model, several analysts have identified the secondary role that it assigns to the military vis-à-vis the civilian elite (to whom the taking of initiatives is always attributed) as one of its most fragile points.

In my opinion, however, what these critics have not perceived is that it is the very "bureaucratic" conception of the military institution that lies at the heart of the "passive" role attributed to the Armed Forces. This point becomes more clearly evident on the issue of changing patterns of military behavior. There, Stepan's analysis of the change in military ideology and the emergence of a new military professionalism seems to be founded on a overestimation of the effects of the 1961-64 Brazilian crisis on military behavior. That critical juncture is seen as having had a double impact: on the one hand, it dissolved the "liberal" scenario in which the elite situated the moderating role of the Armed Forces; on the other hand, it sharpened the military's sense of institutional insecurity resulting from the presence of threats to military unity. These processes led to a change in the military's attitude regarding politics. And, as an analytical framework, it lends support to the central argument behind my critique of Stepan. It brings to the forefront an evident underestimation of the previously established ideological orientation of the Brazilian Armed Forces[11] In such a view, the situation is portrayed as if it were only at this point that the Brazilian military as a corporatist entity "discovers" political ideologies. Thus, notwithstanding his reservations regarding Huntington's professional model, Stepan's conception of the military attitudes that characterize the moderating pattern seemed to be founded on a view of these sectors as a "professional" or "bureaucratic" elite.

This attribute stands out clearly in the second effect of the 1961-64 crisis on military attitudes: institutional reaction to political and social uncertainty. Referring to the military perception of the uncertainty reigning prior to the coup, in a text in which he reproduces Stepan's arguments, O'Donnell asserts: "organizations try to reduce uncertainty perceived as

---

[10] I refer here to the characteristics of role exclusivity, military specialization, ideological neutrality and homogeneization through professionalization that are present in the "professionalization pattern".

[11] For more on this question, see João Quartim (1985, p. 177) on the substition of "politics within the Army" for a "politics of the Army", as well as a discussion of the importance of the anti-Vargas sentiments that since 1945 were a component of the ideology of the Brazilian military.

affecting the internal state and/or viability of the organization. ... the organization's directors operate through concepts and strategies which reflect their bias in perception and evaluation, as well as the patterns of decision-making which result from organizational specialization in certain types of activity". (O'Donnell, 1986, p. 118)

Through these observations I have advanced the central elements of my critique. In both Stepan and O'Donnell, there is a prevailing definition of the military as basically an elitist and bureaucratic group, with modifications in military ideology as a result of the ascendance of the National Security Doctrine. Emphasis placed on elements of variation undermines the importance of that which is held constant. This point established, we can go on to take a look at the effects that this paradigm has on the analysis of the military dynamics that follow the coup.

Other scholars have also perceived the tendency pertaining to the explicitly organizational paradigm to overestimate the homogeneity of the military and to put the divisions within the military camp in the background, whether before or after their coming to power. From my point of view, emphasis on military homogeneity is one of the most visible results of the bureaucratic and elitist paradigm.

Further demonstration of my argument would require a deeper examination of such results both for the "moderating" as well as the post-coup periods. In the first example, it takes me back to the notion of the military as a "professional group" and to the centrality of such a notion for Stepan's idea of the unilateral civilian co-optation of the military. For my purposes here, it seems more relevant to focus attention on the effects that the elitist and bureaucratic paradigm have over the analysis of the post-coup military dynamics. The aspect to be emphasized is the need that such a model creates to identify a *paradigmatic elite* corresponding to the ideal type that underlies it and that materializes its premises of the homogeneity, rationality and foreseeable behavior associated with the military and bureaucratic elite. This in my opinion is the bases of the analyses that take the ESG, the group represented by the *Escola Superior de Guerra*, as the main actor behind the coup movement, followed by the choice of the *Castelista* current as the paradigmatic elite and central agent of post-64 processes.

The fundamental point here is that the search for a paradigmatic elite leads these authors to overestimate a series of aspects including military project, discourse and ideology, in detriment to another series of processes linked to the practices, conflicts and actual balance of forces within the Armed Forces. In my opinion, therein lies the basis of the over-estimation of the role of chosen sectors of the military as paradigmatic: in the Brazilian case, the group belonging to the *Escola Superior de Guerra*.[12] Such studies tend to lose sight of the complex configuration of the whole of the Armed Forces during the military period and the specificity of the practices of the various political currents of the military. At the same time, it is precisely the need to recover aspects ignored by dominant paradigms that justify the search for an analytical alternative for understanding the political and military dynamics of the post-64 Brazilian regime.

---

[12] In this regard, see O'Donnell's view of the Ongania administration as a "demilitarized military government" and his emphasis on the role of the "paternalist" current as the Argentine paradigm of military professionalization.

AN ALTERNATIVE HYPOTHESIS

In the simplest terms, the perspective that I advocate here emphasizes the military aspect of military bureaucracies. In opposition to the thesis of a bureaucratic elite – which gives salience to bureaucratic homogeneity – I try to reveal the nature of the specifically military heterogeneity, internal division and fluidity that characterize military political practice.

In general terms, this viewpoint is not new in the field of analyses on the role on the Armed Forces in countries such as Brazil. For example, this seems to be the sense that is given to the concerns of authors who proposed the hypothesis of military parties in order to take up the specificities of the political behavior of the military institution. As the French sociologist Alain Rouquié notes: "The Armed Forces may be seen as political forces that carry out, through different means, the same basic functions as political parties and that include – just as parties do, but with a different logic – processes of deliberation, of decision-making and even of social articulation and unity." (Rouquié, 1991, p. 12)

In proposing this type of idea such analysts seek to question "the common sense notion (encouraged by the military itself) of the Armed Forces as a unified, if not monolithic action. This notion was inspired by a simplistic sketching of the organizational traits that characterize military institutions (discipline, hierarchy, verticality)". (Rouquié, 1991, p. 13)

The hypothesis of military heterogeneity only makes sense when complemented by an analysis of the particularity of the specifically military features that serve to define the military's political action. According to Rouquié himself, the Armed Forces, a "hierarchical and bureaucratic institution", do not react as a political party, and its intervention in political life is neither the "impersonal, mechanical and unanimous action of a monolithic structural organization nor the docile instrument of formal hierarchical leaders." Military and political cleavages "obey properly institutional mechanisms: thus their fluid boundaries and tendencies." (Rouquié, 1978, p. 661)

The processes that Rouquié analyzed for the Argentine case seem relevant for those who study the Brazilian military. The analysis of the first Brazilian military governments should reveal the relevance of characteristics such as the following: principles of co-optation and verticality that preside in military promotion and nomination and the relation they maintain to the creation of networks of loyalty and the formation of a veritable "clientele" within army ranks; the political reformulation of military hypothesis elaborated at the highest levels as a basis for the contradictory and essentially negative character of military opinion; the military vision of the strategic enemy as the basis of the fluidity of military divisions; the influence of the martial conception of the social universe on military ideology and concerns with unity and unanimity (Rouquié, 1978, p. 662-670). Following in a similar vein, several empirical studies demonstrate it is impossible to understand military practice simply in terms of bureaucratic characteristics (Peixoto, 1991; Varas, 1992).

Nonetheless, the acceptance of these theses on the specific nature of military political practices, according to the hypothesis of my work, depends on the re-examination of the problematic of the relationship between processes of political crisis and structural forms of State power. In other terms, it is not enough to assert the specificity and autonomy of the military: it has to be understood that the action of military parties takes on different meanings in different forms of State and regime. In order to make this fundamental point clearer, we need to return to the question of the forms of State of crisis or of "exception", as it appears in

Poulantzas' work (1978a). There we can find some basic distinctions that, although maintaining a high level of abstraction, point to the fundamental processes for an analysis of the political crises of dictatorships. We should begin with an examination of Poulantzas' distinction between the fascist and Bonapartist or military dictatorship forms of States of exception. For Poulantzas, the dominance of the fascist party, as an ideological State apparatus, allows the fascist State a specific stabilizing element; the military and Bonapartist dictatorships in which dominance is dislocated to a branch of the repressive apparatus (specifically, to civil administration and the Armed Forces) do not possess this specific stabilizing element.

Next, we go on to consider the opposition that Poulantzas establishes between the entirety of forms of the State "of exception" and the democratic form of capitalist State. According to that hypothesis, what distinguishes parliamentary democracies is their ability to allow "organic representation" or the "organic circulation of hegemony". In other words, to use "a skeletal organization that allows for the functioning and organic circulation of hegemony through fractions of the bloc that is in power, through their political representatives, and even a certain regulated ventilation of power within the ruling classes and dominant fractions". In crisis forms, "such a situation is completely impossible". (1978, p. 72)

These two structural distinctions make it possible to put forth the central hypothesis that I have but outlined in the first part of this article: the political crises of military dictatorships maintain a characteristic specificity. Returning to Poulantzas: "the political crises that mark States of exception are feared much more by the latter than they are within parliamentary democracy, which usually possess the institutional means to manage such crisis".(1978, p. 72) But the political instability that characterizes dictatorial forms acquires special significance in the case of military regimes. In this case, the inability to articulate their hegemony, which is common to crisis forms, joins the absence of a fascist party as a stabilizing element and is accentuated by the role of the Armed Forces, as the "dominant apparatus" in these arrangements (1978, p. 82) This new role played by the Army distinguished dictatorships of this type from fascist ones. As Poulantzas says:

> "the internal contradictions of these regimes were manifested par excellence within the military apparatus (which, precisely and further, possesses the power of armaments) and not within the party and the bureaucracy, which are the dominant apparatuses of fascist regimes. These makes the internal contradictions of the former type of regime much more fearsome in their case than in the latter type." (1978, p. 82)

On this point, however, an important distinction should be made that points precisely to the peculiarity of dictatorships of the Brazilian type. In his analysis of European cases, Poulantzas asserts that the crisis of hegemony that led to the emergence of military dictatorships corresponded to important dislocations in the relationship of social forces, a process that was carried out, within the State, through a profound change in its apparatuses: Thus, he argues, "it is essentially toward the Army, or more precisely those who are at its head, toward whom the role of the political parties of the bourgeoisie is re-located, making this former group the political party of the entire bourgeoisie under the guidance of its hegemonic fragment." (1978, p. 82)

In an analysis of the new types of dictatorship in Latin America, such observations must be considered with some fundamental reservations. In these countries, it is not that the military should not be considered as making up the political party of the bourgeoisie, if we consider their role in the maintenance of the bourgeois order and the phenomenon that some Marxist theoreticians have referred to as "substitutionism". Nonetheless, study of the Brazilian case leads to some frontal questions regarding the feasibility of interpreting this intra-military division as intra-bourgeois divisions. In other words, I don't think it is viable to analyze post-1964 Brazilian military parties as an expression in the military realm of wider social divisions, as Poulantzas does for the Greek, Spanish and Portuguese cases or O'Donnell for the Argentine case. In this case, it is impossible to interpret these military currents as political parties of the bourgeoisie.

Further explanation of this issue allows us to move forward on the central hypothesis of this article. In effect, one of the characteristics that stands out in our examination of the political conflicts surrounding the consolidation phase of the Brazilian military regime is precisely the critical unity of the Armed Forces once it was purged of popular and nationalist elements. This unity was built through a unanimous opposition, amongst officials and hierarchy, to returning power to civilian hands. This characteristic brings out a feature that is peculiar to societies of the Brazilian type. Within the latter, given the nature of the process through which popular masses have been brought into political life – referred to generically as "populism" – the emergence of a military ideology based on a strong rejection of civil politics was possible. The latter were seen as the equivalent of a "populist demagogy" that was associated with social instability and risks of a breakdown of order.

This equation of "politics" and "populism" came to express itself, after the Brazilian military took power, in a particular military impenetrability regarding divisions emanating from the "civil world'. In other words, the preventive strategy of refusal of any possibility of a populist "return to the past" created a scenario of military unity which was to define, in the broadest sense, the political dynamics of the post-1964 regime. On a first level, the unitary process led to increasing militarization each time a threat to the military regime was perceived; the same can be said regarding the processes of division within the Armed Forces themselves, that is, with each successive political and military crisis. The crucial unity thus created in opposition to the "political world" thus coexists with constant military strife. It is in effect, a situation of unity within division. In more specific terms, this refers to two relatively separate processes: disunity expresses itself differently within the hierarchy (discord regarding presidential succession) and within officialdom (divisions in the barracks, related to expectations of direct influence on the government).

Thus qualifying Poulantzas' observations and providing clarifications for my own hypotheses, I think the moment is ripe to introduce what I believe to be an essential point: the military dictatorships of the new type, in spite of the myth of their stability, do not just constitute crisis forms of the State because they emerge from specific crises, but can also be considered as critical State forms because they are marked by a specific kind of instability. Understanding this instability requires the study of their intra-military dynamics. Finally, it is the examination of these dynamics that allows us to critique the hegemonic model of analysis of the post-1964 intra-military conflicts. Within this model, the military world is understood through the lens of a dualistic and dichotomous hypothesis based on the notion of an opposition between two fundamental camps: a "liberal", "moderate" or "legalist" sector, bearer of an internationalist economic orientation, and a wide arena of "hard-liners", "ultras" and "radicals", spokespersons for military nationalism. The clash between these two camps is seen as defining the regime's intra-military dynamics. However, a critique of this perspective would take us beyond the scope of this article.

REFERENCES

Antunes, R. 1988. *A rebeldia do trabalho*. Campinas/São Paulo, Unicamp-Ensaio.

Bacchus, W. 1990. *Mission in Mufti*: Brazil's military regimes, 1964-1985. New York, Greenwood Press.

Borón, A. 1977. "El fascismo como categoria histórica: en torno al problema de las dictaduras en América Latina". *Revista Mexicana de Sociologia*, v. 39 n. 2, p. 481-528, abril-jun.

Campos Coelho, E. 1976. *Em busca da identidade*: o exército e a política na sociedade brasileira. São Paulo, Forense-Universitária.

Cardoso, F. H. 1975a. "Estado e sociedade no Brasil". In _____. *Autoritarismo e democratização*. Rio de Janeiro, Paz e Terra.

Cardoso, F. H. 1975b. "A questão do Estado no Brasil". In _____. *Autoritarismo e democratização*. Rio de Janeiro, Paz e Terra.

Cardoso, F. H. 1979. *O modelo político brasileiro*. São Paulo, Difel.

Cardoso, F. H. 1982. "Da caracterização dos regimes autoritários na América Latina". In D. Collier (ed.) *O novo autoritarismo na América Latina*. Rio de Janeiro, Paz e Terra.

Cardoso, F. H. 1984. "A democracia na América Latina", *Novos Estudos*, v. 10, p. 45-56, out.

Carvalho, J. M. de. 1983. "Forças Armadas e política, 1930-1945". In Vários Autores, *A revolução de 30*: seminário internacional. Brasília, Ed. da UnB.

Collier, D. 1982a. "Resumo do modelo autoritário democrático". In D. Collier, *O novo autoritarismo na América Latina*. Rio de Janeiro, Paz e Terra.

Druckman, D. and Vario, E. 1983. "Regimes and Selection of Military Leaders: Brazilian Cabinet Ministries and Generals", *Journal of Political and Military Sociology*, v. 11, p. 301-324, Fall.

Feit, E. 1973. "Pen, Sword and People: Military Regimes in the Formation of Political Institutions", *World Politics*, v. 25 n. 2, p. 251-73, January.

Fiechter, G.-A. 1975. *Brazil since 1964*: modernization under a military regime. New York/Toronto, John Wiley and Sons.

Guimarães, C. 1988. "Domínio burguês incompleto: a teoria do autoritarismo em Marx". In N. V. de Carvalho (ed.), *Trilogia do terror*. São Paulo, Vértice.

Huntington, S. 1968. *Political Order in Changing Societies*. New York/London, Yale University Press.

Jaguaribe, H. 1968. "Brasil: estabilidad social por el colonial-fascismo?". In Furtado, C. *et alii*, *Brasil Hoy*. México, Siglo XXI.

Linz, J. 1970. "An Authoritarian Regime: Spain". In E. Allardt e S. Rokkan (eds.), *Mass Politics*: studies in political sociology. New York, Free Press.

Linz, J. 1973. "The Future of an Authoritarian Situation or the Institutionalization of an Authoritarian Regime: the Case of Brazil". In A. Stepan, *Authoritarian Brazil*: Origins, Policies and Future. New Haven, Yale University Press.

Linz, J. 1978. *Crisis, Breakdown and Reequilibration*. Baltimore/London, Johns Hopkins University Press.

Martins, C. E. 1977. *Capitalismo de Estado e modelo político no Brasil*. Rio de Janeiro, Graal.

Mendes, C. 1966. "Sistemas políticos e modelos de poder no Brasil". *Dados*, v. 1 n. 1, p. 7-41.

Mendes, C. 1967. "O governo Castelo Branco: paradigma e prognose". *Dados*, v. 1 n. 2/3, p. 63-111.

O'Donnell, G. 1973. *Modernization and Bureaucratic-Authoritarianism* – Studies in South American Politics. Berkeley, University of California Press.

O'Donnell, G. 1977. "Corporatism and the Question of the State". In J. Malloy (ed.), *Authoritarianism and Corporatism in Latin America*. Pittsburgh, University of Pittsburgh Press.

O'Donnell, G. 1980. "Desenvolvimento político ou mudança política?". In Paulo Sérgio Pinheiro (ed.) *O Estado autoritário e movimentos populares*. Rio de Janeiro, Paz e Terra.

O'Donnell, G. 1982. "Reply to Remmer and Merkx". *Latin American Research Review*, v. 17 n. 2, p. 41-50.

O'Donnell, G. 1986a. "Modernization and Military Coups: Theory, Comparisons and the Argentine Case". In A.Lowenthal e S. Fitch (eds.), *Armies and Politics in Latin America*. Revised ed. New York, Holmes and Meies.

O'Donnell, G. 1986b. "Tensões no estado burocrático-autoritário e a questão da democracia". In _____. *Contrapontos: autoritarismo e democratização*. São Paulo, Vértice.

O'Donnell, G. 1987. *Reflexões sobre os Estados burocráticos-autoritários*. Sao Paulo, Vértice.

O'Donnell, G. 1988. *Bureaucratic-Authoritarianism*: Argentina, 1966-73. Comparative Perspectives. Berkeley/Los Angeles, University of California Press.

Oliveira, E. R. de. 1978. *As forças armadas*: política e ideologia no Brasil 1964-69. 2a. ed. Petrópolis, Vozes.

Peixoto, A. C. 1991. "O Clube Militar e os confrontos no seio das Forças Armadas 1945-1964)". In A. Rouquié (ed.) *Os partidos militares no Brasil*. Rio de Janeiro, Record.

Perlmutter, A. 1969. "The Praetorian State and the Praetorian Army", *Comparative Politics*, v. 1 n. 3, p. 382-404, April.

Poulantzas, N. 1977. *Poder político e classes sociais*. São Paulo, Martins Fontes.

Poulantzas, N. 1978. *A crise das ditaduras*: Espanha, Portugal, Grécia. 2ª ed. Rio de Janeiro, Paz e Terra.

Poulantzas, N. 1978a. *Fascismo e ditadura*. São Paulo, Martins Fontes.

Poulantzas, N e Miliband, R. 1982. "O problema do Estado burguês". In Blackburn, R. (ed.), *Ideologia na Ciência Social*. Rio de Janeiro, Paz e Terra.

Quartim, J. 1971. "La nature de classe de l'État brésilien". *Les Temps Moderns*, Paris, v. 304/305, p. 651-675 and p. 853-78, nov./dec.

Quartim, J. 1985. "Alfred Stepan e o mito do poder moderador". *Filosofia Política*, v. 2, p. 163-199.

Remmer, K. and Merkx, G. 1982. "Bureaucratic-Authoritarianism Revisited", *Latin American Research Review*, v. 17 n. 2, p. 3-40.

Roett, R. 1973. "Un ejercito pretoriano en politica: el cambio de rol de los militares brasileños", *Revista Paraguaya de Sociologia*, v. 26 n. 26, p. 79-119, enero-abril.

Rouquié, A. 1978. *Pouvoir militaire et société politique en Republique Argentine*. Paris, Fondation Nationale des Sciences Politiques.

Rouquié, A. 1984. *O Estado militar na América Latina*. São Paulo, Alfa-Omega.

Rouquié, A. 1991. "Os processos políticos nos partidos militares do Brasil". In A. Rouquié (ed.) *Os partidos militares no Brasil*. Rio de Janeiro, Record.

Rowe, J. W. 1966. "The 'Revolution' and the 'System': Notes on Brazilian Politics". *American Universities Field Staff Reports*, East Coast South America Series, v. 12, May-Aug.

Saes, D. 1982. "O conceito de Estado burguês: direito, burocratismo e representação popular". *Cadernos IFCH/Unicamp*, v. 1, dez.

Saes, D.. 1987. *Democracia*. São Paulo, Ática.

Schmitter, P.. 1973. "The Portugalization of Brazil?" In Stepan, A. *Authoritarian Brazil*: Origins, Policies and Future. New Haven, Yale University Press.

Schmitter, P. 1974. "Still the Century of Corporatism?" *The Review of Politics,* v. 36 n. 1, p. 85-131, jan.

Schneider, R. 1971. *The Political System of Brazil*, New York and London, Columbia University Press.

Serra, J. 1982. "As desventuras do economicismo: três teses equivocadas sobre a conexão entre o autoritarismo e desenvolvimento". In D. Collier (ed.) *O novo autoritarismo na América Latina*. Rio de Janeiro, Paz e Terra.

Skidmore, T. 1988. *Brasil*: de Castelo a Tancredo. Rio de Janeiro, Paz e Terra.

Stepan, A. 1973. *Authoritarian Brazil*: Origins, Policies and Future. New Haven, Yale University Press.

Stepan, A. 1973a. "The New Professionalism of Internal Warfare and Military Role Expansion". In _____ (ed.). *Authoritarian Brazil*: Origins, Policies and Future. New Haven, Yale University Press.

Stepan, A. 1974. *The Military in Politics* – Changing Patterns in Brazil. Princeton, Princeton University Press.

Varas, A. 1982. "Fuerzas Armadas y gobierno militar: corporativización y politización castrense". *Revista Mexicana de Sociología*, v. 44 n. 2, p. 397-411, abr.-jun.

Velasco e Cruz, S. and Martins, C. E. 1984. "De Castelo a Figueiredo: uma incursão na pré-história da abertura". In Sorj, B. e Almeida, M. H.T. de (eds.). *Sociedade e política no Brasil pós-64*. São Paulo, Brasiliense.

Werneck Sodré, N. 1979. *A história militar do Brasil*. 3a ed. Rio de Janeiro, Civilização Brasileira.

Zirker, D. 1986. "Civilianization and authoritarian nationalism in Brazil: ideological opposition within a military dictatorship". *Journal of Political and Military Sociology*, v. 14, p. 263-274, Fall.

In: Brazil in Focus: Economic, Political and Social Issues   ISBN: 978-1-60456-165-4
Editor: Jorge T. Almeida, pp. 99-122   © 2008 Nova Science Publishers, Inc.

Chapter 6

BRAZILIAN TRADE POLICY AND THE UNITED STATES*

J. F. Hornbeck

ABSTRACT

As the largest and one of the most influential countries in Latin America, Brazil has emerged as a leading voice for developing countries in setting regional and multilateral trade agendas. The United States and Brazil have cultivated a constructive relationship in pursuit of their respective efforts to promote trade liberalization, including attempting to broker a compromise with the European Union in the World Trade Organization (WTO) Doha Round and forming bilateral working groups on trade (and other) issues. Still, they approach trade policy quite differently, are at odds over how to proceed regionally with the Free Trade Area of the Americas (FTAA), and share concerns over specific trade policies and practices.

Brazil's trade strategy can be explained only in part by economic incentives. Its "trade preferences" also reflect deeply embedded macroeconomic, industrial, and foreign policies. Whereas U.S. trade strategy emphasizes the negotiation of comprehensive trade agreements on multiple fronts, Brazil is focused primarily on market access issues as they pertain to its economic dominance in South America. Brazil exercises this priority in all trade arenas, such as pursuing changes to agricultural policies in the WTO, expanding the Southern Common Market (Mercosul) in South America, and resisting the FTAA for lack of a balance conducive to Brazilian interests.

Brazil has a modern, diversified economy in which services account for 53% of GDP, followed by industry and manufacturing at 37%, and agriculture at 9%. Agribusiness (commodity and processed goods) account for some 30% of GDP, explaining Brazil's emphasis on agricultural policies in trade negotiations. Brazil is the world's largest producer of sugar cane, oranges, and coffee, and the second largest of soybean, beef, poultry, and corn. It is also a major producer of steel, aircraft, automobiles, and auto parts, yet surprisingly, a relatively small trader by world standards. The United States is Brazil's largest single-country trading partner.

Brazil is critical of U.S. trade policies such as the Byrd Amendment (repealed, but program in effect until October 1, 2007), which directs duties from trade remedy cases to affected industries, the administration of trade remedy rules, and what it considers to be

---

* Excerpted from CRS Report RL33258 dated February 3, 2006.

discriminatory treatment in the U.S. expansion of free trade agreements in Latin America. It also objects to product-specific barriers such as tariff rate quotas on sugar, orange juice, ethanol, and tobacco; subsidies for cotton, ethanol, and soybeans; and prolonged antidumping orders on steel and orange juice. U.S. concerns focus on Brazil's comparatively high tariff structure, especially on industrial goods, Mercosul's common external tariff program, and Brazil's refusal to address issues of critical importance to the United States such as services trade, intellectual property rights, government procurement, and investment.

Despite these differences, both countries recognize the potential for important gains to be had from mutually acceptable trade liberalization at all levels. As a developing country with an opportunity for considerable growth in both exports and imports, however, Brazil may have the most to gain from addressing both foreign barriers to its trade, and unilaterally opening its economy further.

As the largest and one of the most influential countries in Latin America (see Figure 1), Brazil has emerged in recent years as a leading voice for developing countries, particularly in setting regional and multilateral trade agendas. Brazil led in the creation of the Southern Common Market (Mercado Común do Sul — Mercosul), is a co-chair with the United States of the Free Trade Area of the Americas (FTAA) negotiations, was a founding member of the Group of 20 (G-20) coalition that represents developing country interests in the Doha Development Round of the World Trade Organization (WTO) negotiations, and meets bilaterally in working sessions with the United States on trade (and other) issues, in part because of its influence in all these groups.[1]

Brazil is the 15th largest U.S. export market, but a distant second to Mexico as the United States' top trading partner in Latin America. For economies of their size, Brazil and the United States actually trade rather little with each other. Trade and investment between the two is growing, however, and the potential for deeper economic relations was a prominent theme in the two meetings that Presidents George W. Bush and Luiz Inácio Lula da Silva have held. During President Bush's visit to Brasilia in November 2005, the two presidents issued a joint communique reinforcing the importance of: 1) building on the many bilateral working groups already established; 2) increasing cooperation on trade matters at the WTO; and 3) taking advantage of the potential to double bilateral trade by 2010.[2]

The United States and Brazil have purposely cultivated a constructive relationship in pursuit of their respective efforts to promote trade liberalization. This is important because as a developing country, Brazil's trade priorities can vary from those of the United States, and the two are often at odds over specific trade practices. This has ranged from disagreements that have halted progress on the FTAA, to ongoing trade disputes before the WTO. For the United States, this means that maintaining a strong working relationship with Brazil is important for making progress with its own trade agenda. To assist Congress in understanding Brazil's stance on regional and global trade matters, this report analyzes Brazil's foreign trade policy and

---

[1] Mercosul is the Portuguese variation of the more widely seen Spanish acronym Mercosur. It includes Brazil, Argentina, Uruguay, and Paraguay, with six other South American countries affiliated as associate members. The FTAA is a proposed free trade area that would encompass 34 countries of the Western Hemisphere (all except Cuba).

[2] Joint Statement on the Occasion of the Visit by President George W. Bush to Brazil. November 5-6, 2005.

how it affects its trade relations with the world and the United States. It will be updated periodically.

Source: Map Resources. Adapted by CRS (K. Yancey 11/28/05)

Figure 1. Map of Brazil.

BRAZILIAN FOREIGN TRADE STRATEGY

David Ricardo postulated the rationale for free trade some 200 years ago when he argued that countries could improve their national welfare if they exploited their comparative advantage by exporting those goods at which they were relatively more efficient at producing and importing the rest. Later arguments for trade pointed to the benefits arising from intra-industry trade (and investment) in which specialized production along with scale economies could lead to even more efficient exchange and innovation-driven productivity increases. These foundational ideas, which recognize the value of both imports and exports, remain valid today for explaining why countries generally wish to pursue freer trade and why trade liberalization has been at the center of the economic reform debate in much of Latin America.

In practice, however, few countries have opted unilaterally to throw open their borders to unfettered free trade, and the call to maintain trade barriers is common even if it is understood that they come with a cost to society as a whole. There are many reasons for this. Perhaps most transparent is resistance by firms and workers who stand to bear most of the adjustment costs of freer trade, even if national welfare is ultimately enhanced through lower priced goods and services, a greater selection of choices from imports, and overall efficiency gains that can lead to higher national income. Less obvious is that countries adopt diverse trade policies based on historically, socially, and politically determined "trade preferences" that cannot be explained solely by a calculus of economic costs and benefits.

The "trade preference" framework helps explain Brazil's trade strategy. It pegs Brazil as a "regional leader" based on its leadership in pressing for South American economic integration, its conditional support of multilateral negotiations, and its reticence to consummate separate trade deals with developed countries.[3] Brazil's trade preferences in order of priority are: 1) expand and strengthen Mercosul, where Brazil is the undisputed industrial hub and political leader; 2) advocate developing country interests in the Doha Round, especially on agricultural issues, and; 3) resist what it views as a welfare reducing, U. S.-designed FTAA, and to a lesser extent, also a preferential trade arrangement with the European Union unless it serves as a counter influence to the FTAA.[4]

Brazil and the United States approach trade liberalization from different perspectives. U.S. trade strategy has been characterized as "competitive liberalization,"[5] where simultaneously negotiating comprehensive multilateral, regional, and bilateral pacts allows gains to be achieved where parties can agree. It is competitive in that gains at one level of negotiation (e.g. bilateral or regional) can create new incentives or pressures to make

---

[3] The "trade preference" framework is developed in Aggarwal, Vinod K. and Ralph Espach. Diverging Trade Strategies in Latin America: A Framework for Analysis. In: Aggarwal, Vinod K., Ralph Espach, and Joseph S. Tulchin, eds. *The Strategic Dynamics of Latin American Trade.* Woodrow Wilson Center Press. Washington, D.C. 2004. p. 4-5. By comparison, Chile with its unilateral reduction in trade barriers and multiple trade agreements would be a "multilateral trader," and Argentina would be a "regional partner" based on its supportive role for regional integration. See pp. 11-12.

[4] Da Motta Veiga, Pedro. Regional and Transregional Dimensions of Brazilian Trade Policy. In: Aggarwal, Vinod K., Ralph Espach, and Joseph S. Tulchin, eds. *The Strategic Dynamics of Latin American Trade.* Woodrow Wilson Center Press. Washington, D.C. 2004. pp. 180-183 and multiple interviews by the author with Brazilian trade officials.

[5] Although this concept is widely associated with Robert Zoellick, first USTR in the George W. Bush administration, it has an intellectual antecedent in: Bergsten, C. Fred. Globalizing Free Trade. *Foreign Afairs.* May/June 1996. pp. 105-106.

breakthroughs at other levels (e.g. regional or multilateral). It is comprehensive by its inclusion of issues that go beyond market access such as services trade, intellectual property rights, government procurement, and investment.

Brazil has a narrower and more cautious tack, restricted largely to market access and dominance in regional trade, where it feels most ready to compete. The perceived benefits of Brazil's strategy include attaining greater bargaining power through the Mercosul coalition, slowing the multilateral trade liberalization process to allow more time for economic adjustment, and enhancing its national influence in the world by protecting domestic economic (industrial) capacity. These "trade preferences" are not randomly determined, but are deeply embedded in the country's industrial, foreign, and macroeconomic policies, discussed below.

Trade and Industrial Policy

The "regional leader" category captures well the influence Brazil's economic development strategy has had on its trade preferences and policy. Brazil adopted its own version of the import substitution industrialization (ISI) model employed throughout much of Latin America in the 20th century. To promote industrial development, Brazil created, and protected from foreign competition, important government sponsored enterprises that still operate today, although some are now privatized. These include the National Steel Company (CSN) founded in 1942; Petrobras, the national petroleum company, established in the 1 950s; the National Economic and Social Development Bank (BNDES), created in 1952; and Embraer, a leading manufacturer of regional jets, incorporated in 1969.[6] BNDES was at the heart of this policy, providing financing for public infrastructure and strategic industries. It continues today as a necessary major source of long-term business financing given the unique structure of Brazil's financial system.

Brazil's industrial policy achieved notable results for decades, but with predictable tradeoffs. The inward orientation of the ISI model shielded domestic industry from global competition, diminishing market incentives to innovate and become more efficient. Trade policy was essentially administered protectionism.[7]

The large state bureaucracy also contributed to inefficiency and the high cost of doing business in Brazil. Although privatization efforts in the 1990s have improved the competitive landscape in Brazil, the so-called Brazil cost or "Custo Brasil" endures, which is one way of saying there are numerous microeconomic distortions introduced by excessive taxation, high

---

[6] Gordon, Lincoln. *Brazil's Second Chance: En Route toward the First World.* Brookings Institution Press, Washington, D.C. 2001. pp. 35 and 44.

[7] This policy was overseen by the Carteira de Comércio Exterior do Banco do Brasil (CACEX), created during the military dictatorship (1964-1985). Trade policy today is set by the President with the Foreign Ministry as the lead agency. The Foreign Trade Board (Câmara de Comércio Exterior — CAMEX), created in 1995, acts as an advisory agency for all government departments. Cross-sectoral business interests are voiced by the Brazilian Business Coalition (Coalizao Empresarial Brasiliera — CEB), established in 1996. NGOs, trade unions, and other independent groups are represented in coalition groups, such as the Brazilian Network for the Integration of People (Rede Brasileira pela Integracao dos Povos — REBRIP). Marconini, Mario. *Trade Policy-Making Process in Brazil.* Mimeo. March 2005. pp. 2-3 and 8-9, and author's interviews with Brazilian trade officials.

interest rates, cumbersome regulations, and corruption.[8] The large untaxed informal economy combined with Brazil's big government, for example, mean that formal businesses pay up to 85% of the tax burden, more than twice that of the United States.[9] These issues directly diminish Brazilian productivity and indirectly deter trade liberalization. Yet, continuing to protect this regulatory regime and Brazil's "national production structure" remains an important aspect of the national trade strategy, a priority Brazil pursues unilaterally and through Mercosul.[10]

Trade and Foreign Policy

As with all countries, Brazil's foreign policy shapes its trade preferences, but compared to the United States it plays a more prominent role. Unlike the United States where trade policy is constitutionally defined as the responsibility of Congress and carried out in a separate cabinet-level agency (the United States Trade Representative — USTR), in Brazil it is undertaken by the executive branch under the purview of the Ministry of Foreign Relations. The most important aspects of trade policy, therefore, are driven less by commercial interests and often are subordinated to a larger foreign policy imperative, primarily, enhancing Brazil's influence in Latin America and the world. In the Western Hemisphere, this implies taking on the United States. In the words of one Brazilian expert, "Brazil's foreign policy over the past four decades is characterized by competition with the United States, and the objective of developing the nation's industrial capacity as a key condition for independent activities within the international system."[11]

Economically, there are two sides to this policy: offensively, it seeks to integrate South America; defensively, it seeks to deter encroaching U.S. economic influence in the region. Brazil's government has taken steps recently to realize this agenda, by establishing in 2004 the South America Community of Nations as a loosely interwoven example of political and economic integration and by limiting progress on the U.S. version of the FTAA. Although intentions may not be overtly adversarial, these two policies do present a challenge to the U.S. trade agenda. By extension, Brazil's leadership in the region is played out at the WTO where it is an unyielding force in pushing for reductions in agricultural barriers in the Doha Round.

The foreign policy aspect of trade policy may also be seen in the emphasis on deepening developing country trade relations. In addition to negotiating for developing country interests in multilateral and regional trade talks, Brazil has also consummated an agreement with the Andean countries, India, and South Africa, and deepened relations with Portuguese-speaking African countries, by concluding various commitments on trade. Progress in the Doha Round, FTAA, and EU negotiations has proven harder to achieve.[12]

---

[8] Globally, Brazil ranks at the bottom for the number of regulations and time it takes to start a new business, and is also known for its cumbersome labor force regulations. See The World Bank. *Doing Business in 2005: Removing Obstacles to Growth.* Washington, D.C. 2005. pp. 19, 28, and 89-97.

[9] Lewis, William W. The Power of Productivity: Wealth, Poverty, and the Threat to Global Stability. University of Chicago Press, Chicago, 2004. pp. 140-41.

[10] Pedro Da Motta Veiga, Regional and Transregional Dimensions of Brazilian Trade Policy, p. 183.

[11] Ibid., p. 177.

[12] Mario Marconini, Trade Policy-Making in Brazil, p. 5.

Trade and Macroeconomic Issues

Macroeconomic challenges have and continue to constrain Brazil's trade policy options. Brazil, for example, is known for its historical accommodation to inflation, having employed for decades a comprehensive system of wage, price, and interest rate indexation as part of its macroeconomic management. Inflation ran at "manageably" high rates for years and was fought, albeit unsuccessfully, with a number of stabilization plans. By the 1970s, however, it eventually spiraled out of control following the oil price shocks. This led Brazil to the 1980s debt crisis along with much of Latin America.[13] By the 1990s, the economy was defined by its growing deficits and debt, failed efforts at stabilization, slow growth (averaging only 2.3% from 1980 to 2004), and reluctance to embrace reforms. An important factor in Brazil's sluggish economic performance was poor productivity growth due to microeconomic policy distortions discussed above, macroeconomic problems, and to some degree, also its closed trade policy.[14]

Brazilian trade policy also had to adjust to encroaching globalization in the 1990s, including multilateral efforts (the conclusion of the Uruguay Round), new regional talks (the FTAA), and U.S. subregional initiatives (the North American Free Trade Agreement — NAFTA). Brazil responded with some unilateral liberalization, the formation of Mercosul in 1991 with Argentina, Uruguay, and Paraguay to consolidate its trade positions in South America, and the adoption of a government-assisted export promotion policy to help address its large and growing external debt. The average tariff in Brazil fell from 51% in 1988 to 14% in 1994, but the selective preferences given under Mercosul belied the liberalization message as Brazil continued to limit trade outside the regional pact, allowing it to manage carefully the degree to which foreign competition would be accepted.[15]

Brazil's trade policy shifted again in 1994 to accommodate the *Real* Plan, a price stabilization policy imposed by then-Finance Minister (and later-President) Fernando Henrique Cardoso. It was named for a new currency that was pegged to the U.S. dollar to serve as an anchor to bring down hyperinflation. The plan actually worked where others had not, but in pegging the *real* to the dollar, the differences in inflation between the two countries caused a large real appreciation of the Brazilian currency, as price levels between the two countries diverged. This resulted in a sudden turn to trade deficits in 1995 (see Figure 2), an economic consequence that ran counter to the political priority given to running trade surpluses. To

[13] In the 1970s, Brazil was a maj or importer of oil, but the government delayed passing on the full price increase to the public, financing the difference with debt. By 1982, this subsidy proved unsustainable and when eliminated, the higher price doubled the annual inflation rate to nearly 100%. Because of indexation, the oil price increase was passed on to wages, which then showed up as more price inflation. Suddenly, it seemed, Brazil was swamped by debt and spiraling hyperinflation, and so began the lost decade of the 1980s. For a good discussion of the economic points, see Dornbusch, Rudiger. Brazil's Incomplete Stabilization and Reform. *Brookings Papers on Economic Activity.* William C. Brainard and George L. Perry, editors. Washington, D.C. 1997. pp. 37 1-374.

[14] Blyde, Juan S and Eduardo Fernnadez-Arias. *Economic Growth in the Southern Cone.* Economic and Social Study Series. RE1-04-004. Inter-American Development Bank. Washington, D.C. April 2004. pp. 1-3, 10, and Lewis, *The Power of Productivity,* p. 138.

[15] Costa Vaz, Alcides. Trade Strategies in the Context of Economic Regionalism: The Case of MERCOSUR. In: Aggarwal, Vinod K., Ralph Espach, and Joseph S. Tulchin, eds. *The Strategic Dynamics of Latin American Trade.* Woodrow Wilson Center Press. Washington, D.C. 2004. pp. 235 and 255-57.

offset the exchange rate effect on the balance of payments, Brazil raised interest rates and redoubled its protectionist policies.[16]

The macroeconomic story was further complicated by a major financial crisis in 1998 that resulted in a currency devaluation and return to a floating exchange rate in 1999, Argentina's financial collapse in 2001, and a financial panic in 2002 exaggerated by the impending presidential election of longtime Worker's Party leader Luiz Inácio Lula da Silva. Today Brazil's macroeconomic priorities still constrain trade and other policy choices. The economy is stable, but growing at inadequate levels to bring about desired development goals. To control inflation, the Lula Administration has had to maintain very high real interest rates, while Brazil's large debt service obligation has required a large primary budget surplus, approaching 5% of GDP in 2005, and a trade surplus.[17]

The cost of this development strategy has been accepting the microeconomic distortions discussed above and inadequate social spending, which raises the prospect for future social and political unrest given the already very high levels of income inequality and poverty. Subordinating trade liberalization to debt reduction and other goals also diminishes Brazil's growth prospects, a key variable in reducing poverty. Therefore, as may be seen, Brazil's "trade preferences," which point to a cautious (some would say protective) and carefully managed approach to trade liberalization, reflect a combination of industrial, foreign, and macroeconomic policy priorities that often outweigh purely trade-related economic arguments, and deters progress in Brazil's long-term development. These points bear remembering when considering specific trade negotiation stances and disputes, discussed later.

BRAZILIAN TRADE WITH THE WORLD

Brazil has a modern, diversified economy, with services accounting for 53% of GDP, followed by industry and manufacturing at 37%, and agriculture at 9%. Depending on how agribusiness is measured, it contributes to some 30% of GDP. Brazil is the number one producer of raw sugar, oranges, and coffee in the world, and the second largest producer of soybean, beef, poultry, and corn.[18] It is also a major producer of steel, aircraft, automobiles, and auto parts. By comparative standards, however, Brazil is actually a small trader, with total trade accounting for only 26% of GDP in 2004, up from 14% a decade earlier, but still a relatively small amount compared to the rest of Latin America. Brazil represents only 0.9% of world trade, a number that has not grown, suggesting that Brazil's trade liberalization efforts have not resulted in any change in its trade openness relative to the rest of the world.

---

[16] Pedro Da Motta Veiga, Regional and Transregional Dimensions of Brazilian Trade Policy, p. 178.

[17] The primary surplus is the fiscal surplus not including interest payments, and theoretically represents the amount available for debt service. Real interest rates (adjusted for inflation) in Brazil have hovered around 10% for years, making them among the highest in the world.

[18] Data from Brazilian Institute of Geography and Statistics and Brazilian Embassy, *Highlights of Brazilian Agriculture,* September 2004.

$ millions

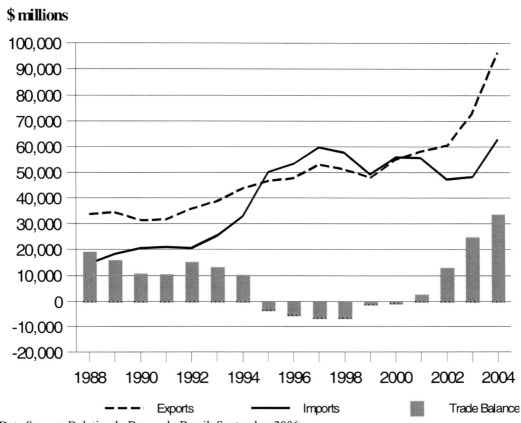

Data Source: Boletim do Banco do Brasil, September 2006

Figure 2. Brazil's Balance of Merchandise Trade, 1988-2004 $ millions.

Brazil's global trade is diversified (see Figure 3), with 25% of exports going to the European Union, 21% to the United States, 20% to Latin America, and 15% to Asia. Brazil's imports mostly from the European Union (25%), Asia (20%), the United States (18%), and Latin America (16%). Brazil's top three trading partners are the United States, Argentina, and Germany. Together they account for over one-third of Brazil's world trade and each, interestingly, is the dominant trading partner of a different region or trade group (NAFTA, Mercosul, and the European Union).

Some 30% of Brazil's merchandise exports are primary products, 14% semi-manufactured goods, and 56% manufactured goods (see Appendix 1). Importantly, natural resource-based goods dominate in all categories. For example, together all steel and aluminum based products, fabricated to varying levels of completion, represent 10% of total exports. Agricultural products, including raw sugar and other products, as well as, manufactured goods like orange juice and refined sugar, and semi-manufactured sugar and soybean products, account for at least 3 0-40% of exports. Soybean and soybean products alone amount to 10% of exports, more than automobile and related parts (8%) and aircraft

(3%).[19] These numbers provide some insight into why Brazil places such a strong emphasis on further opening developed country markets to its agricultural products.

Brazilian imports fall into five categories: capital goods (17.6%); consumer goods (10.8%); durable consumer goods (4.9%), fuels (16.4%); and intermediate goods (50.3%). Brazil imports capital and intermediate goods in support of its own industrial and agricultural growth, development, and export. These goods range from aircraft engines to chemicals and pharmaceuticals that are used in processing other goods. Raw materials for farming, foodstuffs, and nondurable consumer goods round out the major imports.

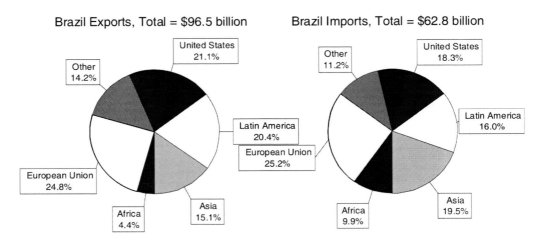

Figure 3. Brazil's Direction of Trade, 2004

Brazil's trade priorities cannot be derived entirely from a calculation of the trade-weighted importance of trade partners. The United States is Brazil's largest single-country trading partner, yet Brazil has resisted increasing trade liberalization with the large U.S. market via the FTAA because the U.S. model of liberalization is viewed as insufficiently balanced to meet Brazilian needs. To appreciate Brazil's approach to the United States and the world with respect to trade negotiations, it is critical to see how its "trade preferences," discussed above, take form in actual negotiations. Mercosul is most important to the economic and political life of Brazil and has taken on perhaps even greater priority under the Lula administration. It is discussed first followed by Brazil's approach to the FTAA and WTO, which will allow for a better understanding of U.S.-Brazil trade relations, as a whole.

Southern Common Market (Mercosul)

Mercosul was created in 1991, the outgrowth of Brazil-Argentine bilateral efforts in the late 1 980s to address longstanding political and security concerns. By including Uruguay and Paraguay, and defining the partnership along economic lines, Mercosul was expected to help the region improve its chances for mutual economic growth and development, and thereby

[19] Data from *Boletim do Banco Central do Brasil.* September 2005 and Jales, Mario. *Brazilian Agribusiness in International Trade and WTO Negotiations.* Presentation made June 12, 2006. Available at [http://www.Iconebrasil.org.br].

stabilize regional political relations as well. Mercosul has succeeded on the political side and also developed as a credible collective voice in the WTO and the FTAA. Its success at economic integration is more questionable.

Mercosul began as a free trade area, but was designed to evolve into a customs union, defined by a common external tariff (CET), and eventually, a common market with the free movement of goods, investment, and labor. To date, Mercosul remains an incomplete customs union with many exceptions to the CET. Early successes were measured by the doubling of intra-Mercosul trade by 1995, as tariffs came down according to schedule, and cooperation remained largely positive. This trend reversed course in the late 1 990s because of financial crises in Argentina and Brazil, and the absence of macroeconomic coordination and other policy problems. Brazilian trade within Mercosul expanded by only 13% from 1999 to 2004, with Brazil's trade balance shifting from a nearly balanced position to an uncomfortably large surplus of $2.5 billion by 2004, as imports from all three Mercosul partners stagnated or declined. Argentina responded with quotas and higher tariffs on certain Brazilian exports and calling for more equitable bilateral trade flows.

In reality, the trade rationale for Mercosul was always limited and fraught with challenges. After 15 years, Mercosul accounts for only 9% of Brazil's exports. The United States and Europe remain the dominant markets for Brazilian manufactures and agricultural goods, respectively, as well as, the major suppliers of capital goods. Argentina and Brazil have both resorted to raising trade barriers against each other in response to sectoral and macroeconomic problems, and Brazil stands alone as the industrial center, so Mercosul offers little competition in technological and innovative-based industries that can bring deeper gains from trade.

The increased intra-dependence fostered by a successful Mercosul also carries certain risks, as seen in the compression of trade and economic growth in Paraguay and Uruguay following financial crises and currency devaluations in Brazil (1999 and 2001) and Argentina (2002). These setbacks merely confirmed what has been widely understood, that Mercosul was really launched as a "political project carried out in the economic and commercial realms."[20] Deeper economic integration, under these circumstances, has proved elusive.

In response, Mercosul turned to broadening its membership rather than deepening the arrangement. Chile and Bolivia acceded to Mercosul in 1996 as associate members (not subject to the CET and other provisions), and after years of negotiation, the Andean Community of Nations (Ecuador, Bolivia, Venezuela, Peru, Colombia) was added in October 2004. Brazil took a further step in organizing the South American Community of Nations in December 2004, which is a very loose arrangement of the twelve major South American countries.[21] In December 2005, Venezuela agreed to become a full member of Mercosul, and has been promised full membership status, except for voting, despite its inability to adopt the CET and other policies. A similar proposal has been suggested for Bolivia following the presidential election of leftist Evo Morales in December 2005. These decisions suggest that Mercosul continues to operate based primarily on political incentives.

---

[20] Costa Vaz, Trade Strategies in the Context of Economic Regionalism, pp. 234-235 and Weintraub, Sidney. Development and Democracy in the Southern Cone: Imperatives for U.S. Policy in South America. Center for Strategic and International Studies. Washington, D.C. February 2000. pp. 12-13.

[21] Details on the various Latin American integration efforts may be found in: CRS Report RL33 162, *Trade Integration in the Americas,* by M. Angeles Villarreal.

Mercosul has been negotiating with the European Union for an FTA for many years. These talks, once considered promising, have bogged down on market access and other issues that have similarly hindered progress on the FTAA. Brazil wants better access for agricultural goods, while the EU wants Brazil to lower tariffs on industrial goods. Brazil is unwilling to make such a commitment until the EU also addresses its agricultural subsidy program. Currently, the talks are stalled, with little expectation of significant movement in the near future, a prospect, as with the FTAA, that may hinge on developments in the Doha negotiations.

Despite the undisputed expansion in Mercosul affiliation, growth in trade has stagnated and after 15 years, by most accounts, the pact still lacks institutional strength and coordination, providing little evidence of enhanced trade-related productivity gains.[22] Still, support for the pact is strong despite its troubles. The smaller economies benefit from preferential access to the large Brazilian market, and Brazil sees a unified Mercosul as being the definitive counterbalance to the United States in FTAA negotiations, where the FTAA is viewed as a complement to, not a substitute for, Mercosul. The technical distinction between a free trade agreement and a customs unions becomes important here. A customs union with a CET implies that its members will negotiate trade agreements collectively with the outside world, or the union becomes largely meaningless.[23]

For these many reasons, Mercosul remains at the heart of Brazil's trade strategy. Brazil relies on the customs union to strengthen its regional economic leadership, and by extension, its trade negotiating position outside of Mercosul. Conversely, Brazil's strength would be undermined if any members of Mercosul opted for FTA status or chose to go their own way with extra-regional negotiations, a position Uruguay flirted with in January 2006, although apparently with no real conviction. Mercosul also serves Brazil's trade strategy precisely because Brazil can set the levels of deepening to ensure a balance between maintaining its industrial policy and co-opting regional voices in approaching the EU, WTO, or FTAA. Finally, Brazil uses Mercosul as a way to ease its transition to trade liberalization in the global economy because it has a ready-made regional comparative advantage in manufacturing.

Free Trade Area of the Americas (FTAA)

The FTAA is a proposed free trade area that would include 34 nations (all except Cuba) of the Western Hemisphere. It has been under consideration for a decade, but talks effectively stalled in late 2003. Problems arose over differences between Brazil and the United States, which as the co-chairs of the Trade Negotiations Committee (TNC), hold the key to consummating the agreement. At the heart of the disagreement are their diametrically opposing positions that reflect not only differences in sectoral and industry issues, but in broader trade preferences as well. The United States remains committed to an agreement that includes negotiating investment, services, intellectual property rights, and government procurement,

---

[22] The limits of Brazil's trade-related productivity gains from Mercosul are analyzed in: Lopez-Cordova, Ernesto and Mauricio Mesquita Moreira. Regional Integration and Productivity: The Experiences of Brazil and Mexico. In: Estevadeordal, Antoni, Dani Rodrik, Alan M. Taylor, and Andrés Velasco, eds. *Integrating the Americas: FTAA and Beyond.* Harvard University Press, Cambridge, 2004. pp. 573-609.

[23] Weintraub, Development and Democracy in the Southern Cone, pp. 6-7.

among other issues. Brazil has not deviated from its more limited support of dealing mostly with market access, and its refusal to engage on these other issues unless the United States concedes to address agricultural subsidies and trade remedy issues.[24]

This impasse resulted in a compromise unveiled at the 2003 FTAA Ministerial meeting in Miami calling for a two-tier agreement under which countries could assume different levels of commitment. The proposed framework, viewed by the United States as an accommodation to Brazil, would include a common set of rights and obligations for all countries along with optional obligations that could be entered into on a plurilateral basis. Defining these various commitments so far has proven unworkable, and the breadth of an emerging resistance to the FTAA became clearer at the fourth Summit of the Americas held on November 4-5, 2005, in Mar del Plata, Argentina. Amid dramatic and sometimes violent public demonstrations against President George W. Bush and the FTAA, it was evident that Latin America was divided over how to proceed. A total of 29 countries supported renewing negotiations, and the United States pushed to set a specific date in 2006.

Brazil, Argentina, Uruguay, and Paraguay (the Mercosul countries) rejected this idea, arguing that the conditions for achieving a balanced and equitable agreement did not yet exist. Taking a more extreme position, Venezuela lobbied to end any further effort on the FTAA and for unified resistance against U.S. policies and presence in Latin America. The Summit declaration called for a time to explore problems in the FTAA process, while awaiting the outcome of the upcoming World Trade Organization (WTO) ministerial, indicating that at this juncture, there is no unified vision on how to proceed with the proposed FTAA. Brazil continues to offer to negotiate market access talks between the Mercosul countries and the United States (the so-called "4+1" option), an overture the USTR has repeatedly declined.

Brazil sees little advantage to an FTAA at this point in time, particularly one that does not address its interests, and so appears content with the status quo for the indefinite future. The United States, by contrast, has been frustrated by an inability to advance a NAFTA-like region-wide agreement. Therefore, it appears that Brazil will continue to reinforce support for Mercosul, while biding its time on the FTAA and attempting to make headway with agricultural issues in the WTO.

Mercosul negotiates the FTAA as a bloc, which may gather strength if Venezuela joins as a full member.[25] Interestingly, most analyses of the economic effects of joining the FTAA point to differences in costs and benefits between Brazil and the other three smaller members. The gains for Mercosul as a whole would come from its comparative advantage in agriculture vis-a-vis the United States, provided barriers to trade in this sector are meaningfully lowered. For Brazil, opening up the U.S. market to agricultural products is critical, but the United States is also its major market for many value-added manufactured exports (frozen orange juice concentrate, steel, aircraft, petroleum). There is, it seems, the potential for considerable commercial gains for Brazil should a far-reaching FTAA be completed.[26]

---

[24] See CRS Report RS20864, A Free Trade Area of the Americas: Major Policy Issues and Status of Negotiations, by J. F. Hornbeck. pp. 5-6.

[25] It has been noted that the addition of Venezuela as a full member of Mercosul consolidates in one bloc all the countries resisting the FTAA, setting up the potential for a maj or political standoff with the United States on this issue. *Latin American Brazil and Southern Cone Report,* December 2005, p. 7.

[26] Weintraub, *Development and Democracy in the Southern Cone,* p. 12, Laens Silvia and Inés Terra. Integration in the Americas: Welfare Effects and options for the MERCOSUR. In Lorenzo, Fernando and Marcel Vaillant, eds. *MERCOSUR and the Creation of the Free Trade Area of the Americas.* Woodrow Wilson International Center

The cost and benefit calculus, however, is more complicated. For the smaller Mercosul countries, an FTAA means giving up preferential access to the large Brazilian market, which could mean a net loss in welfare for some sectors. The FTAA would also mean greater access to the U.S. and other Latin American markets, and reduced costs for capital goods and other imports that no longer face a high Mercosul CET (e.g. 35% in the case of automobiles). The smaller economies might also consider the effects of any future economic setbacks from potential macroeconomic problems in Brazil or Argentina. Brazil also is reticent to push for an FTAA precisely because with Mercosul (and more so with a functioning South America Community of Nations), it is the hub and industrial center of a major preferential trade arrangement, which would certainly change in importance if the FTAA comes to be.

With an FTAA, Brazilian manufacturing industries that compete directly with more efficient U.S. firms (e.g. machinery and chemicals) could lose in the short run. Combined with possible trade restructuring that other Mercosul countries might face, Brazil's comparative advantage might shift, to some degree, from industrial products in a regional economic union to more agricultural goods in a hemispheric one. Given the economic and political strength of the United States, the FTAA might alter the balance of power in the region, to the possible detriment of Brazil's regional leadership. The potential for these relative changes, compounded by Brazil's concerns over its ability to conform to provisions covering enforceable intellectual property rights, services trade, and investor protection, point to why Brazil remains reluctant to advance an FTAA, particularly if U.S. agricultural protection remains relatively untouched. Stated more succinctly, although an FTAA could provide commercial (and certainly consumer) gains to Brazil, it may come at a cost to industrial and foreign policy priorities.[27]

For the United States, even a two-tier FTAA may make sense, particularly if the alternative is an FTAA without Brazil. With a two-tier FTAA, most of the hemisphere would be integrated, including Brazil, at least nominally. It may be viewed as a way to co-opt Brazilian reticence, or at least diminish the stalemate approach that can also extend to other Mercosul countries. Given Brazil's deeply held concerns that reflect its "trade preferences," however, the status quo (impasse) seems to be Brazil's preferred position between moving ahead with the FTAA negotiations or killing them outright.[28]

World Trade Organization (WTO)

Brazil has also been a vocal leader of the G-20 that represents developing country interests in the WTO. Even prior to forming the G-20 group, Brazil stood up for including matters critical to developing countries in the WTO including the most pressing issue, barriers to agricultural trade, as well as, the treatment of rules covering antidumping and

---

for Scholars, Washington, D.C. 2005. p. 107, and Masi, Fernando and Carol Wise. Negotiating the FTAA between the Main Players: USA and MERCOSUR. In: Lorenzo and Vaillant, *MERCOSUR and the Creation of the Free Trade Area of the Americas*, p. 323.

[27] Lorenzo and Vaillant, eds., *Mercosur and the Creation of the Free Trade Area of the Americas*, various chapters, pp. 4, 38, 152, and 324.

[28] The future of the FTAA remains unclear from the Brazilian perspective. At the conclusion of the WTO Hong Kong Ministerial in December 2005, Ambassador Adhemar Bahadian, Brazil's FTAA co-chair representative, suggested that the FTAA may be put off for at least another year. He was, however, replaced soon thereafter as the co-chair, and Brazil has signaled that it is still interested in negotiating with the United States in 2006.

pharmaceutical data protection, among others.[29] In particular, Brazil has insisted on addressing the reduction of barriers to agricultural trade, particularly export and production subsidies. The United States is working in the WTO negotiations with Brazil to find a way to reduce agricultural subsidies, resists addressing antidumping rules, but is generally sympathetic to finding a solution to developing country concerns over providing drugs for HIV/AIDS and other emergencies.[30]

The implication for Brazil-U.S. trade relations is that the WTO is an arena where the two countries can find areas of both commonality and disagreement. For many issues, the United States has indicated that the multilateral forum is the preferred or only venue for issue resolution (domestic agricultural subsidies) and so progress in addressing Brazilian concerns in the FTAA are contingent, at a minimum, upon success at the WTO. Brazil has taken similar stands with respect to services trade, intellectual property rights, and other issues. Hence, it is important to integrate the various factors that drive Brazilian trade priorities at the different levels of negotiation to be able to interpret Brazil's underlying intent and perhaps offer some understanding of why U.S. negotiators have been frustrated in their attempts to move forward on some critical U.S. trade policy initiatives, especially the FTAA.

At the latest WTO ministerial in Hong Kong, Brazil played a leading role in continuing to represent developing country interests in the Doha Round. It's voice was prominent in becoming a member of the latest group of would-be brokers of a Doha Round agreement known as the Group of Six (EU, U.S., Japan, Australia, Brazil, and India). The WTO remains an important forum for Brazil, which could be a major winner if barriers to agricultural trade are significantly reduced. In the post-Hong Kong period, Brazil has expressed a readiness to offer reductions in barriers to trade in industrial goods and services, if the United States can convince the European Union to move forward on agricultural barriers. The current level of cooperation between Brazil and the United States bodes well for making headway in multilateral talks that could "trickle down" to regional and bilateral accommodations. This outcome, however, is far from assured.

U.S.-BRAZIL TRADE RELATIONS

Brazil and the United States are two independent political and economic leaders in the Western Hemisphere, and is reflected in their trade relationship. First, unlike much of Latin America, Brazil does not have a preferential trade arrangement with the United States such as NAFTA, the CBI, or the Andean Trade Preference Act, although it is protective of its U.S. preferences provided under the Generalized

System of Preferences (GSP). Second, although there is consistent effort to maintain constructive engagement between the two countries at all levels of negotiation, much attention turns to areas of disagreement. Indeed, progress on the FTAA has crept to a halt, bilateral disputes have left some interests dissatisfied, including those represented in the U.S.

---

[29] Fishlow, Albert. Brazil: FTA or FTAA or WTO? In: Schott, Jeffrey J., ed. *Free Trade Agreements: US Strategies and Priorities.* Institute for International Economics. Washington, D.C. 2004. pp. 285-287.

[30] For a comprehensive discussion of WTO issues, see CRS Report RL33 176, *The World Trade Organization: The Hong Kong Ministerial,* coordinated by Ian F. Fergusson.

Congress, and key issues in the multilateral realm remain largely unresolved. A look at U.S.-Brazil trade and the issues that confront the two countries help explain this situation.

U.S.-Brazil Trade Trends

Brazil is the 15th largest U.S. export market, but a distant second to Mexico as the United States' largest trading partner in Latin America. For economies of their size, Brazil and the United States actually trade rather little with each other. Total merchandise trade (trade turnover) in 2004 between the United States and Brazil was $35 billion, or 8.2% of U.S. trade with Latin America. The United States purchased 21% of Brazil's exports and supplied 18% of its imports. The ebb and flow of U.S. bilateral trade with Brazil reflects a number of factors including their respective macroeconomic growth trends, Brazil's 1999 and 2001 devaluations (note rise in U.S. imports and fall in U.S. exports in Figure 4 — data presented in Appendix 2), and after 2002, Brazil's enhanced export promotion policy.

Brazil and the United States are far from achieving their full bilateral trade potential. It is clear that over nearly two decades, beginning before either NAFTA or Mercosul came into being, that the growth in U.S.-Brazil trade has lagged compared to U.S. trade with Latin America and especially Mexico, a close trader with the United States. As seen in Table 1, in 1987 Brazil accounted for 1.8% of total U.S. trade, compared to 5.3% for Mexico and 12.4% for Latin America as a whole. U.S.-Brazilian trade grew by 195% from 1987 to 2004, a meager amount compared to the 422% growth in U.S.-Latin American trade and the 665% growth in U.S.-Mexican trade. By 2004, Brazil had lost ground, making up only 1.5% of total U.S. trade compared to Mexico's 11.7% and Latin America's 18.7%.

Nonetheless, the United States is still Brazil's largest single-country trading partner, rivaling total trade with the European Union (EU) and exceeding Brazil's trade with Latin America. A simple analysis of Brazil's trade with the world suggests that the United States could play a more important role. This point is supported by more sophisticated estimates as well. One study using a gravity model simulation suggested that Brazil's trade with the United States in 1999 was only 44% of what the model estimated it should have been.[31]

Table 1. U.S. Trade with Brazil, Mexico, and Latin America

	% of Total U.S. Trade 1987	% of Total U.S. Trade 2004	Total U.S. Trade 2004 ($ millions)	% Growth in Trade 1987-2004
Brazil	1.8	1.5	35,057	195
Mexico	5.3	11.7	266,737	665
Latin America	12.4	18.7	426,849	422

Source: CRS computations from U.S. Department of Commerce data

---

[31] This point is developed in Schott, Jeffrey. J. *U.S.-Brazil Trade Relations in a New Era. Institute for International Economics.* November 2003. pp. 4-5. [http://www.iie.com]

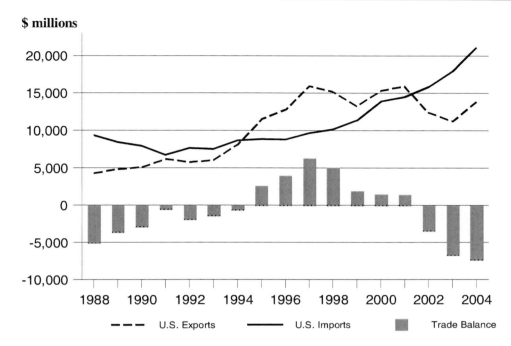

Data Source: Boletim do Banco do Brasil, September 2005.

Figure 4. U.S.-Brazil Merchandise Trade, 1988-2004.

The United States exports mostly capital goods to Brazil; the top three categories composing over half of U.S. exports are:

- *machinery* (gas turbines used in the manufacture of Brazilian aircraft, computers, office machinery and engine parts);
- *electrical machinery* (integrated circuits, radio, television, and telephone parts); and,
- *organic materials* (such as industrial chemicals).

The United States is also the largest market for Brazilian manufactured goods, which are included in the top three U.S. import categories and compose nearly one-third of U.S. imports from Brazil. These include:

- aircraft (regional jet airplanes);
- electrical machinery (cell phones, radio, and other transmission apparatus); and,
- machinery (automobile engine parts).

Other important U.S. import categories include mineral fuel, iron and steel, automobiles, and footwear (see Appendix 3 for bilateral services trade data, not discussed in this report). Treatment of Brazilian agricultural products, conspicuously absent from top categories of U.S. imports, are among Brazil's major bilateral issues.

U.S.-Brazil Foreign Investment

Trade liberalization is also important because it tends to encourage increased foreign direct investment (FDI). Permanent and predictable trade rules induce FDI because the flow of trade will be less likely to be interrupted by government actions. If a trade agreement also includes an investment chapter, which typically assures foreign investors that they will receive national treatment and have recourse to an impartial dispute settlement process, there is further inducement for FDI. This an important issue because the United States does not have a Bilateral Investment Treaty (BIT) with Brazil, another way to secure U.S. investor rights with developing countries.

The stock of U.S. FDI in Brazil was $33.3 billion in 2004 (see Appendix 4). This figure actually declined from a peak of $37.8 billion in 1998. U.S. investment in Brazil, the largest economy in Latin America next to Mexico, is relatively small, representing only 1.6% of U.S. FDI in the world and only 10.2% of U.S. FDI in Latin America (Mexico has twice this amount). In addition, Brazil invests little in the United States, with the stock of FDI amounting to $1.3 billion in 2004. Although this is double the previous year's level, it accounts for less then one-tenth of one percent of FDI in the United States. Brazilian investment is growing, however, concentrated in industries of strategic interest to its economy that face formidable U.S. barriers to entry, such as citrus and steel.

U.S.-Brazil Bilateral Trade Issues and Disputes

Brazil and the United States have a number of specific trade issues that are taken up at all levels of trade negotiations. As with all countries, the United States and Brazil practice some form of protection, although they are very different. The United States is most concerned over Brazil's high average tariffs, particularly on industrial goods, and multiple non-market access issues including intellectual property rights (IPR) enforcement, services trade, government procurement, and investment rules. The United States Trade Representative (USTR) considers the common external tariff (CET) a major barrier to U.S. agricultural exports, distilled spirits, and computer equipment.[32]

Brazil has raised its major concerns over broad U.S. policies such as the Byrd Amendment, which directs duties from trade remedy (antidumping) cases to affected industries, the calculation of antidumping margins, and what it considers to be discriminatory treatment inherent in U.S. expansion of preferential trade agreements in Latin America (NAFTA, Chile, CAFTA-DR). The Byrd Amendment was found to be in violation of WTO rules. Although repealed by Congress on February 1, 2006, the program remains in effect until October 1, 2007. The other two complaints face no challenge in the WTO. Brazil also objects to product-specific barriers that include restrictive tariff rate quotas (TRQs — sugar, orange juice, ethanol, and tobacco), subsidies (cotton, ethanol, and soybeans), and trade remedy cases (steel and orange juice). The U.S. 2002 Farm Bill that effectively increased agricultural subsidies further aggravated the situation. As of January 1, 2006, there were 17 U.S. antidumping and countervailing duty orders in place against Brazil.

---

[32] United States Trade Representative. *2005 National Trade Estimate Report on Foreign Trade Barriers.* Washington, D.C. March 2005, p. 30.

Tariffs Structures

One significant difference between Brazil and the United States is their tariff structure. As shown in Table 2, Brazil has comparatively high average tariffs. Although the difference in average agricultural tariff is small, Brazil's average tariff on industrial products is three times that of the United States, the major product category of U.S. exports to Brazil. It follows that market access discussions between the two countries usually find the United States focusing on reduction of industrial tariffs, whereas Brazil emphasizes U.S. peak tariffs on agricultural imports subject to TRQs. The high out-of-quota tariffs are meant to deter imports to protect U.S. producers, which are, for example, 350% for tobacco and 78% for sugar, and reflected in the comparatively large standard deviation in U.S. agricultural tariffs. Brazil notes that the U.S. average agricultural tariff can mask the high cost Brazil faces from out-of-quota peak U.S. tariffs.[33]

Table 2. U.S. and Brazil Average Tariff Rates

Country	All Products		Agricultural Products		Industrial Products	
	Avg. Tariff*	Standard Deviation#	Avg. Tariff*	Standard Deviation#	Avg. Tariff*	Standard Deviation
United States	4.3%	11.3	8.5%	30.2	3.7%	5.1
Brazil	10.9%	6.8	10.2%	6.0	11.0%	6.8

Data source: Inter-American Development Bank via personal correspondence. * Simple average tariff for calender year 2004.

\# Standard deviation as measure of how much tariffs can vary from average

Brazilian Complaints against the United States

Brazil's major product-specific complaints are summarized briefly below.

Sugar. As part of U.S. support for the domestic sugar growing and processing industry, quotas are set under U.S. commitments made under WTO rules to restrict the amount of sugar imports that may enter the country. The purpose is to maintain the domestic price of sugar above a set minimal level. The United States Department of Agriculture (USDA) allocates quotas among eligible countries, with Brazil receiving approximately 13% of the world total. In-quota imports are subject to a very low duty. Amounts entering above the quota are subject to a tariff computed by the USITC to be 78% ad valorem in 2003.[34] Brazil has expressed concern over the small increases in quotas given to the Central American countries under the CAFTADR, suggesting it bodes poorly for future negotiations with the United States, given that Brazil is the world's largest producer of raw and refined sugar.

Cotton. Cotton is a protected crop in the United States, benefitting from direct payments, counter-cyclical payments, subsidized loans and other federal programs. Subsidies averaged $1.7 billion per year for fiscal years 1991 to 2004.[35] Brazil successfully challenged portions

---

[33] Brazil's positions in this section are summarized from: Embassy of Brazil. *U.S. Barriers to Brazilian Goods, Services, and Investment.* October 2002 and the summary update of the same publication printed in March 2005.

[34] For details of the sugar program, see CRS Issue Brief IB95 117, *Sugar Policy Issues,* by Remy Jurenas. Brazil calculates a much higher ad valorem equivalent of 221% for 2004.

[35] See CRS Report RL3257 1, Background on the U.S.-Brazil WTO Cotton Subsidy Dispute, by Randy Schnepf.p. 1.

of the U.S. cotton program under WTO dispute settlement rules, requiring the United States to change or withdraw these prohibited support programs. Although the United States missed the deadlines to correct these programs, Brazil, unlike some other countries, did not take retaliatory measures. Congress repealed two of the offending programs as part of the FY2006 budget reconciliation conference bill on February 1, 2006, but Brazil remains critical of remaining cotton support programs.[36]

Steel. The steel industry files more antidumping and countervailing duty cases than any other U.S. industry, the subject of repeated complaints by Brazil.[37] As of January 1, 2006, there were 16 such orders in place against Brazil, some dating back to 1986. The steel issue was further exacerbated in 2002 when the United States imposed special safeguard duties of up to 30% on various steel imports, until successfully challenged in the WTO and withdrawn. Brazil estimates that the total cost of these measures exceeds $2 billion in lost sales, and with the United States as one of its most important export markets, is eager to see restrictions reduced, if not eliminated.

Ethanol (corn). For years, both Brazil and the United States subsidized heavily the development of ethanol production from sugar and corn, respectively. Currently, Brazil's subsidy program has ended and it maintains a highly efficient ethanol production process. Brazil's exports of ethanol face two barriers to the U.S. market. First, U.S. corn production is subsidized by various U.S. programs, and some 13% of total corn production is used for ethanol. Second, there is a U.S. import duty on ethanol plus an additional 54 cents per gallon designed to offset a tax reduction all ethanol receives to offset the federal gasoline excise tax levied at the pump on all fuels.[38] Brazil continues to press for changes in both programs.

Orange Juice. Brazil argues that the U.S. tariff on orange juice concentrate is equivalent to 65% on an ad valorem basis and 18.4% on non-concentrated juice. In addition, the most recent U.S. antidumping order against Brazil was placed on orange juice on January 1, 2005. In January 2006, the U.S. Department of Commerce made a preliminary finding of dumping against Brazilian frozen concentrated orange juice, which Brazil has vowed to fight in the WTO.

Tobacco. Also subject to tariff rate quotas and very high over-quota tariffs, Brazil would like to see the U.S. market open more to greater imports of the product from Brazil. Tobacco represents only 1% of total U.S. imports from Brazil on a dollar value basis.

Soybeans. Brazil, the second largest producer of soybeans in the world, must compete against U.S. subsidies on soybeans ranging from $1.5 to $3.2 billion annually between 2004 and 2006. Brazil is evaluating whether to challenge these subsidies in the WTO, as it did with cotton.

Shrimp. On January 27, 2005, the United States imposed an antidumping duty order on frozen or canned shrimp, and prawns from Brazil, decreasing imports from shrimp farmed in the poorer northeast portion of the country.

Beef and Chicken. U.S. sanitary certification for Brazilian chicken has not been approved, and for beef was only approved in 2005, subject to a TRQ.

---

[36] International Trade Reporter. House Approves Budget Measure Containing Byrd Amendment Repeal. February 1, 2006.

[37] CRS Report RL32333, *Steel: Price and Availability Issues,* by Stephen Cooney. pp. 8 and 29.

[38] CRS Report RL30369, *Fuel Ethanol: Background and Public Policy Issues,* by Brent D. Yacobucci and Jasper Womach. pp. 2-3 and 17.

U.S. Complaints Against B razil[39]

The USTR lists a number of complaints against Brazil, ranging from cumbersome import administrative procedures to outright restrictions on certain imports. Of equal importance is the inability to make more progress in areas where the United States is most competitive such as protection of intellectual property rights and services trade.

High Tariffs. Between Brazil's higher average tariffs (especially on industrial goods) and Mercosul's CET (exacerbated by a surcharge from 1997 to 2004), Brazil's tariff regime hurts U.S. exports of agricultural products, distilled spirits, computer and telecommunications equipment.

Prohibited Imports. Restrictions apply to various consumer goods, with a safeguard measure currently issued against certain toys.

Intellectual Property Rights. Although Brazil has numerous IPR laws on the books, the USTR is critical of many and notes that enforcement issues are a serious problem.[40] There is a 5-6 year backlog in processing patent applications, and data confidentiality protection for pharmaceuticals is not covered by law. Brazil lacks copyright enforcement leading to significant piracy losses for U.S. businesses (particularly video and audio cassettes). Despite Brazilian attempts to rectify the problem with a new task force and other initiatives, it lacks the resources to tackle the problem fully at this point in time. Brazil, therefore, is reluctant to sign on to an FTA that contains enforceable IPR provisions. The United States held up review of Brazil's eligibility for benefits under the Generalized System of Preferences (GSP) because of concerns over piracy issues, but the United States decided against taking action in recognition of Brazil's attempts to address piracy. Still, Brazil acknowledges its piracy problem, realizing the implications for its own producers and tax revenues as well. The Brazilian Congress conducted a study on the issue in 2004, which noted that piracy constituted nearly 60% of music sales and that Brazil had failed to close legal loopholes and counteract the problem more effectively, including its lack of organizational capacity and resources.[41]

Onerous Licensing and Regulatory Requirements. Importers complain of the high costs associated with meeting business registration and other requirements in Brazil.

Sanitary and Phytosanitary (SPS) Barriers. The USTR argues that SPS restrictions, including those that apply to beef, the prohibition of poultry imports (also a reciprocity issue), and certain types of wheats from various U.S. states are unfounded.

Government Procurement. Brazil is not a signatory to the WTO Agreement on Government Procurement and there are multiple preferences given to local businesses.

Export and Financing Subsidies. Through various programs at the National Social and Economic Development Bank (BNDES), Brazil promotes the purchase of domestic equipment and machinery and helps finance export activities.

Services Trade and Investment. There are restrictions on industries such as audio visual, telecommunications, financial (insurance), and express delivery services. Brazil has expressed concern over investor-state provisions, standard language in U.S. free trade agreements, and

---

[39] For Brazil's trade barriers, see United States Trade Representative. *2005 National Trade Estimate Report on Foreign Trade Barriers.* Washington, D.C. March 2005. pp. 30-37.

[40] USTR, 2005 National Trade Estimate Report on Foreign Trade Barriers, pp. 33-37.

[41] Federative Republic of Brazil. Chamber of Deputies. *Legislative Investigation Committee on Piracy (CPI) Report.* Brasilia, 2004. pp.127 and 267-269.

possible U.S. reaction to some of its subsidized financing programs conducted under BNDES. Brazil has not signed a bilateral investment treaty with the United States.

OUTLOOK

Brazil trades relatively little for an economy of its size and diversity and would benefit from trading more. It has embraced export promotion, which generates foreign exchange and can contribute to growth in economic output, but has shied away from deeper commitments to lowering barriers to imports, which are key to gains in productivity, per capita income, and development. This strategy is consistent with Brazil's short-term financing needs and its trade preferences, which are driven by a combination of macroeconomic, industrial, and foreign policy priorities.

For the United States, this presents a delicate policy conundrum because economic reciprocity may not be the only key to successful trade negotiations with Brazil. For example, even if significant progress could be made on agricultural issues in the Doha round, and Brazilian trade complaints could be ameliorated in bilateral working groups with the United States, Brazil may still choose not to liberalize areas where either it cannot easily fulfill the provisions of an FTA (enforcing protection of IPR), or where the United States has a distinct comparative advantage or particular interest (industrial goods, services, investment). This has been made clear in statements by Brazilian officials and by formal trade negotiation positions.

To illustrate, in speaking on the FTAA, a former Brazilian Ambassador to the United States and noted trade expert wrote:

> The Brazilian position is not merely a tactical reaction to the U.S. negotiating strategy regarding the so-called systemic issues. In fact, Brazil has a clear interest in preventing hemispheric disciplines on topics such as investment, intellectual property, government procurement, and services from curtailing its ability to formulate and implement public policies that are in its highest national interest.[42]

This attitude is reinforced by evidence questioning the economic logic of Brazil's anti-FTAA position based on the U.S. preference for addressing subsidies in the WTO. For example, studies point out that ending agricultural subsidies would increase FTAA agricultural trade little compared to a far bigger gain for Brazil from eliminating tariffs.[43] Brazil seems to realize this on some level or it would not continue to offer the "4+1" market access talks as an alternative to the FTAA.

As such, U.S. trade negotiators may be frustrated because there is perhaps little they can do to nudge Brazil off its course of continuing to advance Mercosul, where the marginal gains from expansion are likely small, and pursuing selective priorities in the WTO, while leaving

---

[42] Barbosa, Rubens Antonio. The Free Trade Area of the Americas. *Fordham International Law Journal*. February 2004. p. 1021.

[43] Salazar-Xirinachs, José M. Development Issues Posed by the FTAA. In Weintraub, Sidney, Alan M. Rugman, and Gavin Boyd, eds. *Free Trade in the Americas: Economic and Political Issues for Governments and Firms.* Cheltenham, Edward Elgar Publishing, Inc. 2004. p. 238. A similar conclusion is drawn for global agricultural trade as well, where some 80-90% of trade-distorting cost is attributed to tariffs rather than subsidies. Congressional Budget Office. *The Efects of Liberalizing World Agricultural Trade: A Survey.* Washington, D.C. December 2005.

the FTAA to flounder indefinitely. Brazil may actually have more to lose, however, because as much as both countries could improve their economic well-being from greater trade liberalization, as a developing country, Brazil seems to have the most to gain from not only reducing foreign barriers to its exports, but unilaterally opening its economy further, particularly as part of completing its ongoing economic reform agenda.

APPENDIX 1 - BRAZIL: TOP 15 EXPORTS AND IMPORTS

(Calendar Year 2004, $ Millions)

Export Product	$ Value	Import Product	$ Value
1. Soybeans	5,395	1. Fuels and lubricants	10,317
2. Iron ore	4,759	2. Chem./Phar. Intermed. Goods	9,638
3. Motor vehicles	3,352	3. Intermediate parts	5,589
4. Soybean oil cake	3,271	4. Mineral products	5,068
5. Airplanes	3,269	5. Accessories for trans. equip.	4,905
6. Meat, chicken	2,494	6. Non-durable consumer goods	3,673
7. Iron/Steel semi finish	2,115	7. Farming, raw materials	3,473
8. Flat-rolled iron/steel	2,007	8. Industrial machinery	3,278
9. Motor vehicle engines	1,972	9. Office/Science equipment	2,679
10. Meat, bovine	1,963	10. Fixed equipment	2,528
11. Motor vehicle parts	1,961	11. Inedible farm products	2,213
12. Footwear	1,899	12. Parts, industrial capital goods	1,518
13. Coffee	1,750	13. Foodstuffs, intermediate	1,517
14. Cane sugar, raw	1,511	14. Pharmaceutical products	1,454
15. Tobacco	1,380	15. Accessories for indust. Mach.	1,065
Subtotal	39,098	Subtotal	58,915
% of Total Exports	40.5%	% of Total Imports	93.8%

Data Source: Boletim do Banco do Brasil, September, 2005

APPENDIX 2 - U.S.-BRAZIL MERCHANDISE TRADE

($ millions)

Year	U.S. Exports	U.S. Imports	U.S.Trade Balance	Trade Turnover	% Growth in U.S. Exports	% Growth in U.S. Imports
1992	5,751	7,609	-1,858	13,360		
1993	6,058	7,479	-1,421	13,537	5.3%	-1.7%
1994	8,102	8,683	-581	16,785	33.7%	16.1%
1995	11,439	8,833	2,606	20,272	41.2%	1.7%
1996	12,718	8,773	3,945	21,491	11.2%	-0.7%
1997	15,915	9,625	6,290	25,540	25.1%	9.7%
1998	15,142	10,102	5,040	25,244	-4.9%	5.0%
1999	13,203	11,314	1,889	24,517	-12.8%	12.0%
2000	15,320	13,853	1,467	29,173	16.0%	22.4%
2001	15,880	14,467	1,413	30,347	3.7%	4.4%
2002	12,376	15,781	-3,405	28,157	-22.1%	9.1%
2003	11,211	17,910	-6,699	29,121	-9.4%	13.5%
2004	13,837	21,160	-7,323	34,997	23.4%	18.1%

Data source: U.S. Department of Commerce

APPENDIX 3 - U.S.-BRAZIL SERVICES TRADE

($ millions)

Year	U.S. Exports	U.S. Imports	Trade Balance	*Trade Turnover	% Growth in U.S. Exports	% Growth in U.S. Imports	% of Total U.S. Trade
1992	2,500	688	1,812	3,188	na	na	1.2%
1993	2,944	744	2,200	3,688	17.8%	8.1%	1.3%
1994	3,732	917	2,815	4,649	26.8%	23.3%	1.5%
1995	4,994	1,176	3,818	6,170	33.8%	28.2%	1.9%
1996	5,208	1,403	3,805	6,611	4.3%	19.3%	1.8%
1997	6,408	1,775	4,633	8,183	23.0%	26.5%	2.1%
1998	6,620	1,962	4,658	8,582	3.3%	10.5%	2.1%
1999	5,641	1,726	3,915	7,367	-14.8%	-12.0%	1.6%
2000	6,309	1,953	4,356	8,262	11.8%	13.2%	1.7%
2001	5,826	1,856	3,970	7,682	-7.7%	-5.0%	1.7%
2002	5,005	1,723	3,282	6,728	-14.1%	-7.2%	1.4%
2003	4,795	1,841	2,954	6,636	-4.2%	6.8%	1.3%
2004	4,997	1,913	3,084	6,910	4.2%	3.9%	1.4%

Data Source: U.S. Department of Commerce. Bureau of Economic Analysis (BEA). * Trade turnover = total trade or exports plus imports

APPENDIX 4 - U.S.-BRAZIL FOREIGN DIRECT INVESTMENT

(in millions of U.S. dollars, historical cost basis)

Year	U.S. FDI in Brazil	% Change	Brazil FDI in U.S.	% Change
1993	16,772	—	726	—
1994	18,400	9.7%	712	-1.9%
1995	23,706	28.8%	864	21.3%
1996	28,699	21.1%	689	-20.3%
1997	35,727	24.5%	698	1.3%
1998	37,802	5.8%	609	-12.8%
1999	37,184	-1.6%	735	20.7%
2000	36,717	-1.3%	882	20.0%
2001	32,027	-12.8%	596	-32.4%
2002	27,598	-13.8%	997	67.3%
2003	31,741	15.0%	667	-33.1%
2004	33,267	4.8%	1,286	92.8%

Source: U.S. Department of Commerce. Bureau of Economic Analysis (BEA)

Note: historical cost data measures the stock of FDI reflecting prices at the time of the investment

In: Economics, Politics and Social Issues in Latin America   ISBN 1-60021-182-8
Editor: Mary P. Lassiter, pp. 123-154   © 2007 Nova Science Publishers, Inc.

Chapter 7

UNIONS AND THE LABOR MARKET IN BRAZIL

Jorge Saba Arbache

Universidade de Brasilia, Brazil

I. INTRODUCTION

Although labor unions are considered one of the most important institutions of modern capitalism (Freeman, 2000), the literature shows that their mode of operation and impact on the economy vary from country to country. Although there is a wide variety of systems, institutions, and union action strategies in the different countries, an important stylized fact in the literature is that labor unions reduce wage dispersion through collective bargaining processes. This has led Metcalf et al. (2000) to refer to them as a "sword of justice." According to Freeman (2000), this phenomenon is actually more widespread than the more thoroughly researched effect of unions on wages, namely their ability to raise the relative wages of their members. The literature shows that: (i) the distribution of wages among unionized workers and/or those covered by collective bargaining is more concentrated than the wage distribution for other workers, even when demographic and productive characteristics are controlled for in the corresponding regressions; and (ii) collective bargaining diminishes the importance of merit in wage formation, thereby narrowing the wage spread between jobs (Freeman, 1980, 1992; Hirsch 1982; Card, 1992; DiNardo et al., 1995; Gosling and Machin, 1995; Blau and Kahn, 1996; DiNardo et al. 1997; Metcalf et al., 2000, among others).

Estimates of the impact of unions on the labor market in Brazil are still very preliminary. The few results available include those obtained by Arbache (1999), who investigates the wage and income-distribution effects of unions among male manufacturing workers; Arbache and Carneiro (1999), who examine the importance and effects of unions on collective bargaining; Arbache (2000), who studies the effects of trade liberalization on unions and collective bargaining; Menezes-Filho et al. (2002) who assesses the impact of trade unions on the economic performance of Brazilian establishments; and Amorim (2000), who analyzes the relationship between unions and indirect pay. Little is known about the effect of unions on employment, productivity or labor market rigidity, and especially on wages and income distribution. Knowledge of the impact of unions on pay dispersion is particularly important for Brazil, given its highly unequal income distribution. If the legal framework that regulates labor relations is a decisive factor in the functioning of unions and collective bargaining processes, then knowing this could help us to understand the effects of unions on the overall economy.

This chapter seeks to answer the following questions: (i) How do employment and union laws affect collective bargaining processes? (ii) Do unions affect wage formation and income distribution? (iii) Do unions increase the rigidity of the labor market? We conclude by making some suggestions for enhancing collective bargaining and unions in Brazil.

The chapter is organized as follows: Section 2 describes labor laws and union legislation in Brazil. Section 3 describes the characteristics of unionized and non-union workers, union density, and the determinants of unionization. Section 4 investigates the effects of unions on wages and income distribution. Section 5 discusses the results obtained and seeks to demonstrate the effects of employment and union laws on collective bargaining processes and union behavior. Section 6 offers some recommendations for improving labor relations in Brazil.

II. LABOR LAWS, UNION LEGISLATION, AND COLLECTIVE BARGAINING PROCESSES

The institutions that regulate labor relations in Brazil have a huge impact on collective bargaining, given the way they are involved in employment contracts, labor disputes and union activity, and the intensity of that involvement. This section provides a historical overview and describes the characteristics of the main institutions governing the country's labor relations. As we shall see, such institutions contribute to adversarial labor relations and curb the development of collective bargaining. We also show that the nature and functioning of those institutions have potential effects on income distribution and on macroeconomic stability.

Labor Laws and Labor Courts

Relations between workers and employers in Brazil are governed by the Consolidated Labor Laws [*Consolidação das Leis do Trabalho*] (CLT). The CLT law is extremely wide ranging and detailed, regulating the most varied aspects of labor relations. The CLT was first introduced in 1943, during the administration of Getúlio Vargas, in order to consolidate the labor laws existing at that time. One of its main aims was to create a system to protect workers from exploitation by employers, and to harmonize labor relations with a view to avoiding direct disputes between the parties. Camargo (2001) points out that the CLT was premised on the existence of asymmetric power relations between capital and labor, and that the role of the law was to protect and regulate workers' interests. The all-embracing and paternalistic nature of the law created an atmosphere that was not conducive to the development of collective bargaining. The CLT also created unstable labor relations, generating disequilibrium by providing excessive protection for workers. The law requires disputes to be settled in labor tribunals rather than in the companies involved, so little space is left for direct negotiations between employers and employees; and it discourages the development of a cooperative relationship between the two parties.

As Camargo (2001) shows, an important feature of Brazil's labor legislation is the coexistence of individual and collective employment contracts. Individual contracts (i.e. contracts involving employment record cards) are agreed into between the company and the worker and deal with issues such as working conditions and wages. Collective contracts, on the other hand, are agreed between the employer and the workers' union, or between the employers' association and the union, and cover minimum working conditions and minimum wages, among other issues. Workers without an individual contract *are not* covered by collective contracts in their job category. Legally, the results of collective bargaining processes are extended to all workers and companies in that occupation or industry, respectively, even if the workers or companies involved are not members of the respective unions negotiating the agreement. This provision attributes great importance to unions in labor relations.

In Brazil, the justice system is required to rule on disputes related to compliance with labor laws, and on those relating to individual and collective employment contracts. It is also called upon to promote conciliation and arbitration in collective bargaining processes. If negotiations between workers and employers break down, the labor court is required to rule on the dispute. If the impasse is the result of a failure to comply with the legislation, the court will merely apply the law in reaching its decision. But if the impasse stems from a lack of agreement on other issues, the tribunal may decide according to the judges' point of view, possibly even using political criteria (Camargo, 2001). The decision of the labor court *must* be complied with by the parties. Accordingly, labor courts have regulatory authority that affords them great power within the collective bargaining and labor relations framework in Brazil. The courts offer many incentives for free-rider behavior by workers, since employers are the ones who bear the onus of the proof. Thus, the paternalism of the law, together with the tremendous power and involvement of the justice system in labor disputes, act as obstacles to the modernization of labor relations by inhibiting cooperation between the parties and fostering disputes between workers and employers.

Union Organization and Collective Bargaining

Under the CLT, labor unions are organized by occupational category, but employer associations are organized by economic sector. Job categories and economic sectors are defined by the Ministry of Labor, on the basis of similar characteristics. Up to 1988, different occupations and economic categories were prohibited from grouping together in a single union. This restriction was lifted in the 1988 Constitution, when the formation of nationwide unions and union confederations was authorized.

In order to control the unions, the law instituted monopoly of representation and the union levy, together with *mandatory extension* of the results of collective bargaining processes to all workers, including non-union members. Once the union has been recognized by the Ministry of Labor, it then has a monopoly in its predefined geographic jurisdiction. The smallest regional base is the municipality, but unions can also have regional, state, or even national jurisdiction. All collective bargaining processes in a given category have to be carried out with participation from the union holding the monopoly representation in the geographic area concerned.

Although union membership is not compulsory, workers and employers *are required* to collect a union levy each year; 60 percent of this is passed on to the respective union by the Ministry of Labor, which is the body responsible for collecting it. The remaining funds are divided between the Ministry of Labor and the federation and confederation for the occupational or economic category concerned. By law, funds transferred to labor unions must be used exclusively for purposes such as recreation, social assistance, education, and consumer cooperatives, but *never* to finance political activities, collective bargaining processes, or strike funds. Only funds obtained through *voluntary* contributions can be used for such purposes.[1]

Collective bargaining is compulsory and must take place once a year, during the "base-date" period, in which the workers' union and the employer's organization or individual company negotiate wages and other employment issues. Base dates vary between occupations and categories, and this results in negotiations being spread throughout the year. It is possible, however, for different occupations to sign agreements on the same day in the same company or economic category, thereby resulting in a collective agreement covering a large proportion of the workers in a given industry. In bargaining processes between employer organizations and worker unions, the result is known as a collective contract *(convenção coletiva)*; if bargaining takes place between the workers' union and a single company, the outcome is known as a collective agreement *(acordo coletivo)*.

Monopoly representation, the union levy, and the extension of collective bargaining results to all workers gave great power to union leaders, but fostered a lack of responsibility among them with respect to workers' interests and situations. There were two reasons for this: firstly, union finances are guaranteed by an assured income from the union levy, which means union leaders do not have to attract members to finance union activities. Secondly, mandatory union participation in collective bargaining processes in their area of jurisdiction, together with compulsory extension of the results to all workers, gives union leaders great power in labor relations, whether union density is high or low. Consequently, as history shows, union leaders have not always been concerned with attracting and maintaining workers affiliated to their unions, or with working on behalf of the most obvious interests in their category. In many cases, union legislation has spawned bureaucrats that have little interest in workers' situations, but who maintain close relations with the Government in order to maintain their power in the unions. Moreover, the monopolistic nature of unions has resulted in collective bargaining taking place on a fragmented basis with no inter-union coordination across the different occupations and economic categories.

When the military dictatorship took power in 1964, amendments were made to the laws governing union organization and pay-setting processes. One of the most important changes was the introduction of a hardline law on strikes, aimed at regulating the right to strike and creating new criteria for strikes to be considered legal. Highly restrictive rules inhibited the outbreak of strikes and restricted union action; in practice, the changes were intended to repress movements in support of claims of any type. These and other measures, such as prison for union leaders, caused the union movement to stagnate until the late 1970s.

---

[1] Up to 1988, the Ministry of Labor could intervene in labor unions for reasons such as misuse of the union levy, or for calling unauthorized strikes or lock-outs.

In the 1960s, a law on wage adjustments was also introduced with the aim of centralizing and regulating the wage-setting process. This gave the Government power to determine the minimum rate of increase for all wages in the economy. The formula and frequency of pay raises changed several times between the mid-1960s when the law was introduced and the end of the 1980s, but it tended to set pay increases below the rate of inflation and even below productivity gains. The lag in pay raises also tended to generate wage erosion because of the accelerating inflation of that period. The law on pay increases was created as an economic policy tool, with wages in practice being used as adjustment variables in stabilization policies. Any pay increases above those stipulated by law had to be negotiated individually between the company and its workers. Given the weakness of labor unions and the centralization of pay-setting processes, the law not only operated as an instrument of wage control, but also inhibited collective bargaining from the 1960s until the mid-1990s, when it was shelved.[2]

A key feature of the period in which the wage law was in force was that, while wages could theoretically be negotiated between workers and employers, in practice the latter would invoke "collective disagreement" during the bargaining process, which meant referring the dispute to the labor tribunal for settlement. As wages were set by law, the courts did no more than applying the corresponding legislation, overriding any attempt to negotiate increases above the correction set by the Government. Thus, although wages were supposed to be negotiable, pay raises in practice adhered to the rates of increase set by the Government, leaving little or no space for collective bargaining over pay. As a result, the tremendous sway of the Government over wage setting for more than twenty years seriously undermined the development and modernization of collective bargaining processes in the country.

Control of wages and repression of the union movement prompted major wage claims in the late 1970s, and gave rise to a new phase in the organization of the union movement. Workers sought greater autonomy, freedom of action, and changes in wage policy. The reorganization of the movement was particularly significant in the wealthiest and most industrialized areas of São Paulo, where many multinationals and large local companies are based. The perception held by workers that companies in the region were extracting monopoly rents possibly contributed to the emergence of this movement. As shown by Booth (1995) and Nickell et al. (1994), unions tend to demand pay raises where there are *quasi-rents* to be shared out. In such a context, the law on wage increases placed a straitjacket on pay in the most developed regions and most dynamic sectors of the economy, where wage increases above the law were supposedly possible; this led to demonstrations that later culminated in the "new unionism" movement (see Camargo, 2001; and Amadeo and Camargo, 1989).

With this additional flexibility, collective bargaining became more important, and the wage adjustment rates determined by law became the floor and no longer the ceiling for pay raises, as it was now possible to negotiate over productivity.[3] Unions now started to bargain over wage increases above the floor set by the law, through negotiations at the company level. Success in bargaining, however, depended on industry characteristics, occupational category, and region. Unions in companies or industries with greater market power, or those that were more concentrated, had stronger bargaining power. Unions in more competitive sectors had

---

[2] See Carneiro and Henley (1998) for a description of the main features of the wage determination process in Brazil over this period.

[3] Carneiro (1998) provides evidence of the presence of productivity effects in the Brazilian wage determination process during the 1980s and 1990s.

little chance of bargaining over productivity, however, and contracts were negotiated in a more individual and less collective fashion.

In practice, as pointed out by Camargo (2001), the bargaining system was hybrid: on the one hand it was partly centralized, since unions in some sectors negotiated wages collectively; on the other hand, the weakness of unions elsewhere meant that wages were bargained in a decentralized fashion, with actual pay raises tending to match the adjustments set by law. This system of labor relations and collective bargaining led to scant cooperation between unions, as bargaining power between them varied widely. Unions in companies or sectors that were more inclined to grant pay increases had little interest in the possibility of centralized negotiations.

Promulgation of the new Constitution led to the overhaul of legislation on collective bargaining, wages, strikes, and unions. Collective bargaining began to be encouraged, the concept of "illegal strike" ceased to exist, prohibition of worker organization at national level was lifted, and unionization of civil servants was allowed, along with other changes making union organization more democratic. Nonetheless, these changes were insufficient to reduce the greatest obstacles to implementing collective bargaining processes in Brazil, since the basic rules governing employment contracts, the powers of labor tribunals, and union organization remained virtually intact.

III. CHARACTERISTICS OF UNIONIZED WORKERS AND UNION DENSITY

This section discusses some of the main socioeconomic characteristics of unionized workers and their non-union counterparts. The aim is to determine who the union members are, and where they are located, along with information on union density and whether there is a correlation between socioeconomic profile and union membership.

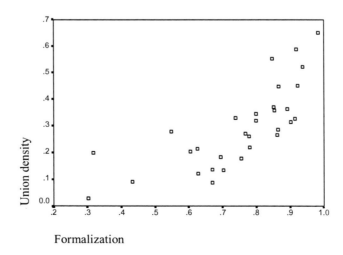

Figure 1. Union Density vs. Formalization, 1999

Our research on unions draws on data from the National Household Sample Survey (PNAD) conducted by the Brazilian Institute of Geography and Statistics (IBGE) for 1986, 1992, 1993, and 1995 to 1999, years for which the "unionization" variable is available. Unions are analyzed by industry at the two-digit level, which covers economic activities ranging from agriculture and manufacturing industry to services and public administration.

The data have been filtered for individuals of 18 to 65 years of age, economically active, and earning a positive wage. We took pay earned in the individual's main activity, and transformed this into a real hourly wage. Although PNAD data are acknowledged to be of high quality, 0.1 percent of cases were suppressed from each end of the real wage distribution as a precaution to avoid outliers arising from measurement errors. As a result of the filter, we have at least 100,000 individuals for each year, about 20 percent of whom are union members.

Characteristics of Unionized Workers

Table 1 shows that the vast majority of unionized workers hold an employment record card (*carteira de trabalho assinada*). While almost 90 percent of unionized workers benefit from the guarantees afforded by a formal work contract, only about 54 percent of non-union workers have this card. As only formal workers are covered by collective bargaining, one might expect that all unionized workers would have a formal contract. The shortfall could arise from measurement error, or unionized workers migrating from formal to informal jobs for some reason. The figures suggest that: (i) workers holding an employment record card have a greater incentive to unionize; (ii) unions are active in guaranteeing workers' rights, thereby reducing the level of informal contracting in the industries where they are strongest; and (iii) unions tend to be concentrated in industries where there is a higher percentage of formal contracting.

These three hypotheses help to explain the higher level of formalization among unionized workers. It is reasonable to assume that formal workers have a greater incentive to join unions, because the costs of union membership for them are less than the benefits. Informal workers do not have incentives to join unions, however, as they do not benefit from the results of collective bargaining.

Figure 1 shows a positive relation between union density and the degree of formalization in the labor force at the industry level, thereby supporting hypotheses (ii) and (iii). It remains to be seen whether there is a causal relationship between the two variables and if so in what direction: i.e. whether greater union activism produces a high level of formalization, or whether greater formalization facilitates union activism.

There seems to be a correlation between union membership and status in the family. About 62 percent of unionized workers are heads of households, compared to just 52 percent of non-unionists. These figures suggest that union membership is a characteristic of more mature workers, and that young people participate in unions less.

Also, there seems to be a correlation between union membership and race: about 61 percent of unionized workers are white, compared to 52 percent of non-union members. In addition, the proportion of men among unionized workers is higher than among non-union members. It can therefore be concluded that either: (i) minorities have fewer incentives to join unions; or (ii) unions are concentrated in sectors or regions where these groups are under-represented.

The distribution of education among unionized and non-union workers is the variable that most clearly distinguishes the two groups. While at least 60 percent of non-union workers are in the first three education brackets (ranging from no education at all to some primary education), at least 50 percent of union members are in the three highest education brackets – covering primary school completed to higher education. This result seems even more remarkable when we analyze the distribution of workers with higher education. Whereas at least 13.7 percent of unionized workers have completed a higher education course, no more than 5.4 percent of non-union workers have done so. If we group the two higher education brackets together (i.e. secondary and tertiary education both completed) we see that in 1999, for example, 47 percent of unionized workers had this level of schooling, compared to just 26.6 percent of their non-union counterparts. Thus, unlike the situation in developed countries (Freeman, 1982; Booth, 1995; Metcalf, 2000), education is a key characteristic of unionized workers in Brazil.

The distribution of workers by size of establishment (a variable not shown in Table 1) shows that nearly 85 percent of unionized workers are in establishments with more than 11 employees, while 58 percent of non-union members work in establishments with 11 employees or less.[4]

Table 2 shows the distribution of unionized workers by region and job category. The proportion of unionized workers in rural and urban areas is quite similar, while unionization is greater in metropolitan than in non-metropolitan areas. The regional distribution shows that the proportion of unionized workers in the southeast – where most of the country's industry and financial center are located – is similar to that in other regions. The proportions of unionized workers in the North, Northeast, and Central-Western regions, are in all cases less than in the other regions combined. In contrast, the level of unionization in the south is considerably higher than in the rest of the country, which suggests that the union movement in this area is relatively more active and enjoys greater bargaining power.

The lower panel of Table 2 shows the distribution of unionized workers by occupational category. Unionization is a clear characteristic of managers, skilled production workers, office workers, and, in particular, professionals. Levels of union membership are substantially above the average in each of these job categories. Among professionals, a group that encompasses all higher-level staff, at least 42 percent are union members; this is much more than the average for other occupations. One possible explanation for this is the regulation and legal control maintained over the practice of higher-level professions through Regional Councils (for example, the *Conselho Regional de Economia*, *Ordem dos Advogados*, *Conselho Regional de Medicina*, etc.), supported by compulsory membership of such bodies as a precondition for professional practice. Often, these bodies operate in traditional areas of union activity, for example regulating fees and establishing wage floors.

---

[4] For this calculation, we used the PNAD variable that classifies the size of establishments in which individuals work as "up to 11 employees" and "over 11 employees".

Table 1. Characteristics of Unionized and Non-Union Workers

(Percentages)

General characteristics	1986		1992		1993		1995		1996		1997		1998		1999	
	Union	Non-union	Union	Non-union	Union	Non-union	Union	Non-union	Union	Non-union	Union	Non-union	Union	Non-union	Union	Non-union
Employment record card	82.3	57.5	91.3	55.2	91.0	54.1	91.4	53.5	90.4	53.8	90.4	53.4	90.5	53.3	89.7	52.4
Head of household	66.8	48.6	64.3	50.7	64.5	50.9	62.8	50.2	62.0	49.7	61.6	50.0	61.3	50.2	61.2	50.2
White	61.5	51.0	61.5	52.0	60.9	51.8	61.1	51.8	62.1	52.5	60.5	51.8	61.2	51.5	59.9	51.7
Male	75.6	63.9	70.5	62.3	69.5	62.4	68.1	61.0	66.7	61.0	66.6	61.5	65.3	61.1	65.2	60.6
Experience (absolute value)	22.9	22.1	22.4	21.8	22.3	21.9	22.6	21.9	22.5	21.7	22.5	21.7	22.6	21.7	22.9	21.7
Age (absolute value)	36.0	33.8	37.0	34.6	37.2	34.7	37.7	34.8	37.9	35.0	38.0	35.0	38.3	35.2	38.5	35.3
Illiterate	11.7	17.0	9.8	15.3	9.1	14.1	7.9	13.0	7.2	12.5	7.7	11.9	6.9	11.1	7.5	10.6
Some elementary education	13.7	19.8	11.5	17.3	10.9	17.0	10.3	16.5	9.2	15.0	9.1	15.4	8.5	14.8	8.4	14.3
Elementary or some primary education	26.4	32.7	26.2	33.0	25.5	33.6	25.4	33.9	23.6	32.7	22.9	32.7	22.3	32.3	21.8	32.0
Primary or some secondary education	13.2	13.1	14.0	14.1	13.7	14.4	13.9	14.7	15.3	16.3	14.8	15.7	14.7	16.3	15.0	16.5
Secondary or some higher education	21.4	13.9	25.0	16.0	25.9	16.5	26.8	17.3	28.1	18.6	28.4	19.2	29.8	20.2	29.6	21.2
Higher education	13.7	3.4	13.6	4.4	15.0	4.4	15.7	4.6	16.6	4.9	17.0	5.1	17.9	5.3	17.7	5.4
Years of schooling (absolute value)	7.2	5.2	7.7	5.7	7.9	5.8	8.1	6.0	8.4	6.2	8.4	6.3	8.7	6.4	8.6	6.6

Table 2. Proportion of Unionized Workers by Region and Occupation

(Percentages)

Geographic region	1986	1992	1993	1995	1996	1997	1998	1999
Urban	22.1	20.2	20.0	19.1	18.7	18.2	17.8	17.4
Rural	22.1	20.0	19.6	17.8	17.7	17.1	16.5	17.2
Metropolitan region	24.2	22.0	22.1	21.2	20.9	20.3	20.0	18.8
Non-metropolitan	20.6	18.8	18.4	17.3	16.8	16.4	15.9	16.4
South-east	22.9	19.1	18.4	17.9	18.6	17.9	17.4	16.7
Other regions	21.7	20.8	20.8	19.5	18.5	18.1	17.7	17.7
North	22.3	16.4	16.2	14.6	15.5	15.4	14.3	14.7
Other regions	22.2	20.4	20.2	19.3	18.8	18.2	17.9	17.6
North-east	19.1	20.8	20.2	18.4	16.6	16.7	16.6	17.2
Other regions	23.4	18.6	19.2	19.2	19.3	18.5	18.0	17.5
Central-western	16.9	17.8	18.7	15.7	16.6	15.2	15.1	15.0
Other regions	23.0	20.5	20.1	19.4	18.8	18.4	18.0	17.7
South	29.8	27.4	26.4	25.5	23.6	23.1	25.5	21.6
Other regions	20.7	18.5	18.5	17.5	17.4	16.9	16.6	16.5
Managers	40.2	34.5	36.0	34.7	33.4	32.2	31.4	30.2
Other occupations	21.6	19.7	19.5	18.5	18.1	17.6	17.3	17.0
Higher-level professionals	52.5	44.8	45.2	45.0	42.3	42.4	43.0	42.2
Other occupations	20.1	19.1	18.8	17.7	17.4	16.8	16.4	16.1
Technical workers	25.2	27.9	29.9	28.4	28.5	28.8	27.4	27.7
Other occupations	22.0	19.7	19.3	18.3	17.9	17.3	17.0	16.7
Office staff	30.8	31.6	32.7	31.1	29.7	29.1	28.7	27.7
Other occupations	21.3	19.2	18.9	18.0	17.7	17.2	16.8	16.6
Sales staff	12.9	8.9	10.1	9.7	10.3	10.0	10.2	9.6
Other occupations	23.8	11.3	21.8	20.8	20.2	19.6	19.2	19.0
Skilled production workers	29.3	19.5	28.3	26.8	26.0	25.3	24.9	24.8
Other occupations	20.6	18.5	18.5	17.6	17.3	16.8	16.5	16.2
Unskilled production workers	15.3	13.9	16.3	12.9	12.3	11.9	11.5	11.4
Other occupations	27.2	25.0	24.9	23.6	23.4	22.8	22.6	22.2

Table 3. Probability of Union Membership

Marginal effects (%)	1986	1992	1993	1995	1996	1997	1998	1999
Some elementary education	18.59	24.27	21.23	26.43	31.21	15.04	16.07	8.81
Elementary or some primary education	62.60	76.04	71.74	81.50	85.27	64.87	68.87	60.22
Primary or some secondary education	149.75	161.31	157.50	174.43	186.89	162.11	164.81	165.31
Secondary or some higher education	287.43	308.45	304.18	327.67	354.47	291.27	312.00	292.32
Higher education	835.15	624.02	680.75	721.92	760.35	633.53	691.90	671.78
Experience	1.38	1.97	1.92	2.25	2.31	2.32	2.44	2.62
Male	24.50	21.91	15.68	18.20	14.74	17.68	12.99	15.82
Head of household	89.43	47.36	51.98	41.20	41.79	39.31	37.09	34.10
Urban region	-13.86	-15.51	-12.41	-9.24	-12.99	-11.87	-9.92	-10.70
Metropolitan region	9.87	12.41	16.32	17.39	21.64	21.87	21.89	12.01
South-east	11.06	-10.12	-19.28	-19.08	1.89	-2.94	-6.76	-13.45
North	19.83	-18.75	-20.74	-27.73	-7.39	-10.23	-16.57	-20.56
Central-western	-20.55	-7.89	-9.23	-21.91	-1.69	-14.45	-13.77	-18.28
South	58.77	45.90	31.47	28.31	37.63	33.18	28.36	15.88
Agriculture	84.91	92.94	119.83	109.82	114.95	107.71	106.25	125.68
Manufacturing	121.24	164.18	178.35	193.99	151.76	134.72	120.43	130.49
Civil construction	-30.66	-19.09	-16.82	-14.54	-26.05	-28.75	-30.20	-33.23
Other industrial activities	187.18	343.72	369.61	442.29	355.15	304.29	310.65	317.70
Services	-48.39	-37.48	-37.16	-38.46	-33.12	-35.44	-37.32	-32.21
Other services	30.16	44.84	44.97	30.16	33.34	31.52	29.09	29.59
Transport and communication services	133.32	255.47	286.31	253.98	244.85	201.06	190.42	218.62

Table 3. Probability of Union Membership (Continued)

Social services	32.26	108.21	141.79	155.10	133.87	150.52	129.10	150.60
Public administration	-12.02	28.39	49.39	74.81	53.48	75.89	66.99	93.66
Other activities	164.23	284.65	328.61	330.09	229.34	237.05	166.07	183.97
N	99 305	104 154	106 285	114 377	111 358	118 135	117 045	120 685

Note: All coefficients are significant at the 5% level, except those shown in *italics*.

Reference categories are: illiterate, north east region, and commerce.

The models were estimated by logistic regression. The standard errors of the estimators are robust

Nonetheless, it is not uncommon to find unions operating in the same location as the these professional councils, and this facilitates and publicizes union activities, promotes union membership, and encourages integration between the two bodies, leading even to some unification of agendas.

About one-third of managers, technical staff, qualified production workers, and office staff are union members, compared to just 12 percent of unskilled production and manual workers – a group covering over half of the entire workforce. Unionization is even lower among sales staff, at around 10 percent[62] This distribution of union membership by occupational group is surprising, as the literature portrays union membership as a characteristic of low-skilled and production-line workers; moreover, workers with higher qualifications presumably have incentives to demand wages related to productivity, rather than based on pre-established pay scales. The occupational distribution of unionized workers in Brazil suggests that unions have the strongest presence in industries that concentrate highly skilled workers, including executives and office staff.

Table 1 and Table 2 therefore suggest that unionization in Brazil is a characteristic of more educated workers, holding the best jobs and working in large establishments; they also tend to be white, male, and heads of households; in addition union members are likely to be in metropolitan regions and to hold an employment record card. This profile suggests that the typical union member is very different from the average Brazilian worker, whose most common characteristic is a low skill level.

Bearing in mind the different characteristics between unionized workers and their non-union counterparts, it is reasonable to assume that socioeconomic variables affect the probability of union membership. To investigate this issue, we have estimated models that identify the contribution of individual characteristics to the likelihood of a unionized worker. Binomial logistic regressions were estimated using the union-membership indicator as the dependent variable. The model's explanatory variables were education, experience, experience squared, gender, head of household, urban/rural, metropolitan region, geographic region, and industry classification at the IBGE 1-digit level. The results appear in Table 3 and show the following:

- The likelihood of union membership rises substantially with schooling; in 1999 for example, an individual who had completed a higher education course was 672 percent more likely than an illiterate worker to be a union member;
- Experience raises the probability of union membership; in 1999 this increased by 2.6 percent with each additional year of experience;
- Men are more likely to be union members than women;
- Heads of households are more likely to be members of unions than other family members;
- Workers in urban areas are less likely to be unionized than those from rural areas;
- Workers in metropolitan areas are more likely to be union members;
- Workers from the south-east, north, and central-western regions are less likely to be union members than workers from the north-east; only workers from the southern region are more likely to be union members than those in the north-east;

- Economic activity seems to have a major influence on the probability of union membership, as the estimates vary substantially between sectors. Workers in manufacturing industry, other industrial activities, transport and communication services, and even agriculture show high probabilities of union membership; while workers in civil construction and services are unlikely to be unionized.

Union Density

Table 4 (bottom line) shows the proportion of unionized workers weighted by the share of each industry in total employment. The figures indicate that union density fell uniformly from 22.2 percent to 17.4 percent between 1986 and 1999, declining by 27 percent during the period. This decline in unionization may be associated with the changes that have taken place in the economy and in the labor market over the last two decades, and particularly in the 1990s when trade liberalization policies were introduced. Other potential explanatory factors include market deregulation, including the labor market, and the privatization of state-owned companies (a sector where unionization was traditionally active), compounded by deep recession in 1990-1992 and a consequent rise in the open unemployment rate. These changes increased competition, undermined profits, and forced companies to adopt cost-cutting measures, potentially affecting workers through a decrease in both the number of jobs and the *quasi-rents* available to be shared out. A drop in union density was an expected consequence of this situation, resulting from higher unemployment and less chance of success in wage claims. Hay (2001) shows that while trade liberalization led to an increase in productivity, the profits of Brazilian companies declined. Arbache (2000) shows that trade liberalization eroded the union wage premium, especially in sectors most affected by imports.

In order to analyze the level of unionization in Brazil, union density was compared with that of other countries for 1994.[63] Blau and Kahn (1999) report that average union density in a group of developed countries excluding the United States was 42 percent that year, whereas the figure in Brazil was 19.5 percent. Density in Brazil only exceeded the figures for the United States (16 percent) and France (9 percent). Differences in union density among countries may be a reflection of the institutions governing unions and collective bargaining processes. In Brazil, legal extension of the results of collective bargaining to all formal workers in the category, even non-union members, must partly explain the relatively low rate of unionization, because it encourages a free-rider behavior. In fact, Nickell and Layard (1999) show that union density is relatively low in countries where the results of collective bargaining are extended to non-union workers, as in France, Spain and Holland.[64]

Table 5 shows union density at the two-digit industry level. Industries are classified into three union-density groups, using the following procedure: the average density of industry i in the period 1986-1999 was compared with the average density economy-wide during the same

---

[62] Not surprisingly, the distribution of occupations between unionized and non-union workers matches the distribution of education.

[63] As there was no PNAD for 1994, we use the average union density for 1993 and 1995 to compare with density in developed countries.

[64] Gosling and Maching (1995) and Fortin and Lemieux (1997) show that the decline in union density in the United Kingdom and the United States caused a decrease in union bargaining power, and this helps to explain the observed increase in wage inequality.

period, namely 19.2 percent. On the basis of this comparison, the union density distribution at the industry level was constructed, and this was then split into three groups as follows:

- Up to one standard deviation – average or low union density;
- Between one and two standard deviations – high union density;
- Three or more standard deviations – very high union density.

Table 4. Union Density

(Percentages)

Industry	1986	1992	1993	1995	1996	1997	1998	1999	Mean
Agriculture	23.6	20.6	20.7	18.5	18.9	18.4	18.1	18.9	19.7
Mining	30.1	22.0	19.6	24.2	15.9	17.0	16.6	16.5	20.2
Oil, gas, and coal	68.3	67.1	71.8	71.7	49.3	64.8	61.1	66.7	65.1
Non-met. products	22.1	19.0	17.5	19.5	17.2	20.1	16.2	15.1	18.3
Metallurgical products	41.0	35.5	38.8	34.9	36.4	30.3	29.7	29.2	34.5
Mechanical products	43.5	40.1	41.7	40.2	31.1	36.6	31.7	31.3	37.0
Elect. and electronic products	47.6	42.4	36.1	38.2	33.6	33.3	33.0	27.1	36.4
Vehicles and autoparts	43.3	47.2	46.5	48.9	46.8	43.2	41.8	42.5	45.0
Wood and furniture	18.2	15.0	10.2	11.2	11.0	9.1	11.2	10.0	12.0
Paper and publishing	36.1	35.1	32.9	32.9	36.0	27.1	27.4	27.2	31.8
Rubber	30.2	28.2	42.9	40.8	28.9	24.6	34.2	31.0	32.6
Chemicals	35.3	30.3	31.1	30.5	31.2	28.2	29.3	34.4	31.3
Oil refining	53.4	63.8	48.7	57.7	49.7	54.6	40.9	48.7	52.2
Perfumes and pharmac.	31.8	23.9	29.0	27.2	26.7	24.0	23.9	26.4	26.6
Plastic products	32.3	28.7	28.4	27.7	31.2	29.4	24.1	27.0	28.6
Textiles	33.1	40.7	38.9	43.3	31.7	33.6	35.3	30.5	35.9
Clothing	8.9	9.4	9.4	9.5	8.2	8.0	8.4	8.7	8.8
Footwear	32.1	30.4	31.5	27.9	22.8	24.2	18.4	21.0	26.0
Foodstuff	26.2	24.1	22.9	22.6	20.9	20.3	20.0	18.1	21.9
Other manufact. products	22.6	16.9	14.6	21.6	20.1	16.2	17.3	13.5	17.9
Industrial services	50.6	66.2	63.3	65.3	60.6	56.6	55.0	54.2	59.0
Civil construction	11.9	10.2	9.5	9.2	8.2	8.0	7.6	6.9	8.9
Commerce	17.9	14.3	13.2	12.2	12.7	12.6	12.7	11.7	13.4
Transport services	34.9	37.1	36.1	32.4	33.1	30.3	29.8	29.4	32.9
Communication	43.3	45.9	52.1	52.2	45.6	41.3	38.9	38.5	44.7
Financial institutions	54.1	60.8	58.7	61.8	53.8	53.8	48.9	49.9	55.2
Social services	14.1	13.9	13.7	12.8	14.0	13.2	13.5	13.0	13.5
Business services	32.1	28.0	28.0	26.1	26.9	25.1	25.4	24.8	27.1
Public administration	24.4	21.1	25.1	19.7	18.0	22.3	20.5	20.2	21.4
Rental and leasing	23.9	26.0	27.9	29.0	28.1	29.5	28.8	29.9	27.9
Other services	4.0	2.7	2.7	2.7	2.8	2.8	2.9	2.7	2.9
Total	22.2	20.2	20.0	19.0	18.6	18.1	17.7	17.4	19.2

Table 5. Union Density By Group

(Percentages)

Group	Mean
1. Medium or low-density (up to one standard deviation)	
Other services	2.9
Clothing	8.8
Civil construction	8.9
Wood and furniture	12.0
Commerce	13.4
Social services	13.5
Other manufactured products	17.9
Non-metallic products	18.3
Agriculture	19.7
Mining	20.2
Public administration	21.4
Foodstuff	21.9
Footwear	26.0
Perfumes and pharmaceuticals	26.6
Other industrial services	27.1
Rental and leasing	27.9
Plastic products	28.6
Chemicals	31.3
Paper and publishing	31.8
Rubber	32.6
Transport services	32.9
2. High-density (up to two standard deviations)	
Metallurgical products	34.5
Textiles	35.9
Electric and electronic products	36.4
Mechanical products	37.0
Communications	44.7
Vehicles and autoparts	45.0
3. Very high-density (three or more standard deviations)	
Oil refining	52.2
Financial institutions	55.2
Industrial services	59.0
Oil, gas, and coal	65.1

Notes: Standard deviation = 15%; overall mean density = 19.2%; mean values between 1986 and 1999.

Industries with densities less than or equal to the economy average include civil construction, commerce, agriculture and clothing, among industries traditionally characterized by low levels of technology and capital and low market concentration.

Industries with union densities between 19.2 percent and 33 percent, include those with a high technology level, such as the pharmaceutical and chemical industries, together with various activities in the service sector. This interval also includes public administration, where union density is slightly above the average for the economy as a whole.

The medium or low union-density group included industries with unionization coefficients ranging from 3 percent to 33 percent; so dispersion in that group is very wide. The high density category includes industries with unionization rates of between 34.5 percent and 45 percent. Industries in this group are characterized by high levels of technology, capital, and market concentration, and they operate in large establishments. The very high density group contains industries with unionization rates above 52.2 percent, including the financial sector, oil drilling and other fuel mineral extraction industries, together with oil refining. These sectors are essentially dominated by the State oil company, Petrobrás, and by large multinationals.

The distribution of employment by union-density group is highly unequal. In 1999, 93.88 percent of workers were employed in medium or low union-density industries, while 66.47 percent were in industries with densities below the economy average; 4.05 percent of workers were employed in industries in the high density group, while just 2.07 percent of the workforce were in very high union-density industries.[65] The very unequal distribution of workers by union-density group is likely to have significant effects on union behavior at the industry level, and hence on the distribution of the rents extracted by them.

IV. UNIONS AND WAGES

How do unions affect wages and the distribution of income in Brazil? Is union bargaining behavior influenced by the institutions that regulate labor relations? How is income distribution affected by the concentration of unions in more sophisticated industries and higher unionization rates among skilled workers? This section seeks to answer these questions.

Union Wage Premium[66]

One of the best-known effects of unions in the economy is their ability to raise wages through collective bargaining. The literature shows that unionized workers with the same characteristics as their non-union counterparts enjoy a wage premium thanks to the action of their unions in pay negotiations. Booth (1995), Abowd and Lemieux (1993), and Nickell et al. (1994) all claim that the success of union activism in raising rates of pay is directly related to the market power of the company and the degree of concentration of the industry concerned. Highly competitive companies or industries cannot pay wages over the odds, for fear of going out of business. A union wage premium will only be seen in companies or industries that generate monopoly rents.

---

[65] The distribution of employment by union-density group in other years is quite similar.
[66] We use the terms "union wage premium", "union premium", "union mark-up" and "union wage differential" synonymously.

To analyze the wage spread between unionized and non-union workers, we have calculated the difference between the logarithm of the real hourly wage of the two groups. The results shown in Table 6 indicate an average wage differential of 58 percent.

Given that union members have a very different socioeconomic profile compared to non-members, the wage differential should next be calculated controlling for individual characteristics. This has been estimated by three methods, namely ordinary least squares (OLS), the Booth method, (1995, p.164), and the Oaxaca-Blinder decomposition.

Table 6. Differential of Log. Of Real Hourly Wages

(Percentages)

1986	55.8
1992	59.1
1993	63.0
1995	57.5
1996	57.0
1997	57.7
1998	57.8
1999	54.2

The results in Table 7 suggest substantially lower union wage premiums than those indicated in Table 6, confirming that individual socioeconomic characteristics are a major factor in explaining the wage gap between unionized and non-union workers. Given that the mean wage differential shown in Table 6 is 58 percent, while the average premium estimated by OLS is just 17.9 percent, we can conclude that nearly 70 percent of the uncontrolled wage differential is explained by differences in worker characteristics.

Table 7. Union Wage Mark-Up

Year	Union dummy (OLS)	Booth method*	Oaxaca-Blinder method**
1986	0.1670	0.1365	0.1281 - 0.1662
1992	0.1772	0.1381	0.1203 - 0.2057
1993	0.2008	0.1682	0.1516 - 0.2316
1995	0.1855	0.1698	0.1581 - 0.2190
1996	0.1813	0.1596	0.1469 - 0.2135
1997	0.1881	0.1702	0.1606 - 0.2134
1998	0.1774	0.1580	0.1479 - 0.2040
1999	0.1574	0.1228	0.1106 - 0.1778

Notes: The explanatory variables in the wage equation model are: education, experience, experience squared, employment record card, urban region, metropolitan region, head of household, race, gender, five geographic regions, and 31 industries.

* Booth (1995).

** Results vary according to the means vector used in the calculations, of non-union and unionized workers, respectively

Average values for the union wage premium are calculated as 17.9 percent, 15.3 percent and 17.2 percent, using ordinary least squares, the Booth method, and the Oaxaca-Blinder method, respectively. The salary differential is greater in Brazil than in several continental European countries, where the premium is around 7 percent, but quite similar to the 18 percent differential seen in the United States (Blanchflower and Freeman, 1992).[67] Although the figures for Brazil and the United States are similar, the determinants of the premium in the two countries are not the same, as the labor market and collective bargaining processes operate very differently in the two countries.

The high union wage premium in Brazil contrasts with generally low union density. One plausible explanation for this is that union mark-ups are very significant in industries of high and very high union density (see Table 5), and this raises the average union wage premium for the economy as a whole. This hypothesis is borne out by the high correlation between union density and the inter-industry wage premium (0.798, significant at the 1 percent level), and the results obtained by Arbache and Menezes-Filho (2000) showing evidence of rent sharing in industries that generate greatest value-added and highest return.

Unions and Wage Dispersion

According to Freeman (2000), the most universal stylized fact in the literature on unions is that wage dispersion among unionized workers is less than that among non-union members. The reasons for this are as follows: (i) unions depart from the principle that there should be a rate of pay for the job, and wages should have little or nothing to do with performance or individual characteristics; (ii) unions defend the existence of rigid job and wage structures, with promotion criteria based on seniority and occupation, and a narrow wage spread over the job hierarchy; and (iii) unions strive to ensure their members do not earn less than the minimum wage for their category or for the overall economy, if one exists, thereby truncating the wage distribution and making it more compact. Consequently, individual characteristics that normally contribute to wage formation, especially human capital variables, have scant influence on rates of pay for unionized workers. The marginal return on schooling, experience and training, for example, will therefore be lower for unionized workers than for their non-union counterparts; and discrimination based on gender, race, age, and so forth, also tends to be less among union members.

The reasons why unions seek rigid pay scales and a narrower wage spread between occupations are as follows: (i) to define clear objectives for collective bargaining processes; (ii) to eliminate competition among worker through wage disputes; (iii) to engender a feeling of solidarity among workers in the search for equal treatment by the employer; and (iv) the power of the median voter, which tends to favor redistribution in favor of the lower paid whenever the median wage rate is below the mean. The most important consequence of union action is that there will be less wage inequality *throughout* the economy, despite union members enjoying a wage premium (Freeman, 2000; Metcalf et al. 2000).

Table 8 shows the dispersion of the logarithm of real hourly wages for unionized and non-union workers. The spread is always *greater* among the former. Figure 2 and Figure 3

---

[67] Blanchflower and Freeman estimated wage models using OLS, with very similar specifications to the model estimated in this paper.

illustrate wage dispersion in 1999, showing that the distribution for non-union workers is a good deal more leptokurtic, with strong positive asymmetry. These results are strange, since they are contrary to the stylized fact that wage dispersion is lower among unionized workers than among non-union members. The most plausible explanation for this is that unions in Brazil do *not* attempt to standardize wages.

Table 8. Wage Dispersion Among Unionized and Non-Union Workers

| | Standard deviation of log. of real hourly wage | | |
Year	Unionized	Non-union	Total
1986	0.9740	0.8914	0.9397
1992	0.9412	0.9076	0.9448
1993	0.9910	0.9229	0.9702
1995	0.9631	0.8936	0.9349
1996	0.9629	0.8949	0.9352
1997	0.9667	0.8926	0.9332
1998	0.9620	0.8751	0.9181
1999	0.9485	0.8636	0.9028

Source: National Household Surveys (PNADs), several years.

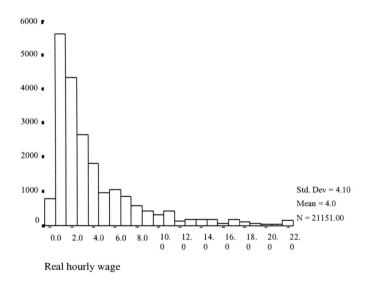

Figure 2. Distribution of Real Hourly Wages – Union Members, 1999

One potential effect of the high wage dispersion among unionized workers is greater wage inequality throughout the economy.[68] This effect will be greater the higher the wage dispersion between unionized and non-union workers, and/or the higher the level of union density. To examine the impact of unions on wage inequality, we use counterfactual analysis

---

[68] Blau and Kahn (1996) show that one of the reasons for greater wage dispersion in the United States compared to other developed countries is the high level of wage dispersion among unionized workers, although this is no greater than dispersion among non-union members in that country.

to simulate what would happen to inequality if the pay of non-unionists adhered to the wage policy in force for unionized workers.[69] If we find that wage formation for unionized workers increases wage dispersion among non-unionists, we will have evidence that unions increase inequality in the overall economy. To confirm the result of the simulation, we examine what would happen with the distribution if unionized workers were to earn the same as their non-union counterparts.

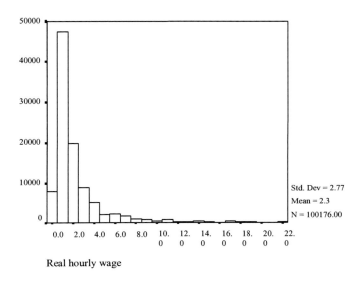

Figure 3. Distribution of Real Hourly Wage – Non-union Members, 1999

The counterfactual for non-unionized workers was implemented as follows:

$$\ln y_i^{ns} = y_i^* + \hat{u}_i^{ns} \left(\frac{\sigma^s}{\sigma^{ns}} \right)$$

Where y_i^* is the simulation of the logarithm of the real hourly wage of the ith non-union worker (the simulation is performed using the β s estimated in the unionized workers wage model); $\hat{u}_i^{ns}$ is the residual from the non-union wage model; σ^s is the standard deviation of the residual from the unionized workers wage model; and σ^{ns} is the standard deviation of the residuals from the non-union wage model.[70]

Table 9 summarizes the effects of unions on the standard deviation of non-union wages, calculated in two stages. Firstly, the standard deviation of the wages of non-union and unionized workers was simulated on the basis of coefficients estimated in the unionized and

---

[69] This could happen if, in order to avoid unionization, companies decided to follow the unionized workers wage policy.

[70] The equation for unionized workers is the same, with the *ns* superscripts replaced by *s* and vice versa.

non-union wage models, respectively. Secondly, we calculated the ratio between the simulated standard deviation and the original standard deviation (calculated without simulation).

The results presented in line 1 of Table 9 show that, apart from 1995, if the unionized worker wage policy was used to set the pay of non-union members, wage inequality would increase by between 5.1 percent and 37.3 percent, depending on the year. This result is unequivocal evidence that unions increase wage inequality in the Brazilian economy, rather than reduce it. Line 2 reports the reverse exercise, using the wage policy for non-union members to set unionized workers' pay. This produces a reduction in wage dispersion of 12.7 percent to 18.7 percent, thereby corroborating the previous evidence. Thus, the effects of unions on wage dispersion in Brazil are precisely the opposite of those reported in the international literature.

Table 9. Simulation of Standard Deviation
of Unionized and Non-Union Workers' Wages

(simulated value/original value %)

	1986	1992	1993	1995	1996	1997	1998	1999
Non-union	13.57	5.08	20.82	-4.64	14.43	11.88	15.79	37.33
Unionized	-13.45	-13.77	-17.45	-12.66	-14.05	-11.97	-14.99	-18.75

Notes: The figures shown in the table represent the ratio of the simulated standard deviation divided by the original standard deviation, expressed as a percentage. The values shown for non-union members refer to the simulated standard deviation obtained using coefficients estimated from the unionized workers wage model. The values for unionized workers refer to the simulated standard deviation obtained with coefficients estimated from the non-union workers wage model.

A very strong factor that may explain the wider dispersion of unionized wages is that merit plays a greater role in setting union members' pay. If so, the coefficients estimated for the productive variables in the unionized wage models ought to be higher than those estimated in the models for non-union members. To investigate this hypothesis, we compared the schooling and experience coefficients in the unionized and non-union wage models.

The results in Table 10 show that the marginal returns on human capital variables in the unionized worker models are always higher than those obtained in the non-union models, which suggests that unions magnify rather than diminish the effects of personal characteristics on wages.[71] These results are counterintuitive and contrary to the literature; they also contradict the idea that unions are sources of wage equalization and standardization.

There are at least three possible explanations for this result. The first relates to dispersion in unionized and non-union workers' characteristics. This could add to inequality insofar as wages are determined by productivity differences. The larger the variance of characteristics within a given group, the higher will be the variance of wages in that group, and vice versa. To test this hypothesis, Arbache (1999) decomposes the variance of unionized workers' wages conditional on the variance of non-union workers' characteristics. The result indicates that 37 percent of wage dispersion among unionized workers is caused by the difference in the dispersion of characteristics between union and non-union members. In fact, on the one

---

[71] The results reported correspond to 1999; qualitative results for other years are similar.

hand, unionization is highly concentrated in certain industries that account for a small proportion of employment, and in certain occupational categories, notably those requiring higher qualifications, which are in short supply in the economy. On the other hand, unionization is substantially lower in traditional industries and among the low-skilled workers who make up the vast majority of the workforce. Thus, the dispersion of characteristics among unionized workers is likely to be large.

Table 10. Returns to Human Capital Variables in Unionized and Non-Union Workers Wage Equations, 1999

Variable	Unionized	Non-union
Experience	0.0347	0.0331
Experience squared	-0.0004	-0.0005
Some elementary education	0.1573	0.1151
Elementary or some primary education	0.3678	0.2888
Primary or some secondary education	0.6414	0.5288
Secondary or some higher education	1.0850	0.9380
Higher education	1.8080	1.7260

Note: All coefficients are significant at the 1% level

The second explanation relates to the median voter theorem. As more highly qualified workers are over-represented in union membership, they wield significant power in defining policies that favor returns to human capital, thereby increasing wage inequality. If unions place a higher value on merit, then more highly skilled workers will seek jobs in sectors where unions have greatest influence in pay-setting processes. Thus, the market would respond to higher wages among unionized workers by allocating the best workers to industries where unions are most active.[72]

The third explanation relates to the scant or non-existent coordination and centralization of collective bargaining processes.[73] This point is discussed below.

Dispersion of characteristics and pay among unionized workers, together with the relatively greater importance of skill in wage formation, suggest that the returns to human capital variables will differ significantly *among* unionized workers throughout the distribution. In other words, the marginal return on education is higher among workers further towards the right-hand tail of the distribution. To examine this hypothesis, we compared the marginal returns on schooling in the unionized and non-union wage models, estimated by quantile regression.

The results, shown in Table 11, reveal three phenomena. Firstly, marginal returns on education rise throughout the wage distribution. A worker in the 90th percentile obtains a greater return from a higher education course than a worker attaining the same level of schooling in any lower income percentile. Secondly, the returns to education are always higher for unionized workers. Thirdly, marginal returns among unionized workers grow

---

[72] This would create a potential sample selection problem. At the limit, selection would tend to reduce wage dispersion as workers would have increasingly similar characteristics.

[73] By "centralization" we refer to the level at which collective bargaining takes place, namely plant, company, industry or economy.

proportionately more as the level of schooling rises. These results are evidence that unions contribute to greater wage inequality, by providing greater relative benefits to workers further to the right in the distribution, as well as workers with more years of schooling.

Table 11. Schooling Coefficients Among Unionized and Non-Union Workers, 1999

Percentile	0.1		0.25		0.50		0.75		0.9	
	Union	Non-union	Union	Non-union	Union	Non-union	Union	Non-union	Union	Non-union
Some elementary education	0.0589	0.0394	0.0961	0.0416	0.1055	0.0465	0.1591	0.0703	0.1560	0.1017
Elementary or some primary education	0.1625	0.1211	0.2180	0.1146	0.2488	0.1175	0.2781	0.1340	0.2656	0.1709
Primary or some secondary education	0.2976	0.2060	0.3428	0.1915	0.3731	0.2244	0.4411	0.2756	0.4790	0.3498
Secondary or some higher education	0.5479	0.4123	0.6510	0.4581	0.7549	0.5674	0.8901	0.7118	0.9513	0.8657
Higher education	1.3916	1.1577	1.5364	1.3185	1.6765	1.5176	1.7903	1.6751	1.7487	1.7513

Notes: Models were estimated by quantile regression. All coefficients are significant at the 1% level. Standard errors were estimated by the bootstrap method. The models' explanatory variables are: gender, urban region, metropolitan region, 5 geographic regions, 31 industries, head of household, employment record card, and schooling.

Unions and Collective Bargaining

One important aspect of collective bargaining processes is their potential economic effect, which goes beyond wage distribution. In the most centralized and coordinated bargaining systems, wage determination tends to be more sensitive to the general conditions of the labor market (Layard et al., 1991) and income distribution tends to be more equal. At the other end of the scale, fragmented bargaining systems that operate at the establishment level tend to be more sensitive to the economic conditions facing the company. In both cases, union demands are tempered by disincentives arising from the effects of inconsistent demands on the workers themselves, such as unemployment, inflation, or a lack of formalization of the employment contract. Discussion on this topic initially analyzed the effects of the crises of the 1970s on the macroeconomic performance of rich countries, and showed that the institutions that regulate collective bargaining play a decisive role in macroeconomic performance (Bruno and Sachs, 1985; Freeman, 1988).

Calmfors and Driffill (1988) show that collective bargaining organized at the industry level, as in Brazil, is the worst possible structure, because workers have few incentives to incorporate into their objective functions the conditions facing the economy and companies, or the external effects on themselves of potentially inconsistent demands. Moreover, the absence of coordination and synchronization among collective bargaining processes in Brazil means that unions are permanently creating pockets of instability, by holding out for wage increases that are inconsistent with macroeconomic balance. This feature of collective bargaining in Brazil has been empirically addressed by Carneiro (1999) and Carneiro and Henley (2000) who argue that the semi-coordinated (intermediate-centralized) bargaining structure currently in place in the country conforms with the insider-outsider hypotheis.[74]

The literature indicates that the most important consequence of coordinated and centralized collective bargaining processes is low wage dispersion. The empirical literature shows that wage differentials are narrower in countries with centralized bargaining processes than where they are more fragmented (Kahn, 1998). Blau and Khan (1996) find, for a set of developed countries, that wage dispersion is lower where collective bargaining is more centralized. Metcalf et al. (2000) discuss and show that the retreat of collective bargaining coverage in the United Kingdom since the 1980s was accompanied by greater wage inequality. Rowthorn (1992) uses the centralization criterion proposed by Calmfors and Driffill (1988) and finds a negative relation between centralization and inter-industry wage dispersion. Thus, the greater the coordination and centralization of bargaining processes, and/or the higher the proportion of workers covered by collective bargaining, the lower the wage dispersion in the economy will be.[75]

The structure of labor relations and union organization in Brazil is highly unfavorable to the strengthening, centralization, and coordination of collective bargaining processes. Unions from the most organized and sophisticated industries are encouraged to adopt individualistic behavior to exploit bargaining power associated with the conditions facing the company or industry. As a result, inter-industry wage differentials may be wider among unionized than among non-union workers. As the rate and composition of unemployment varies from region to region, unions from a single industry but in different localities will have different degrees of bargaining power, leading to potentially greater inequality in the wages of unionized workers.

The effects of the structure of collective bargaining processes in Brazil are particularly important, given the country's highly unequal income distribution and the severe macroeconomic instability it has been experiencing for at least two decades. Negotiations at the industry level and by geographic area mean that unions have less incentive to internalize the effects of the trade off between wage/employment and wage/formal employment contract. Consequently, there will be: (i) high dispersion of inter-industry wages – this will rise with the heterogeneity of technology and market power between industries, and the heterogeneity of bargaining power between unions; (ii) a prolongation of and/or increase in the costs of stabilization processes and/or coordination of macroeconomic policies, with potential effects on unemployment and inflation.

To investigate the effects of the collective bargaining structure on inequality, we compared the standard deviation of the inter-industry wage differential between unionized and non-union workers. Inter-industry wage differentials relate to that part of wages not

---

[74] That is, larger employment today leads to subsequent wage moderation.

[75] It should be borne in mind that wages agreed upon in more centralized collective bargaining systems affect the vast majority of workers, including non-union members, either because the result of the bargaining process is legally extended to everyone, or because companies take the negotiated wage rate as a benchmark for constructing their own pay scale. In either situation, wage dispersion among workers covered by the bargaining process should be less than among those who are not covered.

explained by human capital, demographic characteristics, regional variables, etc., but associated with the industry to which the worker is attached. Thus, the higher the industry wage premium, the higher will be the wage received by the individual in that industry *vis-à-vis* the representative worker. Insofar as industry wage premiums and profits are positively related (Arbache and Menezes-Filho, 2000), it is reasonable to expect a positive relation between union activism and the industry wage premium, because unions negotiate where there are monopoly rents to be shared out. As collective bargaining processes usually occur at the industry level, union pressure for higher pay could lead to greater inter-industry wage dispersion.

We estimated inter-industry wage premiums and calculated the respective standard deviation using the Haisken-DeNew and Schmidt (1997) procedure. Table 12 shows that the dispersion of industry wage premiums among unionized workers is greater than among non-union members. This confirms that union bargaining power at the industry level is quite heterogeneous, a situation that tends to be boosted by fragmentation and a lack of synchronization among collective bargaining processes. Little cooperation between unions can therefore be expected on wages and coordination in collective bargaining processes is unlikely.

Table 12. Standard Deviation of the Inter-Industry Wage Differential

Year	Unionized	Non-union	Total
1986	0.2491	0.1827	0.2023
1992	0.2640	0.1713	0.2061
1993	0.2741	0.1619	0.2002
1995	0.2631	0.1614	0.1934
1996	0.2456	0.1652	0.1892
1997	0.2375	0.1685	0.1898
1998	0.2310	0.1605	0.1796
1999	0.2313	0.1625	0.1818

Notes: (1) The inter-industry wage differential and standard deviation were estimated by the Haisken-DeNew and Schmidt (1997) method. (2) The models' explanatory variables are: education, gender, experience, experience squared, employment record card, head of household, urban region, metropolitan region, regions, and 31 industries (IBGE two-digit level).

V. DISCUSSION

This chapter has addressed the following questions: (i) How do labor and union laws affect collective bargaining processes? (ii) Do unions affect wage formation and income distribution? (iii) Do unions increase rigidity in the labor market? Upon reaching the end of the chapter, we realize we have not found unequivocal answers to these questions. The complexity of the topic and the limitations of relying on economics alone to provide answers may help explain the shortcomings of our findings. Nonetheless, the chapter offers several pieces of evidence that elucidate the issues addressed.

Possibly the most important lesson to be drawn from the study is that institutions are fundamental in explaining union actions, along with their effects on income distribution and macroeconomic stability, and on the current state of collective bargaining in Brazil. The answer to question (i) is closely linked to the institutional apparatus. As we have seen, labor and union legislation – particularly through the union levy, monopoly representation and labor courts – create disincentives for the development of collective bargaining and cause problems for macroeconomic coordination.

The mandatory union levy creates contract problems between the union and the worker. As the union thus has an assured income, the bureaucrat will not always need to obtain additional funds from voluntary affiliations to run the organization. This may result in the relaxation or even disappearance of the contractual relation between the two parties, in which the union member (the principal) would expect "contractual" attitudes and decisions from the union bureaucrat (the agent). Consequently, union leaders may perform their union activities with less commitment, and this may lead to a weakened relationship between the union and its workers. The assured income, which is often sizeable, gives enormous power to the union bureaucracy, and nurtures bitter disputes for leadership of the organization.

In the period prior to the 1988 Constitution, when the State was given great freedom to meddle in union affairs, the contractual relation between union leaders and workers was often tenuous, and union bureaucracy essentially strove to keep itself in power by forging ever closer relationships with Government. More recently, the distribution of funds by Government for unions to use in training and labor intermediation programs has fostered a further strengthening of relations between union leaders and government authorities.

The contract problem created by the union levy means that union leaders do not always feel committed to the most obvious interests of the worker; this inhibits a strengthening of the relationship between worker and union, thereby impairing the development of collective bargaining.

Monopoly representation is another institution that may interfere with the actions of unions in collective bargaining processes. The monopoly guarantees union bureaucracy enormous power in its geographical jurisdiction, giving it major prerogatives such as mandatory participation in discussions on any issue relating to the interests of the category it represents. A problem of union involvement in all negotiations is that it tends to inhibit bargaining between employers and employees at the company level. In addition, excess power linked to the contract problem may also influence the behavior and actions of union leaders in bargaining processes.

The regulatory power of labor courts, together with the paternalistic character of labor legislation and in many cases the justice system itself, prevent workers and employers from entering into direct negotiations with one another. Employees, protected by legislation and the culture of appealing to the court, are encouraged to use to the justice system to resolve disagreements with employers. Employees frequently have appealed to the justice system even before proposing or presenting their allegations or claims to their employers. The latter, either as a way of delaying payments owed, exploiting the opportunity cost of the worker, or increasing the transaction cost of access to amounts supposedly owed, also has incentives to appeal to the courts rather than negotiating with the worker. Direct negotiations are thus replaced by the institutionalization of indirect negotiations through the labor court system.

With regard to question (ii), pertaining to the effects of unions on pay setting and the wage distribution, we find a variety of econometric evidence. Unions clearly contribute to wage formation, by establishing a wage premium that enables union members to earn more than their non-union counterparts with the same individual characteristics and industrial affiliation. In principle, the existence of the wage premium is unexpected, since the law requires the results of collective bargaining processes to be extended to all workers in the occupational category concerned. Thus, any pay raise negotiated by the union must be given to all workers in that category. Possible explanations for the empirical verification of union wage premiums include the following: (i) automatic extension of gains may not have taken place, meaning non-compliance with the law; (ii) wage negotiations may predominantly be carried out at the company rather than the industry level, as we investigated in this study, which would not require extension of bargained results to other workers in the industry; (iii) unions may essentially be negotiating pay floors rather than actual wage rates, thereby giving space for companies to negotiate wages above the floor; and (iv) there may be a wage differential between workers in a given category, but in different *municipios* or jurisdictions of unions or their federations. Unfortunately, shortcomings in union data prevent us from testing these hypotheses. Nonetheless, we would not be surprised if future calculations using company and/or municipal-level data produced lower union wage premiums.

We find evidence that unions do affect income distribution; but contrary to the view prevailing in the literature, unions in Brazil are associated with more rather than less wage inequality. Several factors appear to explain this. Firstly, higher-skilled workers and those in better jobs are proportionately more unionized than less skilled workers. This is counterintuitive, since better qualified workers would not have an incentive to be paid standardized wages. On the contrary, as they are more skilled they ought to prefer their pay to be performance-related rather than predetermined.

Our results suggest that the higher rates of unionization among more skilled workers encourage unions to adopt strategies favoring this group. This is consistent with the median voter theorem, the greater mobilization power of like-minded people, or insider power. The finding that marginal returns on human capital variables are higher among unionized workers and those to the right of the wage distribution, compared to non-union members, is remarkable. Given that the country is so lacking in skilled labor, unions would therefore seem to be exploiting labor scarcity to magnify the returns to skill, thus benefiting workers with more human capital and/or those holding better posts in the job hierarchy. This issue becomes even more important if unions are insensitive to the wage/employment and wage/informal sector trade-offs.

One possible explanation for the higher rate of unionization among highly skilled workers may be the regulation of higher-level professions by regional councils, which, to some extent, behave or end up behaving in a similar way to unions. As we showed above, an example of this is the publication of fee scales and the establishment of pay floors by these institutions. On the other hand, the unions in the respective categories, which often work in conjunction with and in the same place as the regional councils, can take advantage of externalities arising from the actions of these bodies, to promote and disseminate unionization among professional people and thereby increase union membership among them.

Secondly, the dispersion of characteristics among unionized workers is greater than among their non-union counterparts, resulting in higher wage dispersion among union members.

Thirdly, the resurgence of unionism at the end of the 1970s in the industrialized and wealthy areas of São Paulo, does not seem to be mere coincidence. Clearly, it is associated with the nature of the companies and industries in that region, which include multinationals and large domestic companies, mostly operating in concentrated, high technology industries.

The conjunction of these two phenomena, namely the extraction of monopoly rents by companies in the region, and the strict law on pay increases, which limited wage hikes, would have encouraged workers to organize and lobby for greater flexibility to facilitate rent sharing. Thus, the reorganization of the union movement in the wealthiest part of the country and in industries using sophisticated technologies and moderately more qualified workers seems to have molded the "new unionism" as an activity associated with workers who are more rather than less qualified.[76]

Fourthly, the fact that occupational categories' base dates are spread throughout the year, compounded by the fragmentation of collective bargaining by region, reduces the chances of centralization and/or coordination of bargaining processes and encourages free-rider behavior. In this context, unions in sectors that extract monopoly rents have incentives to act in a decentralized fashion, exploiting circumstances that are favorable to them, in accordance with the characteristics of the industry and/or region in which they are located. On the other hand, the weakness of unions in more competitive sectors means they have less chance of bargaining success. As union density is higher in the more concentrated and sophisticated industries, we consequently find greater inter-industry wage inequality associated with unions.

Another major consequence of the fragmentation of bargaining processes is the difficulty this raises for macroeconomic coordination. A fragmented system of negotiations, with highly variable bargaining power between unions, encourages free riding and inconsistent wage demands, constantly generating potential pressure on prices. But the effects of fragmentation become even more acute as unions in more organized sectors show scant concern for the wage/employment and wage/informal sector trade-offs, provoking potentially negative consequences for the level and quality of employment, and harming outsiders in particular.

As for the relation between unions and labor market rigidity posed in question (iii), we find evidence that union action on wages tends to increase rigidity and segmentation in the labor market. The union wage premium, together with an over-valuation of human capital, raise labor costs, creating entry barriers for less skilled workers in certain industries and encouraging segmentation. *Broadly speaking*, this produces one group of industries with higher union density, higher wages, and more skilled workers; and another group of industries with lower union density, lower wages, and less skilled workers.

VI. RECOMMENDATIONS

In the light of the above discussion, we now make some recommendations for encouraging and strengthening collective bargaining processes, ideally turning them into the key instrument of labor relations in Brazil. We believe the following measures should be adopted: (i) abolish the union monopoly; (ii) abolish the mandatory union levy; (iii) abolish the regulatory power of the labor tribunal system; (iv) organize unions by economic activity rather than occupation; (v) strengthen representation at the workplace; and (vi) change

---

[76] It should be noted that the concept of skill in a country with a high proportion of illiterate or functionally illiterate workers, such as Brazil, is different from that of a country with a higher average level of education. Thus, even an individual who has not completed second grade, for example, could be considered to have formal education well above the national average.

collective bargaining base dates so as to reduce fragmentation and encourage centralization and/or cooperation between unions in bargaining processes. We believe these measures would enhance unions and give them greater independence; the measures would also strengthen them and elicit more committed engagement from them on issues pertaining to workers' interests. The current structure of collective bargaining in Brazil reflects and reveals scant consensus among the agents involved in improving and modernizing the country's labor relations.

Given the paucity of research on unions in Brazil, investigation of their impact on employment, productivity, profits, and working conditions, together with studies of the differences between unions in the public and private sectors, and at the company and regional level, would be particularly welcome in order to shed further light on the issues raised in this paper.

REFERENCES

Abowd, J.M. and Lemieux, T. (1993), 'The effects of product market competition on collective bargaining agreements: the case of foreign competition in Canada', *Quarterly Journal of Economics*, 108: 983-1014.

Amorim, B.M. (2000), Salários indiretos e sindicatos no Brasil, Campinas: *Anais do XXVIII Encontro Nacional de Economia*.

Arbache, J.S. (1999), 'Do unions always decrease wage dispersion? The case of Brazilian manufacturing', *Journal of Labor Research*, 20: 425-436.

Arbache, J.S. (2000), 'Does trade liberalization always decrease unions bargaining power?', *Proceedings of the 2000 EALE/SOLE World Conference*, Milão.

Arbache, J.S. and Carneiro, F.G. (1999), 'Unions and wage differentials', *World Development*, 27: 1875-1883.

Arbache, J.S. and Menezes-Filho, N., (2000), 'Rent-sharing in Brazil: Using trade liberalization as a natural experiment', Rio de Janeiro: *Annals of the V Annual Meeting of the Latin American and Caribbean Economic Association*.

Blanchflower, D.G. and Freeman, R.B. (1992), 'Unionism in the United States and other advanced OECD countries', *Industrial Relations*, 31: 57-79.

Blau, F.D. and Kahn, L.M. (1996), 'International differences in male wage inequality: institutions versus market forces', *Journal of Political Economy*, 104: 791-837.

Blau, F.D. and Kahn, L.M. (1999), 'Institutions and laws in the labor market', in O. Ashenfelter and D. Card (eds.), *Handbook of Labor Economics*, Amsterdam: Elsevier.

Booth, A. (1995), '*The economics of the trade unions*', Cambridge: Cambridge University Press.

Camargo, J.M. (2001), '*Sindicatos e justiça do trabalho no Brasil*', mimeo, Departamento de Economia, PUC-Rio.

Calmfors, L. and Driffill, J. (1988), 'Centralization and wage bargaining, *Economic Policy*, 3: 14-61.

Card, D. (1992), '*The effect of unions on the distribution of wages: redistribution or relabelling?*', NBER Working Paper 4195.

Carneiro, F. (1998). *Productivity Effects in Brazilian Wage Determination. World Development* vol. 26(1), pp. 139-153.

Carneiro, F. and A. Henley (1998). *Wage Determination in Brazil: The Growth of Union Bargaining Power and Informal Employment. The Journal of Development Studies* vol. 34(4), pp. 117-138.

Carneiro, F. (1999). *Insider Power in Wage Determination: Evidence from Brazilian Data. Review of Development Economics* vol 3(2), pp. 55-169.

Carneiro, F. and A. Henley (2000), *Real Wages and the Lucas Critique: Can the Government Tax Policy Influence Wage Growth in Brazil?*, Brazilian Review of Econometrics, Vol. 20(1):89-113.

DiNardo, J., Fortin, N.M. and Lemieux, T. (1995), 'Labor market institutions and the distribution of wages, 1973-1992: a semiparametric approach', NBER Working Paper 5093.

DiNardo, J., Hallock, K. and Pischke, J.S. (1997), 'Unions and managerial pay', NBER Working Paper 6318.

Fortin, N.M. and Lemieux T. (1997), 'Institutional changes and rising wage inequality: is there a linkage?', *Journal of Economic Perspectives*, 11: 75-96.

Freeman, R.B. (1980), 'Unionism and the dispersion of wages', *Industrial and Labor Relations Review*, 34: 3-23.

Freeman, R.B. (1982), 'Union wage practices and wage dispersion within establishments', *Industrial and Labor Relations Review*, 36: 3-21.

Freeman, R.B. (1988), 'Labor market institutions and economic performance', NBER Working Paper 2560.

Freeman, R.B. (1992), 'How much has de-unionization contributed to the rise in male earnings inequality?', in S. Danzinger and P. Gottschalk (eds.), *Uneven tides*, New York: Sage Press.

Freeman, R.B. (2000), 'Single peaked vs. diversified capitalism: the relation between economic institutions and outcomes', NBER Working Paper 7556.

Gosling, A. and Machin, S. (1995), 'Trade unions and the dispersion of earnings in British establishments, 1980-90', *Oxford Bulletin of Economics and Statistics*, 57: 167-184.

Green, F., Dickerson, A., and Arbache, J.S. (2001), 'A picture of wage inequality and the allocation of labor through a period of trade liberalization: the case of Brazil', *World Development*, 29:1923-39.

Haisken-DeNew, J.P. and Schmidt, C.M. (1997), 'Inter-industry and inter-region differentials: mechanics and interpretation', *Review of Economics and Statistics*, 79: 516-521.

Hay, D. (2001), 'The post 1990 Brazilian trade liberalization and the performance of large manufacturing firms: Productivity, market share and profits', *Economic Journal*, 473:620-641.

Hirsch, B.T. (1982), 'The interindustry structure of unionism, earnings and earnings dispersion', *Industrial and Labor Relations Review*, 36: 22-39.

Kahn, L.M. (1998), 'Collective bargaining and the interindustry wage structure: international evidence', *Economica*, 65: 507-534.

Menezes-Filho, N., H. Zylberstajn, J.P. Chahad, and E. Pazello (2002), '*Trade Unions and the Economic Performance of Brazilian Establishments*', Paper Presented at the 2002 Latin American Meeting of the Econometric Society, São Paulo, Brazil.

Metcalf, D., Hansen, K., and Charlwood, A. (2000), 'Unions and the sword of justice: unions and pay systems, pay inequality, pay discrimination and low pay', mimeo, Center for Economic Performance, London School of Economics.

Nickell, S.J., Vainiomaki, J. and Wadhwani, S. (1994), 'Wages, unions and product market power', *Economica*, 61: 457-474.

Nickell, S.J. and Layard, R. (1999), 'Labor market institutions and economic performance', in O. Ashenfelter and D. Card (eds.), *Handbook of Labor Economics*, Amsterdam: Elsevier.

Rowthorn, R.E. (1992), 'Centralization, employment and wage dispersion', *Economic Journal*, 102: 506-523.

INDEX

D

F

J

K

N

O

P

V

W

Y